*J.K. LASSER'S™*

# WINNING WITH YOUR 403(b)

## Look for these and other titles from J.K. Lasser™—Practical Guides for All Your Financial Needs

*J.K. Lasser's Pick Winning Stocks* by Edward F. Mrkvika Jr.

*J.K. Lasser's Invest Online* by LauraMaery Gold and Dan Post

*J.K. Lasser's Year-Round Tax Strategies* by David S. De Jong and Ann Gray Jakabin

*J.K. Lasser's Taxes Made Easy for Your Home-Based Business* by Gary W. Carter

*J.K. Lasser's Finance and Tax for Your Family Business* by Barbara Weltman

*J.K. Lasser's Pick Winning Mutual Funds* by Jerry Tweddell with Jack Pierce

*J.K. Lasser's Your Winning Retirement Plan* by Henry K. Hebeler

*J.K. Lasser's Winning with Your 401(k)* by Grace W. Weinstein

*J.K. Lasser's Strategic Investing after 50* by Julie Jason

*J.K. Lasser's Winning with Your 403(b)* by Pam Horowitz

*J.K. Lasser's Winning Financial Strategies for Women* by Rhonda M. Ecker and Denise Gustin-Piazza

# J.K. LASSER'S™

# WINNING WITH YOUR 403(b)

## Pam Horowitz

**John Wiley & Sons, Inc.**

New York • Chichester • Weinheim • Brisbane • Singapore • Toronto

Published by John Wiley & Sons, Inc.

Published simultaneously in Canada.

*Library of Congress Cataloging in Publication Data:*

ISBN 0-471-41211-2

Printed in the United States of America

10  9  8  7  6  5  4  3  2  1

Winning with Your 403(b) *is dedicated to*
*my four special winners:*
*Charlotte and Isabel Horowitz, and*
*Charles and Catherine Lindsay,*
*with the hope that they will navigate*
*life's financial paths*
*with confidence and success.*

*It is also dedicated to*
*Mary St Cyr,*
*a special friend and extraordinary mentor*
*who gave me support and encouragement*
*when I needed it most.*

# Contents

# Preface

**M**aking the best use of your 403(b) plan means that *you* have to take charge. Like it or not, retirement is about money; the more you put away now, the more you'll have later. And a 403(b) is one of the best possible tools for building a nest egg. First, however, you have to educate yourself about 403(b) options. *Winning with Your 403(b)* is a complete reference guide to everything you need to know about those options—including how to comparison-shop for the right plan and the investments in it. Unfortunately, it's up to you; no one else can or will do the job for you.

# Acknowledgments

I'd like to offer my thanks to David Horowitz for his help with the charts and graphs. And thanks to Mark LoGiurato for introducing me to Peter Krass, author of several excellent books about finance, who, in turn, put me in touch with my exceptional agent, Ed Knappman.

Last but not least, a special thank you to Sedona for just being there.

# Introduction

For many years I thought I had my ducks in a row and my finances under control. I was making monthly contributions to my 403(b), a retirement savings plan for employees of non-profit organizations and following the investment advice of the man who sold it to me. So I wondered why I was seeing such dismal returns in a booming, double-digit market. It didn't take me long to find out. This book is the result of my efforts to unravel the 403(b) mystery.

*Winning with Your 403(b)* is for everyone like me who ever had 403(b) anxiety: those nagging financial doubts that keep you awake at night. "I'm contributing faithfully to my 403(b), but am I contributing enough? My 403(b) has more downs than ups; I have a feeling it could be doing better. . . ."

Those voices in the night were my wake-up call. I knew I had to become more knowledgeable about my 403(b) plan so that I could learn to use it wisely. But try as I might, I couldn't find anyone to explain it to me. There's no shortage of information on 401(k) plans for the employees of for-profit businesses. I could find out everything I ever wanted to know about them in books, magazines, and on the Internet. But with so little information out there on 403(b)s, I realized I was pretty much on my own. So I decided to start at the top.

I wrote to the CEO of Vanguard Mutual Funds, John Brennan, about my 403(b) frustration. I told him I wasn't in the right plan, that I knew there were much better plans out there, but I had no idea how to access them. Mr. Brennan responded with, "The tale you tell about your own experience is not new to us. Far too many teachers take the 'safe option' and invest in programs that are too high cost because they are aggressively sold to them."

How right he was. Investing on your own can feel very scary. Because information about 403(b) plans isn't easy to find and most employers offer little support, it can be comforting to put your trust in the hands of the 403(b) vendor with the reassuring smile. Unfortunately, he'd be the last one to tell you his plan costs too much.

Some of you are probably where I used to be. You know your employer offers a 403(b) plan, you think you should be taking advantage of it, but you don't know how. Others may be at the next level. You were approached by an aggressive salesperson, opened a 403(b) account, but have no idea where it's going. You knew little about the 403(b) concept and perhaps even less about the investments in it. Essentially, you were investing blindly and hoping for the best.

Several years ago I knew a 403(b) plan was probably a good idea, but that's *all* I knew. With retirement looming in my not-too-distant future, I was sure I should be saving more and thought a 403(b) plan could help. But I didn't know how to get started. Then fate stepped in and sent an annuity salesman to my door.

I listened politely as he told me why a variable annuity was the key to 403(b) success and how I could contribute to it. Guaranteed interest? Sure. Growth and income? Sounds good. I didn't ask a lot of questions because I didn't know the right ones to ask, and I didn't want to reveal my ignorance. So I signed on the dotted line, feeling like I'd just become a member of a secret club for retirement mavens.

I still didn't understand 403(b) plans. All I knew was that I now had one and that it was in something called an annuity. At that time, my 403(b) "research" consisted of checking the returns in my monthly annuity statement. It was the early '90s; the stock market could do no wrong. But the returns from my annuity were lackluster, and I was sure I was investing in the market from Mars.

Many negative returns later, I decided I was in the wrong plan, so I stopped contributing to the annuity and went in search of 403(b) plan number two. My first step was to consult a colleague who recommended the company that managed *his* 403(b) plan.

And so began my affair with Mr. Rep from the financial services company. "Help is on the way," he told me. "Franklin Templeton to the rescue . . ." I didn't know he got a commission from the Franklin Templeton mutual fund company; I didn't know Franklin Templeton had only "loaded" funds with extra fees to buy or sell them. Obviously I was still no Warren Buffett.

Like the annuity man, my new knight in shining armor was very persuasive, so once again I signed on the dotted line. Unfortunately, 403(b) plan number two was also not a winner. It, too, produced less-than-thrilling returns and since my rep received commission from each contribution, I seemed to be losing more than I saved.

Even with 403(b) benefits of before-tax dollars and deferred taxes, my piggy bank was beginning to look better and better. At least I couldn't lose money there. My investments outside the 403(b) were fine, but those within it were another story. And I still didn't know what was wrong. I became determined to get to the bottom of this 403(b) business. Either I would master it or I would head straight for Las Vegas.

Going into educator mode, I did some homework and slowly but surely began to peel away the layers of confusion. I hunted for 403(b) reading material and called retirement specialists from mutual fund companies to ask endless questions. But eventually, finally, and amazingly it all came together, and I was no longer at the mercy of commission-hungry 403(b) salesmen. I could do this myself (drum roll!). I could manage my own 403(b).

When I put my third plan into place, I knew I had finally gotten it right. It was a 403(b)7, the "7" meaning my contributions went directly to a mutual fund family. They did not pass go nor get chipped away by big bad salesmen along the way.

*Winning with Your 403(b)* will show you how you can have it all: You can invest before-tax dollars, get respectable returns, and defer taxes on the growth. I finally did it with 403(b) plan number three, and you can too—without going through the hassle of plans one and two.

# CHAPTER 1

# Ten Questions to Ask about Retirement

I started investing in a 403(b) plan several years ago, but it wasn't until I invested outside the plan that I realized my 403(b) returns were much smaller than my other investments. As a retirement savings plan for employees of non-profit organizations, I knew a 403(b) offered tax-deferred investment growth and realized it could be a powerful tool in planning my retirement—but only if I learned how to use it properly. Thus began my 403(b) education process.

Unlike savings deposited directly into a bank, contributions to a 403(b) plan are often made through outside vendors. You have to choose a vendor from your employer's list of options; that vendor then becomes your 403(b) "vehicle" and is responsible for handling your 403(b) account.

Basically, it's a three-step process:

1. Select a 403(b) vehicle.
2. Choose mutual fund investments from available options in the vehicle.
3. Decide on the monthly amount you want to contribute to your 403(b).

Your 403(b) vehicle can be an annuity, a financial company, or a mutual fund family. The vehicle you select may be the most important piece of the 403(b) puzzle.

Because I had no knowledge of the 403(b) process, I opened an account with the first vendor who came along. It was not until much later that I learned the consequences of investing blindly. By trusting the salesperson who sold me a high cost, commission-based plan, I lost many valuable investing years and thousands of retirement dollars. That's why it's so important to ask the right questions and become 403(b) savvy *before* you sign up; you have to understand all the options and make sure your money is invested in the right place from the beginning. You can't recover money lost to inferior 403(b) plans, nor can you get back years lost in the market due to bad investment decisions.

The purpose of *Winning with Your 403(b)* is to help you understand your 403(b) and give you the tools necessary to make the best use of it. I learned the hard way that no one else would do the job for me, and my retirement nest egg will be forever diminished by the years I lost while trusting others to manage it. Here are some of the questions I wished I'd asked before plunging into the 403(b) world without a parachute.

## 1. Am I Saving Enough for a Comfortable Retirement?

If you're a late bloomer like me, you're probably wondering if you have enough time left to save enough money. But just how much *is* enough? There are many variables that determine how much you will need for retirement. Unfortunately, most of them are beyond your control.

You don't know what the economy will be like when you retire; you can't predict your life-span, so you can't know how many years your retirement savings will need to last. You can be sure inflation will take a bite out of your investment dollars, but you don't know how big a bite. You may end up with other sources of retirement income but that, too, is hard to calculate until you get there. With so many beyond-your-control factors, it's pretty difficult to come up with an exact amount that will ensure a comfortable retirement.

One thing you *can* control is how you deal with money *now*. Obviously if you spend every cent and max out your credit cards, you won't have to worry about a comfortable retirement because you won't be able to retire. On the other hand, if you have fairly stringent saving habits, you're on the right track. If you've managed to stash away some savings dollars, the most important thing is where you put them. Are they under a mattress or in a retirement plan, such as a 403(b), where they can reap the benefits of tax deferral and compounding interest?

In order to build a substantial nest egg, you should invest some money in the stock market. Returns from other investment options such as bank savings accounts, bonds, and CDs can't compare to the average stock market return of between 10 percent and 12 percent a year. Yes, stocks can be volatile and there will always be bull and bear markets, but in the long run, stock market investments have proven their prowess in the battle against inflation.

While it's difficult to place a dollar amount on retirement requirements, the more you save and the sooner you save it, the better off you'll be when gold watch time rolls around. Every year that you postpone saving for retirement will shave thousands of dollars off your bottom line. In Chapter 5 you'll read about the "miracle of compounding"—the longer you leave your savings invested, the more time it has to accrue interest; it's that simple. If you invest $2,000 a year for 10 years ($20,000 total) and let it sit there for 40 years or so, your $20,000 will grow to $650,000 (assuming an average market return of 11 percent).

## 2. How Secure Is Social Security?

The big Social Security question is will it be around when you retire? The answer is probably, in one form or another. According to *Worth* magazine, "The Social Security administration can't maintain the current level of benefits past 2030 unless changes are made in the system." Unfortunately, it's too soon to tell what those changes will be.

In the year 2000, maximum Social Security benefits were $17,984, and the average yearly benefit was $12,362. But even at the maximum level, you can be sure Social Security won't provide enough retirement income to support the lifestyle of your preretirement days. Most people envision their retirement as a carefree time for hobbies, travel, and new adventures. It's clear that a supplementary retirement plan is needed to make this vision a reality. "Your Social Security benefits are the foundation on which you can build a secure retirement. You'll need to supplement your benefits with a pension, savings or investments."[1] That's where your 403(b) comes into play.

With its built-in tax-deferred savings and tax-reducing components, a 403(b) plan is the ideal complement to Social Security benefits and/or a pension plan. Unlike fixed benefits from pensions or Social Security, however, 403(b) retirement savings plans are dependent upon decisions made by you, the individual investor. This book was written to guide you through those decisions so that you can take maximum advantage of the 403(b) retirement savings tool.

## 3. Should I Invest in a 403(b), an IRA, or a Roth IRA?

All retirement vehicles offer some form of tax break as an incentive to encourage people to save for their retirement years. The difference between them comes down to allowable contribution amounts and type of tax advantage.

### Regular IRA

A regular IRA (as opposed to a Roth IRA) is a retirement savings plan that allows you to invest a maximum of $2,000 in the mutual funds of your choice. Your IRA savings grow tax-deferred until you begin withdrawing, at which time you will owe taxes on the growth based on your income tax bracket at that time.

### Roth IRA

Such a deal! The gains in a Roth are tax-free forever! You pay tax on the initial investment, but after that the entire growth on that investment is yours to keep. Your dollars compound tax-free until you begin taking withdrawals. Like a traditional Roth, your maximum yearly Roth investment can't exceed $2,000 and contributions to it won't reduce your taxable income. Not everyone is eligible to open a Roth IRA. See Chapter 2 for detailed information on Roth eligibility.

### 403(b) Plan

A 403(b) retirement plan has several advantages. Contributions to it are automatically deducted from your earnings; you don't see them, so you can't spend them. The growth on your earnings is tax-deferred and each contribution reduces your taxable income for that year.

**BEFORE-TAX DOLLAR BENEFIT**

Your 403(b) contributions are taken off the top, reducing your taxable income by the amount of those contributions. For example, if you contribute $8,000 to your 403(b) and your gross salary is $60,000, you'll pay taxes on $52,000 for that year. IRA investments, on the other hand, are made with earned income that has already been taxed and usually won't reduce your taxable income.

**LARGER MAXIMUM CONTRIBUTIONS**

In the year 2000, 403(b) contributions could be as much as $10,500 with even greater allowable contributions predicted for the future. Under present law, you can contribute only $2000 a year to a regular IRA. That $2,000, however, can be invested in the mutual funds of your choice, unlike a 403(b) plan that limits you to the options on your employer's list.

See Chapter 2 for an in-depth look at how a 403(b) compares with other retirement plans.

# 4. Why Do I Need a 403(b)?

Because retirement comes around faster than you think. . . . Social Security and pension plan payments are the foundation for retirement income, while your 403(b) plan is the frosting on the cake.

You need a 403(b) to supplement your retirement income, to help ensure financial comfort throughout retirement. Many retirees find out too late that they didn't save enough and that Social Security and/or a pension plan can't do it all. When your earning years are over, a 403(b) plan can make a significant difference in your quality of life. Remember, there is no turning back if you fail to take advantage of a 403(b) during your earning years.

As an employee of a non-profit, your 403(b) can and should be the cornerstone of retirement planning. By contributing to a 403(b), you're taking an active role in your own future. You choose your 403(b) vehicle and the investments in it. Your money then continues to grow, tax-free, until withdrawal. With compounding interest and a little TLC, your 403(b) will take good care of you during your retirement years.

*Winning with Your 403(b)* will guide you through the process of choosing the right 403(b) vehicle and selecting the funds in it. You'll learn the three categories of options available in most plans:

annuities, financial services companies, or direct investing through a mutual fund family. And you'll learn how to select the funds in that vehicle based on your personal goals and risk factors. Chapter 4 contains detailed information on choosing your 403(b) vehicle, while Chapter 5 presents an overview of mutual funds and how to pick the best ones for your portfolio.

## 5. How Much Should I Contribute to My 403(b) Plan?

You should try to contribute the maximum, because a 403(b) is the best retirement savings option for employees of non-profit organizations. In 2000, the maximum contribution was $10,500 or the maximum exclusion allowance (MEA) based on salary and years of service—whichever was larger. For more information on the MEA, see Chapter 2. Consider contributing the maximum to your 403(b) plan for the following reasons:

- **Tax-deferred dollars**—All 403(b) contributions are tax-deferred. Your contributions grow tax-free until you start making withdrawals at retirement. Every penny of your investment can compound without any tax consequences during the growth phase.

- **Income tax reduction**—Your gross income (total amount of your salary before deductions) is calculated *after* 403(b) contributions are taken out. If you contribute $5,000 to a 403(b), you will owe no taxes on that $5,000 at the end of the year.

- **Forced savings**—With a 403(b) plan in place, you're following one of the basic principles of saving: Pay yourself first.

- **Regular contributions**—The amount you designate goes directly into your 403(b) account at the same time each month. This is called "dollar cost averaging" in which the amount you contribute remains the same, but the number of shares your contributions buy varies according to the current share price. That translates to a win-win situation where you're buying more shares when the market is down and thereby boosting returns when the market rises.

- **Choices**—Unlike many employer-controlled pension plans, a 403(b) lets *you* make the decisions. You select both the 403(b) vehicle and the investments in it.

## 6. What Should I Consider When Choosing Investments for My 403(b) Account?

### Goals

We all hope for financial security and independence in our golden years. The amount you'll need to meet your goals depends on how lofty they are. If, for example, owning a second home is part of your retirement dream, you need to project that into your long-term savings plan.

### Time Horizon

How many years do you have left until your projected retirement? The more years you have, the more aggressive your portfolio can be. You can consider investments that have some risk, but also the potential for greater reward. That's because you have plenty of time to weather the ups and downs of the market and still end up with a substantial nest egg. However, if retirement is in your short-term future, you need to be more conservative. You can't afford to lose assets because there may not be enough time to recover from market plunges. Investment choices based on a timeline of years remaining until retirement can be found in Chapter 6.

### Risk Tolerance

If you're a market watcher and the stock market's roller coaster rides make you queasy, you might sleep better with more conservative investments. Aggressive funds often have high risk associated with high return. Their highs can be stunning; their lows can be devastating.

In the 1990s, for example, double-and triple-digit returns in tech funds were the norm. The "wealth effect" was felt from coast to coast and many investors regarded the stock market as a personal gold mine. Then came 2000 when the economy faltered, many dot-coms died, and funds with triple-digit returns plunged into negative territory. Those who didn't pull out in time saw their investments drastically diminished on a day-to-day basis.

On the other hand, you're taking a risk by taking no risk at all. If you invest only in "safe" investments like bonds or money markets, you're limiting long-term growth potential. A balanced portfolio is the only solution to survival in both bull and bear markets. Read more about balance and how to achieve it in Chapter 9.

### Financial Situation

Are you a saver or does money burn a hole in your pocket? How stable is your job and how long do you plan to work there? What is the net worth of your current assets? If you own a home, car, stock and bond investments, CDs, or savings accounts, you're on the right track to financial security in later years. If your present financial picture is stable and you're not worried about bagging groceries to stretch your retirement dollars, then you can afford to take some risk in your investment choices. But if you're a borrow-from-Peter-to-pay-Paul kind of person, chances are you can't afford to lose money so your investing style needs to be somewhat conservative.

Chapter 6 contains detailed information on planning and saving for retirement by looking at your current assets and future goals.

## 7. What Kinds of 403(b) Plans Are Available to Me?

Most employers offer three ways in which employees can invest in 403(b) plans but take little or no responsibility for educating them about which one to choose. "You're on your own to find out what you should be doing," says one bewildered 403(b) investor.

The three options are:

1. *Tax-sheltered annuity (TSA)*—An annuity is an insurance policy wrapped around an investment portfolio of mutual funds. You choose investment funds based on the choices available within the annuity. Essentially, you're buying an insurance policy and then buying the funds in it. The key word here is "buying." There are two layers of costs: annuity fees and operating expenses for the mutual funds, and those costs are reflected in the form of lower returns on your investment.

   An annuity is tax-deferred, but the growth on 403(b) investments is already tax-deferred; you pay no tax on your 403(b) contributions until you withdraw them. So there's no need to house your 403(b) in an annuity to get that tax-deferral benefit. In fact if you do, you'll pay unnecessary annuity management fees along with mutual fund fees and high surrender fees if you want to get out. And those extra fees can quickly turn positive gains into negative returns.

   The insurance benefits of a 403(b) held in an annuity are

questionable. Chapter 4 will tell you why. Investors can usually achieve far greater returns if their insurance policies and retirement investment plans are kept separate.

2. *Financial Service Companies*—Employer lists of 403(b) options usually contain at least one or two financial service companies like Merrill Lynch or Salomon Smith Barney. A salesman from the financial services company "manages" your 403(b) account; your designated 403(b) dollars go directly from your employer to him; he then sends them to the mutual funds you have selected from his company's choices.

   Don't be fooled into thinking you're getting free—or even good—advice from the financial representative who comes calling. Nothing is free, especially in the investment world. Chances are that rep will steer you into loaded funds that require extra fees to buy or sell them. Moreover, he or she takes a commission off the top of each 403(b) contribution you make. Remember that those extra, unnecessary fees translate into lower returns and a smaller retirement nest egg.

3. *Direct investing*—Many institutions offer direct investing with at least one mutual fund family. That means that your contributions go directly to the funds you select within that family. The only costs to you are the expense ratios (operating expenses) of the funds you've chosen. There are no extra fees such as annuity management charges or salesperson commissions. Your cost is no more than normal fees paid by anyone investing in that fund, inside or outside of a 403(b) plan.

   Keep in mind that all mutual funds charge management fees and there can be vast differences in amounts from one to the other. For example, you can pay as little as .25 percent for an index fund, while an actively-managed fund can have operating expenses of as high as 3 percent. Bottom line: The less you pay in fees, the more you get to keep for yourself.

   Not all employers offer direct investing in mutual fund companies. Annuity companies are very aggressive and have managed to retain the lion's share of 403(b) investment dollars. You can, however, take the initiative to get a mutual fund family included in your employer's list of options. See Chapter 12 for suggestions on how to add new 403(b) providers to your employer's list.

## 8. How Do 403(b) Fund Fees Affect My Returns?

A lot! Paying a mere one percent fee can really add up. That seemingly tiny percent can diminish your returns by as much as 30 percent over a 40-year period. On a $10,000 investment, for example, paying an extra one percent annual fee can cut your nest egg by almost $200,000. That's because the growth of investment dollars depends on the principle of compounding. Suppose you invest $500 in a fund and it grows at the rate of 10 percent a year. In the second year, your $500 investment becomes $550, and the third year you'll see a growth of 10 percent on $550 = $605, based on compounding interest.

Conversely, if you invest $500 and your 10 percent return is diminished by a 2 percent fee, your actual return becomes 8 percent and your investment is then worth only $540 in the second year and $583.20 in the third. Compounding interest works in your favor, while compounding fees work against you. Chapter 5 gives a detailed explanation of this important investing principle.

To determine the fees in your plan, you first have to look at your 403(b) vehicle. If it's a variable annuity, you'll pay, on average, 2.09 percent in fees and expenses. According to fund tracker Morningstar, the average mutual fund costs approximately 1.4 percent to own, and many are even less.

Also, if your 403(b) dollars are being filtered through an investment company, you are paying management fees. When I used a "middleman," one percent of each contribution I made went directly to him (or his company). Moreover, he put me in loaded funds, so I was paying extra fees just for the "privilege" of owning them.

"Stop contributing to the variable annuity in your 403(b) plan," advises investment professional Dr. Don Taylor. "There's a host of reasons not to own an annuity in a tax-deferred account like a 403(b). Continued contributions to an annuity within a 403(b) is a belt, suspenders, boxers, and briefs approach toward investing for retirement."[2]

While you can't control market swings or inflation, you do have a say in the amount of fees you're willing to pay to own an investment. And choosing lower-cost investing can make a significant difference in the size of your retirement nest egg. Chapter 5 contains the tools you need to select low-cost investments for your 403(b) plan.

## 9. Can I Make up for Lost Time?

Probably not, but you can give it your best shot. Investment gurus maintain that you can't time the market; it's time in the market that matters. My late entry into the investment world made me think that a buy-and-hold strategy might not work for me. Many investing years had slipped by, and I didn't want to waste the rest of them with slow-moving, mediocre funds.

Keeping the idea of balance in mind, I took a more aggressive approach with some of the funds in my portfolio. I don't hesitate to move in and out of funds because 403(b) plans allow you to do that without penalty. If, for example, your 403(b) plan is directly invested with a fund family like Vanguard, there's no charge to switch allocations. There's also no charge to move among funds in an annuity; in fact, most annuity companies have 24-hour hot lines that allow you to change your mind any hour of the day or night. 403(b) accounts managed by financial service companies can be a different story. Mutual funds in those accounts will carry loads (if they're A, B, or C shares). In that case, you will be charged extra fees when you buy or sell them.

I would recommend a buy-and-hold strategy for investors who don't want to spend a lot of time monitoring the market. Even if you're willing to curl up with the Wall Street Journal or have a daily encounter with a money dot-com, there's still no guarantee you'll pick a winner. You have a better chance, however, if you make educated investment decisions. That said, if you're intrigued by tech and motivated to monitor, Chapter 8 will show you how.

## 10. Can I Make 403(b) Decisions on My Own, or Do I Need a Financial Advisor?

Never forget that people who call themselves "financial advisors" have to earn a living, and they don't do it by giving free advice. The slick salesperson in the silk suit sitting in the company cafeteria is not your best friend. He's there for the sole purpose of making a sale.

There are many fee-only financial planners who charge a flat fee or hourly rate for investment advice. If you're afraid to invest on your own, you might want to consider consulting one. Fee-only planners can design customized, comprehensive programs that include estate planning, life insurance, tax advice, and so forth. If a fee-only planner sounds appealing, you can learn more about choosing one in Chapter 11. However, my hope is that you won't need a financial planner. After reading *Winning with Your 403(b)*, you should have all the tools necessary for successful retirement investing on your own.

## Chapter 1 Homework

1. Contact your employer for answers to the following questions:

   - Am I eligible for a pension plan?

   - What factors determine how much my pension plan will be worth?

   - Is Social Security deducted from my paycheck?

   - Do you have any literature about 403(b) plans?

   - Which 403(b) vehicles are available to me?

   - What forms do I need to activate my 403(b) account?

2. Go to www.jumpstart.org for a Web site that offers basic, easy-to-understand financial literacy skills geared toward young adults.

# CHAPTER 2

# What is a 403(b) and How Does It Compare to Other Retirement Plans?

## 403(b) Retirement Plans

The 403(b) concept was created by the government in 1954 with a provision added to the Internal Revenue Code; it has since become a major source of retirement income for millions of Americans. The combination of pre-tax dollar contributions and tax-deferred earnings on their growth makes a 403(b) plan one of the best investment bargains.

### Pre-Tax Contributions

Pre-tax contributions to a 403(b) plan reduce your taxable income. For example, if your gross income for a year is $50,000 and you

### A 403(b) Plan Is . . .

A 403(b) plan is a tax-deferred investment program that enables employees of non-profit organizations to save for retirement with before-tax dollars. Contributions to a 403(b) grow and compound entirely tax-free until investors begin taking withdrawals.

contribute $7,000 to a 403(b) retirement account, you will only pay income taxes on $43,000 for that year.

Because each contribution is deducted from your earnings *before* taxes, your take-home pay isn't reduced by the total amount of each contribution. Figure 2.1 shows, for example, that if you contribute $500 a month, your paycheck is decreased by only $360.

The second half of the tax equation is that your investment dollars grow and compound with no taxes due until you begin to withdraw them. Table 2.1 indicates the difference in the growth of an investment held in a taxable versus tax-deferred account. If, for example, you are in the 28 percent tax bracket and invest $2,000 in a tax-deferred account with a 9 percent return, after twenty years that money will grow to $111,500. On the other hand, that same investment held in a taxable account will grow to just $82,500.

It's important to view 403(b) investments as long-term savings. There are stiff penalties for early withdrawals—sometimes from the 403(b) vehicle itself, always from the IRS, who will impose a 10 percent penalty for withdrawals taken before retirement or age 59½.

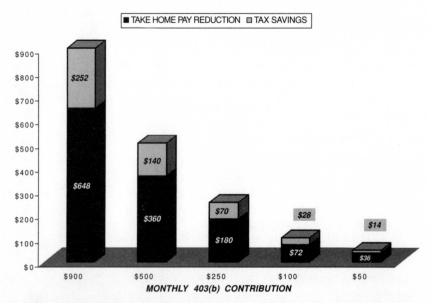

**FIGURE 2.1**   How 403(b) Contributions Can Reduce Your Current Federal Income Taxes and Increase Savings.

**TABLE 2.1** Growth in Value of a Taxable versus Tax-Deferred IRA Account

| Investment Period (Years) | Value of Taxable Account | Value of Tax-Deferred Account before Taxes | Value of Tax-Deferred Account Adjusted for Taxes |
|:---:|:---:|:---:|:---:|
| 15 | $51,400 | $64,000 | $54,500 |
| 20 | $82,500 | $111,500 | $91,500 |
| 25 | $125,100 | $184,600 | $146,900 |
| 30 | $183,300 | $297,200 | $230,800 |

Assumes $2,000 nondeductible annual investment, a 9% return, and a 28% tax rate.

403(b) plans are restricted to mutual funds rather than individual stocks, so it's important to have some idea of how funds work. A mutual fund can hold stocks, bonds, or cash (money markets similar to bank savings accounts) investments. With the exception of index funds, each fund has a manager who's responsible for making decisions about what to buy, sell, or hold. Because few investors have the time to monitor their investments daily, a skilled fund manager can be a major asset.

Mutual fund investing has less risk because a fund holds an assortment of stocks. If one plunges, there are others to compensate for the fall. Monies invested in mutual funds are automatically diversified, and spreading the risk produces a comfort level that may be hard to find when your financial future is riding on individual stocks.

Chapter 5 provides detailed information on mutual funds and how to choose them.

## Three Types of 403(b) Vehicles

Employers contract with mutual fund companies, annuities, and other financial vendors to offer 403(b) plans in three flavors:

1. Contributions that go directly to funds in a specific mutual fund family.
2. Contributions that go indirectly to funds inside an annuity.
3. Contributions that go indirectly to funds offered by a financial services company.

Investors must choose a "vehicle" for their 403(b) from these three options and decide how much money will be allocated to specific funds inside the vehicle. Unlike dollars deposited directly into a savings account, 403(b) dollars can only reach their destination by going *through* an annuity, financial services company, or mutual fund family.

It's important to do some homework before selecting your 403(b) vehicle because not all choices on your employer's list are created equal. Most non-profit institutions don't do a lot of screening; they will accept practically any insurance or financial services company that seeks them out. That often translates to an overwhelming amount of mediocre choices, and weeding through them to find the good ones can be quite difficult.

Corporations, on the other hand, often have only one provider who handles all of their 401(k) accounts. Either the provider or a member of their human resources department is usually available to meet with investors and answer their 401(k) questions. Sadly, 403(b) investors—who are often educators themselves—don't have the benefit of that educational component.

### Mutual Fund Family

If you choose direct investing with a mutual fund family, your allocations will go to one or more funds within that family. You might opt for a single fund or you may prefer a mix of several, such as equity, sector, or index. Your contributions are then distributed among the funds you select using the percentages you have designated. (Chapter 5 contains detailed information about each type of mutual fund.)

A monthly contribution of $200, for example, can be allocated several different ways: the entire amount to only one fund; $100 each to two funds; $50 to four funds, and so on. This division of contributions is called your "asset allocation."

### Variable Annuity

You can also invest in mutual funds through a variable annuity. Taking your 403(b) vehicle on this route will cost you unnecessary fees that compound along with your investment. You'll be paying for the insurance component of the annuity, as well as the costs to manage the mutual funds within it, and those extra fees will wreak havoc on your bottom line.

If, for example, you invest $10,000 in a fund with an 11 percent return, after 40 years that investment will turn into $650,000. But paying an extra fee of just one percent will reduce your return to 10 percent and your $10,000 initial investment will be worth only $450,000 after 40 years. The effect of compounding fees can't be ignored when a mere one percent can mean a $200,000 loss.

Since their inception, 403(b) plans have been structured as an arrangement between the employer, the employee, and an outside provider. That's essentially how annuity (insurance) companies got their feet planted firmly in 403(b) soil. Until 1974, all 403(b) plans, by law, had to be annuity-based. The law changed after 1974, but many people still don't know that, and annuity companies aren't eager to get the word out.

Being able to invest outside an annuity was a tremendous breakthrough for 403(b) investors. Without extra annuity management fees, investment returns could be significantly higher. And without annuity exit fees, investors could move to better 403(b) plans without penalty. Unfortunately, too few investors break free from annuity bondage because they don't know that they can.

### Financial Services Company

A third 403(b) vehicle option often included on employers' lists is financial services companies such as Merrill Lynch and Salomon Smith Barney. Unfortunately, what you won't find on the list are discount brokers like Charles Schwab because they don't handle 403(b) or 401(k) retirement accounts.

A commission-based salesperson from a financial services company will gladly pay you an in-person visit and handle all the paperwork required to set up your 403(b) account. He or she will also give you allocation choices from the mutual fund families his or her company represents.

My second attempt to find the "right" 403(b) plan led me to a small investment company from my employer's list. When I asked the representative for some no-load fund options, I was out of luck because funds without loads don't pay commission. Instead, he put me in loaded funds that charge fees to buy and sell them, and once again I was blindly investing in funds with less-than-stellar returns.

## Contributing to a 403(b)

A 403(b) plan is the best defense against the inevitable evils of taxes and inflation, so it's important to know how a 403(b) works. The more money you invest and the earlier you start, the more you'll have later. Retirement can seem a long way off when you're 25—so far in the future that many people put off making 403(b) contributions for years. The end result, as Figure 2.2 clearly illustrates, is that you can't make up for lost time.

Investor A began investing at age 25 and invested $2,000 a year for

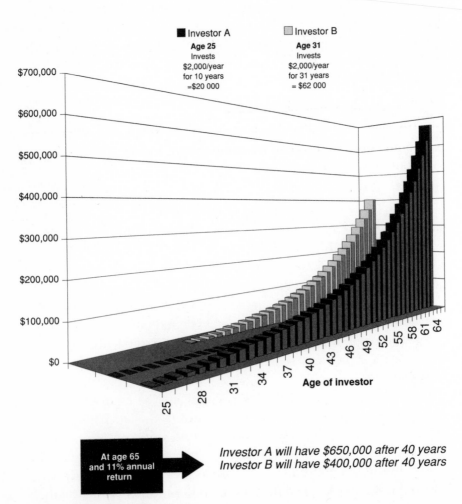

FIGURE 2.2 Compounding Interest.

ten years (a total of $20,000). Even though she stopped investing after that ten year period, by the time she reached 65, her investment had grown to $650,000.

Investor B didn't begin investing until age 35 and invested $2,000 annually for 31 years. His total investment was $62,000, yet when he reached 65, his nest egg was only worth $400,000.

Although Investor B invested more than three times as much as Investor A over a period that was three times longer, getting a late start cost him approximately $250,000. Behold the miracle of compounding!

Contributions to a 403(b) come directly from your salary and are made with pre-tax dollars. They're officially referred to as "salary reduction contributions." Matching employer contributions are possible, but not nearly as common as they are in 401(k) plans.

## Maximum and Minimum Contributions

The IRS sets the ceiling on 403(b) contributions and calculating maximum contributions can be complicated. In 2000, the maximum contribution was the lesser of:

- $10,500
- The MEA (maximum exclusion allowance) based on your salary, years of service, and previous contributions to your 403(b) plan.

To calculate your maximum contribution:

*Step One*

$10,500 maximum contribution

*Step Two*

1. Total years of service with current employer
2. Gross income
3. 20 percent
4. Multiply 1, 2, and 3
5. Subtract all 403(b) contributions from previous years
6. Subtract answer 5 from answer 4

*Step Three*

1. 25 percent
2. Gross income
3. Multiply 1 and 2

The lesser of the three calculations is your maximum contribution (MEA).

Determining your MEA is a complicated process. You may want to contact a tax advisor or the administrator of your retirement plan (i.e., the mutual fund, investment, or annuity company in which your account is held) for help with the calculations.

403(b) accounts usually have no required minimum investment. While fund families would like you to contribute at least $50 monthly, they will accept as little as $10. Of course, it's in your best interest to save as much as you can. A few sacrifices now will yield tremendous dividends later.

### The Bottom Line

Keep in mind that 403(b) contributions are long term; withdrawals can't be taken until retirement or age $59^1/_2$, whichever comes first. You're stashing away money for future security, so don't invest dollars that will be needed sooner. If you withdraw 403(b) assets before the law allows, the 10 percent penalty imposed by the IRS can erase much of the gains you've made.

## Borrowing from a 403(b)

The key to building a substantial nest egg: Keep your retirement money intact. It can only continue to grow if you contribute to your 403(b) on a regular basis and allow the interest to compound untouched. Once you borrow from a retirement account, you're depleting investment dollars and the compounding interest they generate, and it's not easy to recoup those losses.

While it may seem appealing to borrow from your 403(b)—after all, it's your money—think again. Like many loans, it has to be paid back with interest that's not tax-deductible. And, although you don't need bank approval and are repaying the loan to yourself, remember that you're using after-tax dollars to pay it back.

That means you're negating the advantage of your original pre-tax savings and when you withdraw the money at retirement, you'll be paying taxes on it again. Double taxation is not the way to grow a retirement nest egg.

## Playing Catch-up

403(b) investors have a "catch-up" opportunity not available to their 401(k) comrades. Called a "catch-up provision," it allows you to contribute as much as $13,500 annually, going forward, to make up for years in which your contributions were less than the maximum. The only "catch" to the catch-up provision is that you must have worked at the same place for at least 15 years.

## Roll-overs

It's possible to relocate your 403(b) account, but it's not always easy. If your 403(b) is in an annuity, you'll have to pay a hefty penalty to get out early. Other plans, however, aren't as restrictive as annuities and allow you to roll accumulated 403(b) money over to a fund of your choosing. Accumulated 403(b) assets can be transferred *inside* or *outside* your employer's list of options. For example, if you favor Fidelity but have been contributing to Calvert, you're free to transfer. The catch is that only previously-accumulated assets can be moved. Future 403(b) contributions must still be directed to a fund, financial services, or annuity company on your employer's list of approved vendors. Moreover, if your assets are in an annuity, you won't be able to move them unless you have passed the annuity exit penalty phase.

For several years Michelle Cota, a high school teacher in Westport, Connecticut, had her 403(b) contributions sent to two funds in the Strong mutual fund family. Then Michelle began to follow some funds outside her 403(b) plan and was especially attracted to the White Oak Growth Fund. A phone call to Oak Associates confirmed that they handle retirement investment accounts, so she was able to transfer her accumulated 403(b) assets from Strong to White Oak without charge. She could not, however, make new contributions to White Oak because it wasn't on her employer's list of approved 403(b) vendors.

## Withdrawals

Withdrawals from a 403(b) plan are called "distributions." They can be taken no sooner than age 55, if you take early retirement, or age 59½ even if you're still working. You have to pay taxes on withdrawals because they're tax-deferred, not tax-free. When you begin to take them, they will be taxed according to your income tax rate at the time.

## How Other Tax-Deferred Retirement Plans Compare

Not all retirement plans are created equal; in fact, there can be vast differences between them. Table 2.2 illustrates how they differ in many ways including eligibility to participate, amount of allowable contributions, and withdrawal regulations.

### 401(k) Plan

401(k) plans are retirement savings plans for employees of for-profit businesses. A 401(k) is similar to a 403(b) with respect to contributions, roll-overs, and withdrawals. Like 403(b) investors, 401(k) holders decide how much they want to contribute from their salary and where those contributions will go. Their choices can include individual stocks, mutual funds, or stock in the company for which they work.

Many 401(k) employers (approximately 80 percent) offer some type of matching contribution; the majority of 403(b) employers do not. In addition to the benefit of matching contributions, 401(k) employers take care of administering individual accounts and teaching their employees how to use them.

Unfortunately, 403(b) investors are responsible for setting up their own plans. That's because non-profit organizations are offering a service rather than a plan. The 403(b) employer is considered a "conduit" and assumes no risk or responsibility for employee participation. On the other hand, 401(k) employers play a "fiduciary" role. They are responsible for educating their employees, as well as for administering the plan itself.

## 403(b) and 401(k) Common Denominators

Both 401(k) and 403(b) plans were established by the government as retirement savings vehicles. Unlike pensions over which the

**TABLE 2.2 Comparing Retirement Plans**

| | Eligibility | Maximum yearly contribution | Pre- or after-tax dollars | Withdrawing | Advantages | Disadvantages |
|---|---|---|---|---|---|---|
| 403(b) | employees of non-profit institutions | $10,500 or MEA | pre-tax | 10% penalty before retirement or age 59½ | catch-up provision tax deferral | limited choices/few matched contributions |
| 401(k) | employees of for-profit companies | $10,500 | pre-tax | 10% penalty before age 59½ | matching contributions tax deferral | no catch-up provision |
| Traditional IRA | anyone under 70½ with earned income | $2,000 | after-tax | 10% penalty before age 59½ | unlimited investment choices tax deferral | small maximum contribution |
| Roth IRA | anyone with earned income; single filers up to $110,000, joint filers up to $160,000 | $2,000 | after-tax | tax-free if over age 59½ and held for 5 years | unlimited investment choices totally tax-free earnings | small maximum contribution |
| Annuity | anyone | unlimited unless part of another plan | pre-tax or after-tax | varies with type | tax deferral | high fees and exit penalties |

Year 2000

worker has no control, 401(k)s and 403(b)s are structured so that employees make the major decisions, including how much to invest and where to invest it. These plans also share other common characteristics.

### Built-in Deductions

Both 401(k) and 403(b) plans have the advantage of pre-determined deductions. Because investment dollars are automatically deducted, you're "paying yourself first," thus eliminating the temptation to dip into designated savings dollars. For the less disciplined among us, automatic payroll deduction is the best way to save. If you don't see it, you won't miss it.

Even small amounts invested regularly go a long way toward building your retirement nest egg. Suppose you can only afford to sock away $20 a week by eliminating a lunch date or joining a car pool. Table 2.3 shows just how valuable that $80 monthly savings can be. After ten years, you will have saved $10,400. Historically, the market has produced average returns between 10 and 12 percent. With an annual compounding interest rate of 10 percent, your retirement account will be $16,702.42 richer. And if your money earns 12 percent interest, you'll have $18,699.93. Well worth the sacrifice of a few ham-on-ryes!

**TABLE 2.3** Investment of $80.00/Month
Compounded Annually

| YEAR | 10% | 12% |
|------|------------|------------|
| 1 | $ 1,048.00 | $ 1,065.60 |
| 2 | $ 2,200,80 | $ 2,259.07 |
| 3 | $ 3,468.88 | $ 3,595.76 |
| 4 | $ 4,863.77 | $ 5,092.85 |
| 5 | $ 6,398.14 | $ 6,769.59 |
| 6 | $ 8,085.96 | $ 8,647.55 |
| 7 | $ 9,942.56 | $10,750.85 |
| 8 | $11,984.81 | $13,106.55 |
| 9 | $14,231.29 | $15,744.94 |
| 10 | $16,702.42 | $18,699.93 |

### Dollar Cost Averaging

Dollar cost averaging is another benefit of both 401(k) and 403(b) plans. Because contributions are automatic, you're investing the same amount on a regular basis. When the stock market is up, you make more money; when the market is down, your dollars buy more shares. Dollar cost averaging eliminates those impulsive decisions that can lead to buying high and selling low.

Suppose you designated $100 monthly to the Couch Potato fund. If Couch Potato is selling at $25/share in January, your $100 contribution will buy four shares. But in February, if the price drops to $20 a share, that same contribution buys five shares. You now own more shares and those shares equal more money in your retirement account when the price of the fund goes back up.

## Other Retirement Plans

### Variable Annuities

Like a 403(b), an annuity is a tax-deferred retirement savings plan; unlike a 403(b), an annuity has an insurance component. The insurance piece of an annuity guarantees that you cannot lose your original investment (principal). However, it's almost

## Typical Fees in a Variable Annuity

Mortality and expense charge (M & E) 1.1%

Administrative charge .14%

Investment management charge .82%

Contract fee $25–$75 yearly

Expense ratios and/or loads of mutual funds in the annuity (varies)

Exit fees:

| | |
|---|---|
| Years 1–5 | 6% |
| Years 6–8 | 5% |
| Years 9–12 | 4% |
| Year 13 | 0 |

statistically impossible to lose principal in long-term invest-ments such as 403(b) plans, and the additional fees for this dubi-ous "protection" benefit can substantially reduce the growth of your investment.

Variable annuities typically invest in mutual funds (called subac-counts). Annuity investors pay the annuity expenses, combined with the costs of running the mutual funds within it. According to Morningstar, the average variable annuity fund costs 2.09 percent, while the cost of the average mutual fund is 1.4 percent or less. That may not sound like a huge difference, but how those fees add up! On a $10,000 investment, for example, an extra 1 percent can cut your return by 30 percent over 40 years and reduce your nest egg by almost $200,000!

Other annuity costs to consider are the high surrender fees if you want to get out early. An annuity can lock you in for 8–12 years with a sliding scale of exit penalties that can be as high as 8 percent for the first year.

Choosing an annuity for your 403(b) vehicle is a losing proposition that can deplete your nest egg by hundreds of thousands of dollars. Keep in mind that a 403(b) is already tax-deferred. You don't need to pay unnecessary fees for a benefit that's already there. Annuities are a retirement savings tool for employees of businesses that don't of-fer tax-deferred investment plans such as a 401(k) or 403(b).

### Traditional IRA

A traditional individual retirement account (IRA) allows you to con-tribute a maximum of $2000 a year to a personal retirement account. By law, you can have a 403(b) and an IRA. Both are tax-deferred, and contributions to them can be made only with earned income.

Unlike a 403(b), an IRA is funded with after-tax dollars. In some cases, however, IRA contributions may be tax-deductible. If you are single and have a gross income up to $31,000 or are married and fil-ing jointly with a combined income of less than $51,000, you can deduct your entire IRA yearly contribution. An IRA also gives you unlimited investment choices While your 403(b) plan is limited to whatever your employer offers, an IRA lets *you* decide where to put your money.

Flexibility is a benefit of both an IRA and a 403(b). You can't withdraw money from either before retirement or age 59½, but you can change your allocations within them. A discount broker like

Charles Schwab may charge a small fee if you hold a stock or mutual fund in your IRA for less than six months, so check with your IRA holder before making a change.

### Roth IRA

A Roth IRA is similar to a traditional IRA with one major difference: You pay the taxes on each contribution up front but then owe no taxes on the growth of your savings when you take withdrawals. Paying taxes now to enjoy tax-free income later is the biggest Roth benefit; the return on your investments will compound, but the taxes won't. The salary limitation allowance on a Roth is also much higher than that of a traditional IRA. Single filers with gross incomes up to $110,000 can have a Roth; married couples (filing jointly) can contribute to a Roth with an income of $160,000 or less.

While you can have both an IRA (or a Roth IRA) and a 403(b), it's usually wise to max out your 403(b) plan first. With a 403(b), you'll reap the benefits of higher maximum contributions from pre-tax dollars. On the other hand, if your employer's 403(b) plan choices are poor and your income qualifies you for a tax-deductible IRA contribution, that may be your best first choice.

There are, for example, nonprofit organizations that offer employees nothing but annuities for their 403(b) vehicle—no mutual fund families into which they can invest directly. In that case, it makes sense to max out an IRA first. You can then invest any remaining savings dollars in "the best of the worst" of your 403(b) choices.

#### ROTH IRA FEES

You need to remember that fees matter, even in a Roth. If you invested $2,000 a year for 35 years in a Roth IRA account with no fees, you would end up with $372,204 (based on an 8 percent annual return). If that same money is invested with a $30 yearly maintenance fee, however, your return decreases to $366,621. Thirty dollars a year doesn't seem like much, but, with compounding, it can make a significant difference.

## Pension Plan

A pension plan is a traditional retirement plan that pays a fixed amount of money each year to retired employees. The benefits are usually calculated by salary and years of service. Some non-profit organizations, such as school systems, offer a pension plan along with the opportunity to contribute to a 403(b).

There are several fundamental differences between a 403(b) and a pension plan. First and foremost, the performance of a 403(b) account depends on the decisions and contributions of its investors. With traditional pension plans, benefits are pre-determined and employees have no input regarding portfolio purchases.

Pension plans also lack the flexibility of 403(b) accounts. Pensions stay within the company, whereas a 403(b) can be rolled over into another 403(b) plan, or even into an IRA.

By itself, a traditional pension plan probably won't provide enough compensation for a secure retirement and will need to be supplemented with additional dollars—such as those stashed away in 403(b) savings.

## Keogh

A Keogh plan is a tax-deferred retirement savings plan for self-employed workers. A Keogh allows much higher maximum contributions than a 403(b)—as much as $30,000 yearly, and like a 403(b), contributions come from pre-tax dollars. Keogh contributions grow tax-deferred until withdrawal begins, at which time they are taxed as ordinary income.

## Making the Most of Your 403(b)

As a 403(b) investor, making your money work to your advantage means taking charge of it. No one else will do the job for you. Walter McBay of PMG Securities says, "Participants need to educate themselves about their options and they need to speak up. You can lobby your employer for better choices in your 403(b) and, most important, when it comes to retirement investments, you have to comparison-shop."[1]

Every dollar you don't have to pay for fees, loads, or commissions in your 403(b) plan is another dollar with compounding power added to your retirement nest egg. Thus it pays to spend time finding the right plan, rather than spending dollars on unnecessary fees to be in the wrong one.

## Chapter 2 Homework

1. Obtain a copy of your 403(b) vehicle options from your employer.

2. Phone three possibilities that you're considering and ask:

   - Which funds are offered in your plan?

   - What is the minimum monthly contribution?

   - Are there fees or surrender penalties if I choose to leave?

   - What is the procedure for opening an account?

3. Log on to www.vanguard.com for a wealth of basic information on 403(b) plans. Some of the information is Vanguard-specific, but much of it relates to all 403(b) accounts.

   1. Click on: "Specialized Sites"

   2. Click on: "Employer-Sponsored Plans"

   3. Scroll down to: "Answers to your plan-related questions"

   4. Click on: "Read frequently asked questions about 403(b) plans"

      The following topics are covered in this section:

      - Learning the Basics

      - Making Contributions

      - Managing Your Investments

      - Receiving Distributions

# 403(b) Plan Secrets

Employees of non-profit organizations are generally eligible to participate in 403(b) plans, but some don't even know about them. Almost everyone has heard of a 401(k), but mention a 403(b) and you get little response.

403(b) plans were born in 1958 as a retirement investment vehicle for non-profit workers. At that time, 403(b) vehicles were restricted to annuities only. Then in 1974, Congress extended 403(b) options to include direct investing with mutual fund families. Unfortunately, the change had hardly any impact at all.

Insurance companies who sold the annuities certainly weren't about to spread the word; they had cornered the 403(b) market and wanted to maintain their stronghold. The truth of the matter was that, to many, a 403(b) was no big deal. Potential participants knew little about this tool for retirement savings and not much was being done to enlighten them. Information was sparse and if people weren't familiar with investing outside a 403(b), they couldn't begin to understand the complexities of investing within one.

Educators are probably the biggest segment of the 403(b) market, yet Spectrum, a market research group, found that only about half were participating in them. Contrast this to the 401(k) marketplace where approximately 80 percent of eligible employees have a 401(k) plan. There is almost $1.4 trillion stashed away in 401(k) plans, while the amount invested in 403(b)s is only $520 billion.

This chapter looks at some reasons for the lack of interest in 403(b) plans and explores the factors that keep eligible investors away. You'll see that there is light at the end of the tunnel. Some change is happening, slowly but surely. We'll look at some ideas on how to hurry it along.

Ignorance about 403(b) plans runs rampant among employees of non-profit institutions. It's one of the best kept secrets that a 403(b) is the key to a comfortable retirement, an additional source of income to supplement the pension check. Yet 403(b) plans remain shrouded in secrecy, and people are naturally reluctant to put hard-earned dollars into something that confuses them.

## 403(b) Confusion

Tax-deferred confusion is one way people view 403(b) plans. There's even confusion in the name itself: TSA, 403(b), 403(b)7.

### TSA—Tax Sheltered Annuity

An annuity is an insurance policy with a tax-deferred savings component. This is very redundant because 403(b) plans are automatically tax-deferred. Holding a 403(b) inside an annuity is like buying a retirement savings plan inside a retirement savings plan. You're paying double but not getting twice the benefit.

### 403(b)

403(b) is actually the number of the tax code that created this retirement savings vehicle. A 403(b) plan can be held in an annuity, managed by a financial representative, or invested with a mutual fund family.

### 403(b)7

If your 403(b) is a 403(b)7, then your 403(b) contributions go directly to a mutual fund family without a broker, the annuity salesperson, or other financial rep acting as middleman.

According to teacher and 403(b) advocate Dan Otter, "Most educators know the 403(b) as a TSA, or the tax-sheltered annuity. It gives the impression that the only place participants can invest their money is in insurance-based annuity products."[1]

Confused? 403(b) nomenclature is just the tip of the iceberg. Fully understanding a 403(b) is like trying to solve a 5,000 piece puzzle of Kermit the frog. After sifting through 75 variations of the color green, you give up in frustration. Comprehending a 403(b) plan is a similar, multi-layered process. Potential participants first have to find out what it is. And once they find out *what* it is, they have to learn how to use it. Unfortunately, 403(b) plans don't come with instruction manuals.

## Step 1: Pick a Provider

Your employer's list of 403(b) providers can be overwhelming, but basically any name on it fits into one of three categories. Annuities, fixed and variable, is one category, often distinguishable by the word "insurance" in the name.

A second category, "middlemen" consists of commission-based financial reps who handle 403(b) accounts. Middlemen are harder to spot unless they're representing well-known companies like Merrill Lynch or American Express.

Behind door number three are the mutual fund companies to which you can send your 403(b) contributions directly. Clues here will be familiar names like Franklin and Fidelity with the words "mutual funds" somewhere in their title.

So what happens after you've successfully categorized all possible providers? You get to pick one. But how do you know which one to choose?

## Step 2: Choose the Investments

Say you solve the provider piece of the puzzle and actually manage to pick one. Now all you have to do is choose the investments in your plan. First you have to find out which funds are available. Once you do that, you need to select fund categories. Is growth better than value? What's an index fund? What about technology?

If you know nothing about investing, it's hard to pick investments. Major mutual fund companies have dozens of fund choices, but without Mutual Funds 101, selecting an investment mix isn't easy. And going the annuity or middleman route won't help much in making your decision. It's unlikely you can master annuity mutual fund subaccounts in one easy lesson, and the middleman working on commission is sure to steer you toward investments that put the most money in his or her pocket.

## Step 3: Determine the Percentages

You've put the fund choices into a hat and picked a few. Now it's on to the third step: What percentage of your 403(b) contributions will go to each one? It's time to get in touch with your inner risk tolerance. How much market volatility are you comfortable with? What percentage of your investments will you allocate to growth stock funds, bond funds, and money markets? Which allocation will give the optimum balance between portfolio growth and portfolio safety?

It's easy to see why the average investor might give up on a 403(b) plan in favor of U.S. savings bonds. It's so confusing that many people decide that a pension plan will have to do.

## 403(b) TLC

Most of us need some guidance and direction when it comes to making major decisions. And a little TLC is always nice. However, most employers offering 403(b) plans won't provide it, because they're not obligated to.

"Many teachers say they aren't told they qualify for a 403(b). Others say they receive little or no information from their school districts about the plans and feel compelled to pick from a limited menu of investments,"[2] say Mary Doclar and Mike Lee in the *Fort Worth Star-Telegram*.

Non-profit organizations have no responsibility to educate employees about the 403(b) retirement tool because they are acting as conduits without fiduciary responsibility. In plain English, their only obligation is to furnish a list of 403(b) providers and see that employee contributions get to the right place. It's up to you to pick a provider and inform your employer, who will then deduct the specified amount and send it to your vehicle-of-choice. According to the law, that's all they have to do.

Compare this to 401(k) plans. Both 401(k)s and 403(b)s are tax-deferred retirement plans, but that's where the similarity ends. Employers offering 401(k) plans have the fiduciary responsibility that's missing from 403(b)s. In some companies, the 401(k) is in lieu of a pension, so it's pretty important. And because of matching contributions, employers have to maintain some control. Their list of 401(k) providers may be small, but you can be sure the choices on it have been thoroughly researched.

401(k) employers also offer their workers a wealth of information on 401(k) procedures, including that all-important personal contact. Often, there's benefit specialists on the premises to answer questions and give guidance. 403(b) holders, on the other hand, are investing in the dark.

## Tax-Reduction Seduction

There are plenty of salespeople out there ready to jump in and offer their version of TLC. You can be sure that their tender, loving advice is slanted toward the financial products they sell. The first ones through the door are often fast-talking annuity sales reps. But they won't talk about extra annuity fees or underperforming subaccounts, and they'll fail to mention locked-in penalties that force you into annuity bondage for as long as eight years.

The average annuity salesperson pitches tax reduction, telling you that an annuity offers tax-reduced, tax-deferred savings. And the innocent 403(b) investor is seduced into signing on the dotted line, unaware that these benefits are already built into *all* 403(b) plans.

"Teachers are seduced by the tax reduction they can achieve and don't realize the underperforming fee-bloated annuity can more than wipe out that benefit,"[3] claims Washington attorney Carol Calhoun.

The following commentary was written by an honest annuity rep, Mike Diersen, in his article *Annuities vs. Mutual Funds Within a 403(b)*.

> Too often, teachers are influenced into believing that annuities are the only investment option available within their 403(b) plan. The methods of influencing teachers into these vehicles vary from mild to extreme levels. Nevertheless, insurance sales representatives have been extremely effective in taking advantage of teachers in this arena.[4]

Indeed, non-profit organizations are happy to delegate the employee education duty to 403(b) providers. Helping workers understand

403(b) plans is a hassle rather than a priority. So the task is usually left to the first salesperson to arrive on the scene.

It's no wonder so many 403(b) holders sign up for unsatisfactory plans, thereby earning tens of thousands of dollars less than their private sector peers. Considering the minimal amount of information they're given—and the often biased source of that information—it's surprising that there are any 403(b) accounts outside an annuity. "As an insurance-licensed representative, I stand to make a handsome up-front commission, as well as trailing commissions, from selling annuities. But I work under the premise that annuities should only be used as a last resort,"[5] adds Mike Diersen, an annuity sales representative with a conscience.

In 1977, 403(b) assets totaled $422 billion. More than half of that is in fixed annuities, while another $139 billion is in variable annuities. Only $64 million is directly invested in mutual funds. So, if annuity plans are the vehicle-of-choice for many 403(b) investors, then dubious credit must be given to the annuity salespeople who do their job so well.

The TLC investors want shouldn't come from salespeople with a product to sell. That's a conflict of interest, and those who stand to lose are the 403(b) investors. Employees of non-profits are entitled to objective advice for the purpose of information gathering and decision making, not profit making for the vendor.

## Matching Motivators

Employees of non-profits work for a paycheck, not for perks such as company cars or stock options. Nor are matching funds a part of the picture—403(b) contributions come out of their pay and aren't usually matched by employer donations.

Larry Putnam is a hospital director who was eligible to contribute to a 403(b) plan for many years but chose to wait. He says that he didn't pay much attention to the 403(b) plan at first and didn't participate because of "not much spare cash at the time to fund both the regular retirement plan (pension) and a 403(b) plan. Car payment, helping children with college, and wedding expenses didn't leave much money to contribute to a supplemental retirement plan."[6]

Like many living on a fixed income, Larry had to stretch his dollars to make ends meet. He might have been motivated to stretch them a little further if he'd had the added incentive of matching contributions. But his 403(b) plan didn't offer that, so Larry opted not to participate—an easy decision when there are too many bills, limited funds, and a reluctance to invest in something you don't understand.

401(k) plans, on the other hand, often come with a strong motivator in the form of matching contributions. Participants view this as a deal too good to pass up. For example, if your employer offers equal matching, then an investment of fifty cents instantly becomes a dollar. Whether the market rises or falls, you're blessed with a 50 percent return from the get-go. 403(b) plans offer no such allure, no flashing lights telling you, "Listen up. I'll double your money."

Yes, you can reduce your taxable income in a 403(b). You can also take advantage of tax-deferment while your dollars compound. But you have to contribute your own hard-earned dollars without the bonus of matching funds. And when you're struggling financially *today*, it's hard to think about saving for *tomorrow*.

## Mediocre Choices

The choice of funds in your 403(b) depends on the vehicle and what it offers, whether that vehicle is an annuity, a mutual fund family, or an investment company. Unfortunately, 403(b) accounts held in annuities or managed by financial reps from investment companies often have very mediocre choices. My first 403(b) plan was an annuity that appeared to have an extensive selection of funds. However, most of them were "clones" of less-than-stellar loaded funds with high operating expenses.

My second 403(b) with an investment company wasn't any better. I was, again, the not-so-proud owner of mediocre, loaded funds and was forced to pay the commissions of the rep who sold them to me.

## The Dog Ate Your Homework

One of the most successful teaching tools—the use of prior knowledge—is absent from most people's 403(b) learning curve. Teachers use past experiences as a base on which to build new knowledge. Few investors, however, have much previous experience with retirement savings plans and may even lack basic investing skills. How much homework are they willing to do to correct the deficiency?

403(b) investors often have responsibilities that extend beyond their jobs, working in helping professions with all-encompassing obligations. Teachers, for example, rarely leave their work behind at the end of the teaching day; nurses care for patients in life or death situations; social workers are problem solvers of the first magnitude; and members of the clergy reach out to the community on every level.

Living your job doesn't leave much time for other things, and it takes more than a little homework to learn the intricacies of a 403(b) plan and how to manage it. Time and energy are precious commodities usually reserved for priority issues. More often than not, 403(b) research doesn't make it to the top of the list.

Too many potential investors still see 403(b) plans as a mystery. Without adequate information or the incentive of matching funds, there's little incentive to sign up. With unawareness comes uncertainty and again, people are reluctant to commit hard-earned dollars to something they barely understand.

## Effecting Change

The good news is that change is in the air. As 401(k) plans gain more prominence, 403(b)s are also getting greater recognition. "When all is said and done, 401(k) plans are becoming the primary savings tool for Americans,"[7] reports Plansponsor.com, a company that specializes in retirement finance issues. And as 401(k)s become the cornerstone of retirement funding in the private sector, 403(b) plans can't be far behind.

Americans are living longer, envisioning more retirement years, and accepting the responsibility for funding them. Some doubt the security of Social Security. Others want payback for years of hard work in the form of grander retirement lifestyles. Indeed, many factors are simultaneously converging to bring new awareness to investor-funded retirement plans.

### Technology

Thanks to advances in technology, managing retirement plans can be done more efficiently. Information is now stored in a computer, simplifying the entire management process. It's much easier to keep accurate records and track discrepancies. A click of the mouse can quickly trace problems, shortening a process that once took days instead of minutes.

Computer technology has also opened information doors previously inaccessible to the average investor. Just a short time ago, you'd wait for the newspaper delivery to find yesterday's fund prices. Now those prices are available from the Internet on a minute-by-minute basis. You can also check out fund managers, Morningstar ratings, and a fund's major holdings instantly, 24 hours a day.

The Internet also contains a wealth of how-to, where-to Web sites. You can plan your entire retirement, including where to spend it, without ever leaving your desk. Enter the parade of Web calculators. There are calculators galore to help you become a number cruncher extraordinaire. You can figure out how much to save for retirement and how to live on what you have if you haven't saved enough. There are calculators to balance your portfolio and even help you find a place to live that's within your budget.

Financial information Web sites also abound. Major mutual fund families such as Vanguard and Fidelity have a wealth of how-to-invest strategies on their sites. Vanguard, for example, hosts the Vanguard University with everything you ever wanted to know about investing. Morningstar rates funds and gives detailed information about them. Fund Alarm has bells and whistles that tell you when to sell.

Technology has clearly broadened investment horizons and chipped away at 403(b) unawareness with information accessible to all. (You can find appropriate calculators and many other helpful Web sites throughout this book.)

### New Rules and Regulations

Laws concerning 403(b) and other retirement plans are constantly being revised as the federal government seeks to give more control to investors themselves. Limitations on maximum contributions have been raised several times, and Congress continues to be an advocate of individual retirement plans, in part due to concerns about the future of Social Security.

### Media

Television, newspapers, and magazines play an indirect but major role in promoting 403(b) awareness. When technology took off, posting unheard of gains in recent bull markets, the media stepped in to capitalize on this new-found love of Wall Street. "Network executives say the economic boom has created a boom in popular interest in Wall Street,"[8] says Keith Alexander, *USA TODAY* columnist.

Several television dramas and films like *Wall Street* and *Boiler Room* have focused on Wall Street, and commercials are constantly bombarding us with cab drivers buying islands, courtesy of their portfolio's hot performance, or the happy yuppie couple securing their child's future with mutual funds. Suddenly the road to Wall Street wealth is open to the masses and an awareness of all things financial has moved up a notch.

### Hear Ye, Hear Ye

Last but not least are the voices of the people. They're asking questions and demanding answers in 403(b) forums across the land. One investor does some research on the Service Provider Agreement and discovers it's the reason for poor fund choices in his plan. He delves deeper and finds that something called the "Hold Harmless" contract is keeping many excellent mutual fund companies away. Essentially, the hold harmless agreement absolves the employer of any responsibility for mistakes or mishandling of 403(b) accounts and places that responsibility entirely on the 403(b) vendor. While insurance companies selling annuities have traditionally signed that agreement, many mutual fund families are reluctant to do so. They believe the hold harmless agreement should be between employer and employee, not employee and 403(b) vehicle. The investor then shares his findings with a few colleagues and they draft a letter to their 403(b) plan administrators, thus starting a new chapter on 403(b) awareness.

> The employees in my school district have to invest in loaded 403(b) funds because the district insists on using the ASBO "Hold Harmless" contract that makes the purchase of the no-load 403(b) Vanguard funds impossible, writes one newly enlightened investor.[9]

The message is clear: They're not gonna take it anymore! Little by little, one voice at a time, increased 403(b) awareness happens. Take, for example, Grant MacLaren who became a champion for better fund choices in his school system. Grant created a series of handouts singing the praises of no-load mutual funds, gained the support of his peers, and succeeded in getting no-load mutual fund families added to his employer's list of options.

Then there's Larry Putnam, a hospital administrator who relocated and moved to a hospital without a 403(b) plan in place. Fellow employees told him they wanted a tax-deferred retirement plan, so Larry went to work. It took three months to draft a proposal that included 403(b) options with load and no-load fund choices, stock and bond funds, and without a single annuity plan. To Larry, the no annuity option meant no Tax Sheltered Annuity (TSA) people allowed in the lunchroom—banned forever from the hospital cafeteria.

Larry was lucky in more ways than one. His position as hospital administrator gave him the power to get a plan in place quickly. Moreover, Larry was starting from scratch, allowing him to construct a 403(b) to his specifications. It's often much easier to start fresh then to undo damage that's already been done. Larry didn't have to worry about pressure from hard-sell sales reps because he simply refused to let them in.

### Get Tough

Some 403(b) investors who felt their voices weren't being heard decided to get tough. They filed class action law suits against insurance companies who promote annuities as the ideal 403(b) vehicle. An attorney in San Antonio representing 403(b) investors claims that "they don't buy things; they get sold them. And what they get sold is the high-commission garbage."[10]

Other law suits contend that some insurance companies gave cash donations to school systems and acted as volunteer tutors. While there are no legal restrictions against salespeople soliciting business on school property, annuity reps coming in to tutor students seems a bit questionable.

Bringing in an attorney is a last resort measure. But some 403(b) holders become so frustrated by unfair tactics that they feel legal action is necessary. And while these law suits will never have the impact of O.J. Simpson's trial, they can certainly help raise awareness about the inequities in 403(b) plans.

### What You Can Do

There are several ways in which individual investors can lobby for changes in the 403(b) system.

- Ask that the current vendor list of 403(b) providers be revised to include a reasonable number of employee preferences and quality choices.
- Request that a 403(b) workshop be presented and hosted by an independent financial expert who receives no compensation from any vendor.
- Ask for written material explaining 403(b) plans and drawing attention to similarities and differences among the three vehicle options:

Annuity

Middleman

On-your-own

- Require that sanctioned vendors make a full disclosure of all fees related to their investment product.

Employees can make a difference, one voice at a time. And little by little, those voices will get stronger and come together. Through letters, conversations with colleagues, or legal intervention if necessary, employees need to send the message that they're no longer willing to settle for inferior choices. And hopefully, those who administer and control our 403(b) plans will start to listen.

## Chapter 3 Homework

TEST YOUR OWN 403(b) AWARENESS BY ANSWERING THE FOLLOWING TRUE OR FALSE QUESTIONS.

True or False:

1. 403(b) plans must be held in tax-sheltered annuities (TSA).
2. To get tax deferral in a 403(b), you must apply for it.
3. You can contribute to both an IRA and a 403(b) at the same time.
4. You can contribute to both a 403(b) and a 401(k) at the same time.
5. A 403(b) plan is the same thing as a pension plan.
6. Before-tax contributions to a 403(b) reduce your taxable income.
7. You can have individual stocks and mutual funds in your 403(b) portfolio.
8. Dollar cost averaging means that you invest the same amount of money over regular intervals.
9. The three possible 403(b) vehicles are annuities, financial services companies, and mutual fund families.
10. 403(b) investors have a "catch-up" opportunity not available in 401(k) plans.
11. The amount you invest is more important than the length of time it's invested.
12. Distributions (withdrawals) from a 403(b) plan can be taken no sooner than age 50.
13. All 403(b) plans held in annuities are subject to surrender fees if you want to leave the annuity before a specified number of years.
14. You can have more than one 403(b) account but can only contribute to one at a time.

# ANSWERS

1. F
2. F
3. T
4. F
5. F
6. T
7. F
8. T
9. T
10. T
11. F
12. F
13. T
14. T

# Choosing the Best 403(b) Vehicle

**W**hen you're ready to begin saving for retirement in your 403(b), the first decision you have to make is which plan to use. Every 403(b) plan is held in some kind of "vehicle," or holding tank for retirement savings. Your employer has a list of various 403(b) providers who receive your contributions and direct them to the investments you've selected. As you read in Chapter 3, you have three choices of 403(b) vehicles: annuity, financial services company, or mutual fund family.

It's important to understand that saving in a 403(b) is a three step process:

403(b) contribution

403(b) vehicle

Funds you've chosen in the vehicle

In the best case scenario, as discussed in this chapter, you will have three possible "homes" for your 403(b) plan. In the worst case, your employer's options may be only one or two of the following vehicles, and you will have to lobby to add others. (Chapter 12 will help you do that.)

## 403(b) Vehicle Options

### Variable Annuity

With this option, 403(b) contributions are invested in mutual funds inside an insurance policy. Cost to you:

- Annuity fees
- Operating expenses of funds inside the annuity
- Surrender fees

### Financial Services Company

A financial group (i.e., Merrill Lynch, Salomon Smith Barney, etc.) handles your 403(b) account and acts as a "middleman" by forwarding your contributions to the funds you've selected from their choices. Cost to you:

- Commission paid to the company rep
- Operating expenses of the funds you select
- Loads (fees to buy or sell the funds)

### Direct Investing

Your 403(b) contributions go directly to one mutual fund family. They do not go through a middleman nor are they packaged inside an annuity (insurance) wrapper. Cost to you:

- Operating expenses of the funds you select

## Variable Annuity

All 403(b) plans offer an annuity option and here's why they do: In 1958, Section 403(b) was added to the Internal Revenue Code, enabling employees of non-profit organizations to contribute a defined portion of their income to contracts that, at that time, were only available through insurance companies; even today, a 403(b) plan is often referred to as a TSA or Tax Sheltered Annuity. The continued use of the term "TSA" for all 403(b) plans is confusing and supports the misconception that a 403(b) and an annuity are one and the same.

A recent article by Christine Dugas in *USA TODAY* defined a variable annuity as "an insurance policy that is wrapped around an investment portfolio, usually of mutual funds. There are layers of insurance fees on top of mutual fund management fees, so you

shouldn't consider an annuity until you have exhausted other, less ⟵
costly retirement options."[1]

Dugas' message is that 403(b) holders who invest in annuities are paying too much to grow their nest egg inside an insurance policy. They're paying the costs of the policy along with the cost of operating the funds within it (expense ratios). She maintains that you shouldn't consider an annuity unless you have no other 403(b) options because:

1. The tax-deferral in an annuity is automatically part of any 403(b) plan, inside or outside an annuity.

2. You're paying extra for an insurance benefit that guarantees you can't lose any of your principal. However, losing principal is an extremely unlikely scenario in any long-term retirement savings plan.

Here is a breakdown of some of the extra fees you'll face if your 403(b) is in a variable annuity—fees that eat into your returns and take a big bite out of your retirement nest egg.

*Maintenance fee*—the cost for administering your 403(b) annuity account (between $25 and $50 a year).

*Fund management fee*—Annual charge for mutual fund management within the annuity (can range from .5 percent to 2.5 percent). Every mutual fund has a management fee whether or not you buy it through an annuity.

*Mortality and expense charge*—An insurance fee to guarantee that you won't lose principal. You pay this whether or not you decide to annuitize, a process by which you're guaranteed a steady stream of income for the rest of your life. Read more about annuitization later on in this chapter.

*Surrender charge*—The cost to exit an annuity before a specified time period (varies between seven and nine years) can be as high as 9 percent, with gradual decreases based on how long you've been in the plan.

A recent letter in *Mutual Funds* magazine sums up annuity frustration:

My employer just started a retirement plan for us, and I was surprised to see it was a variable annuity with an annual 1.3% fee for the annuity. This fee, of course, is on top of the expense ratio of the mutual funds. That 1.3% annuity fee will amount to tens of thousands of dollars for a young person like me putting in $9,500 annually.[2]

This financially-savvy investor is concerned about her employer's choice of an annuity-based retirement plan—and rightfully so. With an annuity as their only option, workers have no choice but to pay extra fees that diminish the growth of their savings.

### Annuity Pros and Cons

Annuities are complicated. To fully understand them, you have to break them down into bite-sized pieces. Following are some pros and cons about variable annuities as they relate to 403(b) investors.

#### ANNUITIZATION (APPLIES TO WITHDRAWALS *DURING* RETIREMENT)

*Pro*: If you take the option to *annuitize* your account at retirement, you're guaranteed a steady stream of income for as long as you live.

*Con*: You're essentially placing a bet with an insurance company that few people want to make. If you live longer than the amount you contributed to the annuity, you win. If you die before using up your assets, they win—the balance reverts back to the insurance company and your heirs get nothing.

#### TAX DEFERRAL

*Pro*: A variable annuity is tax-deferred. You pay no taxes on contributions or growth until you begin taking withdrawals.

*Con*: A 403(b) is already tax-deferred. You don't need to pay the higher costs of an annuity to get that benefit.

#### PRINCIPAL PROTECTION

*Pro*: An annuity guarantees that you won't lose any of your investment principal.

*Con*: You're paying a lot in extra fees for a benefit that is probably useless. Unless a catastrophe like the Great Depression occurs, it's practically impossible to lose principal in a long-term investment program such as a 403(b).

#### TRANSFERS

*Pro*: You can change investment choices within an annuity easily and without penalty.

*Con*: Switching out of an annuity early can cost you a bundle in surrender charges. You could pay as much as 9 percent to exit in the first year, 8 percent in the second, 7 percent in the third, and so on. On average, you have to remain in an annuity for eight years before the surrender fees disappear altogether.

## FUND CHOICES

*Pro*: Annuities include many funds from which to choose in their plans. At first glance, a new investor may be quite pleased at the number of choices.

*Con*: After careful analysis however, you begin to realize that the choices represent quantity, not quality. A typical annuity offers funds with loads that charge extra fees to buy and sell them. You won't see these fees upfront and may be totally unaware of them. However, they will be reflected in your investment returns.

My first 403(b) plan was an annuity that offered choices from the MFS fund family, among others. They sounded good; after all, MFS is a respected, been-around-for-years name in the mutual fund world. However, MFS offers at least fifty funds, but only two of them were available in the annuity. No high-performing, five-star rated options here!

In an annuity, you'll often have to settle for "the best of the worst." You wouldn't choose them outside the annuity, and with the myriad of excellent no-load funds out there, you shouldn't be limited to below average choices.

## CLONES

*Pro*: Annuities offer what are referred to as clones of mutual funds. In the annuity industry, these are known as "subaccounts" and their attributes can closely resemble the fund they're cloning.

*Con*: Cloned funds may or may not be run by the manager of the real thing and their returns can be vastly different from the original.

According to an article by Walter Updegrave in *Money* magazine, "The Hartford Capital Appreciation mutual fund, managed by Saul Pannell, returned an annualized 31% for three years. By contrast, the Hartford Capital Appreciation subaccount in the Hartford Director Variable Annuity, also managed by Pannell, earned an annualized 16.4%."[3] Subaccounts are affected by the annuity's higher expenses and can include very different holdings in their portfolios, accounting for the large discrepancy.

### THE BEST OF THE WORST

*Pro*: Most annuities have a 24-hour hotline to provide you with the current performance of your investments.

*Con*: It's very difficult to compare the performance of ordinary mutual funds with funds in a variable annuity. That's because annuity performance is calculated in unit values, while mutual funds outside an annuity are measured in dollars.

If your 403(b) plan is in an annuity, it pays to track the performance of the funds you hold within it. If you follow your funds for awhile and find they're underperforming compared to others in the annuity, consider upgrading: buying winners and selling losers. An annuity charges nothing to trade funds, so a simple phone call is all it takes to make a change.

### LIFE INSURANCE

*Pro*: An annuity guarantees that if you die before you begin taking withdrawals, your heirs will receive no less than the total sum you invested in the annuity. However, if you've opted for the annuitization option referred to earlier, whatever is left in the annuity goes back to the insurance company and your heirs get nothing.

*Con*: This isn't much of a benefit. Few long-term investors ever lose their original investment (principal) through long-term investments in mutual funds either inside or outside an annuity, because the longer you hold any investment, the more it usually increases in value.

## *Beyond Annuities*

In 1979, Congress added Paragraph 7 to the 403(b) section, allowing investors to establish 403(b) accounts directly with mutual fund families. This new direct-investing option was officially called a 403(b)7. With the addition of Paragraph 7, 403(b) owners finally had a green light to take the direct investment route. They could send their retirement savings to a mutual fund without having an annuity as the gatekeeper. Again, the insurance companies who sell annuities were not anxious to publicize this. And if employers didn't recognize the change and add mutual fund families to their 403(b) provider list, then workers still couldn't benefit from the new law. Even today, more than 20 years later, many 403(b) owners think tax-sheltered contributions have to be held in a tax-sheltered annuity.

And many employers continue to use the TSA heading in 403(b) literature they give their employees; seeing "Tax-Sheltered Annuity" at the top simply perpetuates the myth that that's all a 403(b) can be.

Don't beat yourself up if, like many others, you succumbed to the sales rep in the silk suit who took you by the hand and said reassuringly, "An annuity is your key to retirement security, so show me your money."

When my annuity salesman came calling, he asked a few questions. "How old are you? Do you think you have an aggressive or conservative attitude toward money?" So I reluctantly confessed my age and told him I liked to shop at flea markets. He then signed me up for a stock and bond combination fund and a guaranteed interest (money market) account. Off I went, annuity papers in hand, thinking I was now on the road to financial security in my senior years.

But later, when I looked at the returns of my funds in the annuity and the performance of my funds in my taxable account, I was shocked at the difference. My annuity was creeping along, while my non-annuity holdings were charging ahead in a raging bull market.

At that point, I plunged into three stages of mourning: shock, remorse, and anger. I mourned my lost returns; I mourned those lost "bull" years, and I got angry enough to do something about it. And you can too. Whether you're a teacher, a nurse, or a minister, you can take charge of your own 403(b) plan. If you've already signed up for an annuity, the following section will show you how to modify that choice.

## Changing Choices

There are three ways in which you can alleviate some of the pain of being in the wrong vehicle.

### 1035 Exchange

If you already own an annuity but are unhappy with its performance, you can roll it over, tax free, into another annuity. That's called a 1035 exchange, because it's under Internal Revenue Code Section 1035. Edie Hoffman, a nurse in Arkansas, was the not-so-proud owner of an annuity from Avanti. Edie did some research and found that she could roll her Avanti annuity over to an annuity from Vanguard without paying exit penalties. So while still tied to the annuity concept, Edie was better off at Vanguard where annuity costs, in general, were lower and she had a much better selection of low-cost funds.

"The least expensive is Vanguard variable annuity, which is no-load, meaning there are no surrender charges, and the annual insurance expenses are only .38% a year,"[4] writes Ellen Schultz of the *Wall Street Journal*.

Some insurance companies offering annuities charge surrender fees even if you transfer to another annuity. If that's the case, you probably won't benefit from an exchange unless you've held the annuity past the specified surrender charge time period.

### Percentage Transfer

Most annuity companies allow you to move 10 percent of your assets every year. You can't withdraw them, but you can transfer them to another 403(b) vehicle with no strings attached. That means you can put 10 percent of your annuity assets into any fund you choose; it doesn't have to be a fund in the annuity or a fund from your employer's list. If your annuity company has this option, ask them to send you the forms necessary to make this transaction.

### Stop Contributing

Simply "freeze" your annuity until the penalty phase has expired. By doing that, you'll avoid the surrender fees and can begin directing new contributions to a better, non-annuity-based plan. By law, you can hold more than one 403(b) account; you just can't contribute to more than one at a time. So if you find a plan that's more appealing, you can reroute your 403(b) contributions to it.

## A Place for Annuities

There is a place for annuities, just not in your 403(b) plan. Because your money is already growing tax-free, it makes no sense at all to pay extra annuity fees that diminish the growth of your returns. While you're still in the accumulation phase—working and growing your assets—an annuity is *not* the place to be.

When you have retired and are no longer contributing earned income to a retirement savings plan, then—and only then—should you consider annuities. An annuity won't provide maximum growth on your assets, but it may be a way to protect them *during* retirement.

When you retire, your 403(b) assets can be converted to an annuity. You can then take the annuitize option that will guarantee a steady stream of income as long as you live. The decision to annu-itize brings peace of mind to some people by ensuring that they can't outlive their assets. But as previously discussed, taking this option also ensures that your heirs will be left with nothing. Annuitization is a bet that few people with loved ones want to make.

## Financial Services Companies

Financial companies like Merrill Lynch or Salomon Smith Barney may also be on your employer's list of sanctioned 403(b) providers. Their representatives are middlemen who act as financial advisors of sorts, recommending funds from the plans they offer and directing your contributions to them.

What's in it for them? Plenty. Not only do they take a fee for manag-ing your money, usually a percentage of each 403(b) contribution, but they also sell loaded funds from which they receive commissions.

What's in it for you? Not much. I've been there, done that. My sec-ond 403(b) account was managed by a rep from a financial services company. He took advantage of my then-ignorance and directed my contributions to Mutual Shares and Mutual Discovery. Both were loaded funds and their performance was less than stellar in a very bullish market.

When I asked the rep why my funds appeared to be sleeping, he accused me of being "performance-driven." He also failed to give me a good reason why he had chosen Franklin funds for my portfo-lio. The words "load," "commission," or "kick-back" never entered our conversation.

"While many representatives do provide good service to employ-ees, some may steer employees into signing up for products with the highest commissions, as opposed to the investments which are best for the employees,"[5] says an article by Alan Feigenbaum entitled *The Fleecing of 403(b) Participants*.

It's up to you to become educated about your retirement plan op-tions. No one can do that for you and there's no shortage of sales representatives who will prey upon your lack of knowledge. You need to know the right questions to ask before committing your re-tirement savings to them. Here are a few:

**Which fund families are you affiliated with?** It's important to know this because a financial services company can only sell the mutual funds of families it represents—and these may very well be lackluster funds with limited potential.

**Are the funds loaded and, if so, will I pay a load coming in, going out, or both?** A front load is an extra charge that's levied each time you *buy* shares in a fund. For example, if you bought shares of Balanced A in BlackRock funds, you'd pay an upfront load of 4.50 percent at the time of purchase. A back load is a fee charged when you *sell* shares. If you bought shares of BlackRock Balanced B, the fee would be 4.50 percent when you sold them.)

**How do you receive your management fee and/or commission?** Usually it's a percentage off the top of each 403(b) contribution you make, in addition to a commission paid by the fund itself.

Once your questions have been answered, it's time to do the math, along with some comparison shopping. At the very least, study the funds your rep recommends. Look at their long- and short-term performance compared to similar funds without loads. There is wide variation in the performance of mutual funds in different categories such as small and large growth and different sectors like energy or healthcare. Obviously, you want to invest in one that excels, rather than one that just plods along. The fund prospectus will tell you if the fund is loaded, its total fees and charges, past performance, and so forth. You can also find that information by visiting the fund family's Web site or by researching the fund on other financial sites such as Morningstar.com or Yahoofinance.com.

Here's how to compare: Suppose you want a growth and income fund and the only one available through your financial services company is Putnam Growth and Income A. Doing some research would tell you that Putnam Growth and Income A (in February 2001) had an upfront sales charge (load) of 5.75 percent and its five-year average rate of return was 13.61 percent. Comparing that to the Vanguard Growth and Income, you'll find that Vanguard had no upfront sales charge (load) and its five-year average rate of return was 18.63 percent.

While we've all heard the disclaimer "past performance is no guarantee of future returns," it is definitely useful information. Without the 5.75 percent load in the Putnam Growth and Income fund, its returns would be almost equal to the Vanguard fund. But because of it, five percent that should be compounding in *your* nest egg is going directly to the Putnam fund family. The danger of loads is that they can severely diminish returns and subtract thousands of dollars from your retirement pot.

You should also be aware of the fact that you're paying extra fees and commissions for a middleman's "advice." That advice is probably not in your best interest because it's limited to the fund families he or she represents. If you conclude, as I did, that you want to take charge of your own 403(b) investments, read on for a step-by-step guide that tells how to do that.

## Direct Investing

By investing on your own, you will eliminate unnecessary fees, loads, and commissions. Look at your employer's list of participating 403(b) vendors for mutual fund families into which you can invest directly. If those options are not on your list, Chapter 12 has suggestions on how to get them there.

If mutual fund families are available, begin by calling their toll-free number and asking for the retirement investing department. They will be happy to answer questions, send information, and walk you through the 403(b)7 sign-up process.

## Step-by-Step Guide to Investing on Your Own

1. Get a list of 403(b) options (participating providers) from your employer.
2. Look for fund families to which you can contribute directly.
3. Decide which funds to buy within the family by looking at:

*Past performance*—returns of the fund for 3, 5, and 10 years (or since the fund's inception)

*Risk rating*—compares a fund's returns to its potential for loss. For example, if a fund is rated: "Return average" and "Risk below average," its returns will be higher than some and less than others in the same category, and the possibility of losing money by investing in this fund is below average when compared to others. (Risk ratings can be found on the Morningstar Web site in their Quicktake Reports.)

*Loads and expenses*—mutual fund operating costs that are passed on to the investor. To keep the most money for yourself, look for funds with the lowest expenses. Continuing to use the two growth and income funds as an example, Vanguard is clearly the better choice with an expense ratio of .37 percent and without loads, compared to Putnam with an expense ratio of .79 percent and a load of 5.75 percent.

*Manager tenure*—how long the current fund manager has been at the helm. Since fund performance depends so much on the investment choices of the manager, think of that person as your personal stock picker and look for a fund with a consistently good track record under the same manager.

4. Track the funds you're considering in the financial section of the *Wall Street Journal*, the *New York Times*, and on the Internet (see for example Table 4.1).

5. Contact the fund family to begin the process of opening your 403(b) account.

## Sample Mutual Fund Table

**TABLE 4.1** Charcate Mutual Fund (Fictitious) as It Would Look in a Newspaper

**FUND FAMILY**

| FUND NAME | TYPE | RATING | NAV | WKLY % RET. | YTD % RET. | 1-YR % RET. |
|-----------|------|--------|-----|-------------|------------|-------------|
| Charcate |  |  |  |  |  |  |
| BIChip | LB | 2/2 | 15 | −0.6 | +5.2 | +14.8 |
| Growth | LG | 4/3 | 9.11 | +1.7 | +10.1 | +22 |
| Tech | ST | 5/3 | 36 | +3 | +14 | +35 |

Using a newspaper financial section to track Charcate Funds TechVal (technology value) will provide the following facts about that fund:

Type of fund (category based on its holdings): ST (sector technology)

Rating (Morningstar): 5/3 (fund is rated a 5 against all types of funds, fund is rated a 3 compared to others in its technology sector),
   Note: 5 is the highest rating possible

NAV (Net Asset Value - cost of one share of the fund): $36

Wkly % return (percent returned by the fund for the current week): +3%

YTD % return (percent returned by the fund from January 1st to the present): +14%

1 year % return (percent returned by the fund for the past 12 months): +35%

6. Find out the minimum monthly contribution.

7. Submit the paperwork, with choices and allocation amounts, to your payroll department.

Before deciding on a 403(b) vehicle, make sure you understand all fees and expenses. If you are investing through an annuity or a financial services company, find out the amount of extra charges for commissions, fees, and loads. The only way to avoid these unnecessary charges is to send your 403(b) contributions directly to a no-load mutual fund family. If your list of approved vendors doesn't include this option, search the list for a plan with the fewest additional charges.

## Summary

The 403(b) vehicle you select is just as important as the mutual funds you choose within it. Fees are fees, whether they come from the fund itself or from the costs to manage it. By eliminating extra fees wherever possible, you'll be able to keep more of your own investment dollars and the compounding growth they generate.

Annuities are a Pandora's box of hidden fees, certain to affect the growth of your nest egg. Investment companies also charge for their services and usually offer a limited selection of loaded funds. That's why your best bet is to bypass the middleman and send your investment dollars directly to a mutual fund family.

### Chapter 4 Homework

1. If you are already contributing to a 403(b) plan, contact your provider for a list of all funds available to you. Use www.morningstar.com to get a "snapshot" of each fund. By doing this, you can see if you've made the best choices or if you should consider switching to other funds.

2. If your 403(b) vehicle is an annuity, contact the annuity company for a list of available investing options. Then compare the unit values of the funds in your annuity. Consider changing funds if the annuity offers better choices than the ones to which you're already contributing.

3. If you don't have a 403(b) plan in place, get a list of sanctioned providers from your employer. Look at the list and weed out the annuity and investment companies. Hopefully, you'll be left with one or two fund families that offer direct investing. Call them for information about which of their mutual funds are available in a 403(b) plan.

# Mutual Funds 101

L ong ago when I began my trip down the financial freeway, I didn't know a mutual fund from a trust fund. I had some bonds that I planned to convert to mutual funds, but I had no idea how to choose from the thousands of funds out there.

To narrow the field I went to a local branch of Charles Schwab, a discount broker specializing in the sale of no-load funds from a variety of mutual fund families. The Schwab salesman couldn't recommend specific funds, but he was able to suggest fund categories. Mutual funds are categorized by the type of stocks in which they invest (sector, growth, value, global, international, etc.), in various sizes (from large growth to micro), and assorted markets (from established to emerging). So I made the big move and bought a large growth fund and an international fund. Watch out Wall Street; here I come. . . .

## A Mutual Fund Is . . .

A mutual fund is a portfolio of stocks, bonds, or other securities owned by numerous investors and managed by an investment company.

I didn't check the managers' tenures; I didn't study the funds' past performance records. When I made my choices, I might as well have been throwing darts at a board (blindfolded). But at least I was now involved in my own hands-on investing experience, and I'm convinced that's the only way to learn. Forget hypothetical portfolios. When real, hard-earned dollars are at stake, you start to get serious.

I followed the progress of my tiny portfolio with the intensity Imelda Marcos used to count her shoes. I even got into the habit of reading the financial section of a daily newspaper. The more I read, the more I questioned and the more I learned.

I read an article about the Miller family in California who had a lot of money invested in technology and I wondered why. Sure I spent a lot of time with my computer, but I never considered investing in it. The Millers were my first exposure to tech sector funds. I was dazzled by the returns of their technology investments and wanted to find out more. And that's how *your* journey into the world of mutual funds will probably begin. Some newspaper headline or magazine article about funds will pique your interest, and you may find yourself browsing the financial shelf at Barnes and Noble.

As an educator, I knew that using prior knowledge and connecting to past experiences were excellent learning motivators. Years of teaching had taught me that students can't learn in a vacuum. For a lesson to be meaningful, it has to have a base, a jumping off point, some connection to their own lives.

Teachers are constantly learning from their students, and it didn't take me long to figure out the power of connecting. Studying the energy crisis, for example, made sense to my class because they could connect it to power failures in their own community.

So while my own prior knowledge about mutual funds was limited, at least I could relate it to past attempts to save money. Those previous efforts became my base. From there I could branch out from the concept of saving money to the notion of investing and growing it.

## Facts about Funds

403(b) plans are limited to mutual funds; no single stocks or individual bonds. There are over 6,000 mutual funds available today, compared to only 500 ten years ago. But don't let that number scare you. As a 403(b) investor, your selection of funds is limited to only those offered through your 403(b) plan. As you read on, you'll see why that can be a good thing.

When you invest in mutual funds, you buy stocks and other equities as a combined effort, pooling your money with others. The fund manager then invests that pool in stocks, bonds, cash, or a combination of each. When choosing a mutual fund, you're essentially selecting a manager to be your financial advisor. He or she has the final say in which companies you will ultimately own shares.

### Mutual Fund Prices

Each share of a mutual fund has a cash value called its *net asset value* (NAV). A fund's net asset value is the cost, in dollars, to buy one share of that fund. If you invest $100 in Fund X, with an NAV of $10, you will own ten shares of that fund. If the NAV of Fund X drops to $8, you still own ten shares, but your total investment is now worth only $80.

You can find net asset values listed in the financial sections of major newspapers and on the Internet. See the homework section of this chapter for the best places to follow your funds.

### How Do Mutual Funds Make Money for You?

1. *Income* through payment of dividends. 403(b) dividends are automatically re-invested.
2. *Capital gains* from profit made when an investment is sold.

#### INCOME

When a mutual fund sells some of its holdings and makes a profit, the gains are passed on to investors in the form of *dividends*. Unlike a *return*, which is what you get when you sell all or part of an investment, dividends represent profits generated and passed on to shareholders. In other words, investors don't have to sell shares to receive dividends. They can be taken as cash distributions to provide a steady stream of income, or they can be reinvested, whereby the investor gives up current income to own more shares. Dividends in a 403(b) plan are automatically reinvested because, by law, you can't draw income from a 403(b) investment until you retire or turn age 59½.

#### CAPITAL GAINS

*Short-term capital gains* are profits made from selling a mutual fund held for less than a year. These gains are then taxed at whatever your income tax rate is for that year. *Long-term capital gains* are profits from investments sold *after* a year's time and are taxed at the lower, long-term capital gains rate of 20%.

The good news is that if your investments are in a 403(b) account, you don't have to worry about taxes of any kind until you begin taking withdrawals. Unlike money in a nonretirement account, your 403(b) gains aren't taxed while they're being earned. Contributions are tax-deferred and can compound without any tax implications.

The bad news is that when you begin taking 403(b) withdrawals at retirement or age 59½, they will be taxed at your income tax rate instead of at the lower capital gains rate.

### How Do Mutual Funds Make Money for Fund Families?

A mutual fund family derives its profit by taking a small portion of each dollar invested. The amounts vary from fund to fund and are distributed among some or all of the following:

Expense ratio

Management fees

12b-1 fee

Loads

#### EXPENSE RATIO

You need to be aware of a mutual fund's expense ratio because it represents your cost to own that fund. The expense ratio refers to the percentage charged by a fund to manage it and can be found in the fund prospectus, newspaper quarterly reports, or on the fund family's Web site. The higher the expense ratio, the greater its negative impact on your returns. The average actively-managed mutual fund has an expense ratio of approximately 1.4 percent, while the expense ratio of a passively managed index fund is often much less. Read more about index funds in Chapter 7.

#### MANAGEMENT FEES

These are costs to investors for managing their money within the mutual fund. The management fee is usually a small percentage of the fund's assets (between .5 percent and 1 percent). That might not seem like much, but consider a fund with a billion dollars in assets. A seemingly miniscule one percent management fee would equal ten million not-so-miniscule dollars. Remember that every percentage point paid out in fees has a negative impact on the return of your investment.

## 12b-1 FEE

In addition to management fees, some mutual funds charge 12b-1 fees to cover the costs of marketing and advertising. The term "12b-1" comes from the section of securities law that allows these fees to be charged. A 12b-1 fee, by law, cannot exceed one percent of a fund's assets. Not all funds charge 12b-1 fees. Index funds, for example, have no need to collect 12b-1 fees because they aren't actively marketed.

## LOADS

Another source of revenue for mutual funds is the sale of class A, B, or C shares. This is a fancy way of referring to the commission paid by investors to own a loaded fund.

**A Shares**—An upfront sales charge deducted from initial investments (ranging from 3 percent–8 percent).

**B Shares**—A back end charge paid by the investor when shares are sold. B share loads can start as high as 6 percent with a gradual decline every year. They usually disappear altogether after six years.

**C Shares**—C shares have no front or back loads, but they have extremely high 12b-1 fees that last as long as you own the fund.

With so many excellent no-load funds out there, it's easy to avoid buying loaded mutual funds with A, B, or C shares. There's little or no reason to own loaded funds with the extra costs they generate.

## THE IMPACT OF FUND FEES

The performance of a fund is clearly affected by its fees. When the market is moving up, investors rally around rising returns and don't focus on fees. Why worry about a few percentage points in extra fees when your fund is reflecting double digit returns? But in a market decline, fees suddenly matter. Suppose Fund X is struggling in a down market and can only manage a 5 percent return. If the fees of Fund X are 2 percent, its net gain will be only 3 percent, and investors come back to the reality that a 2 percent loss is significant.

In 1998, Robert Frick did a study for *Kiplinger's Personal Finance Magazine* to assess the long-term damage of high fund costs. Frick found that "if you dropped $10,000 into a higher expense, long-term growth fund five years ago, you'd have about $1500 less today than if you'd invested in a fund with a lower expense ratio."[1] He calculated that over an even longer period of 25 years, you would have 50 percent more with the lower expense fund, based on a 10 percent return for the high expense fund and a 12 percent return for the low. While you have no say in a manager's picks, you can certainly control the amount you're willing to contribute toward his or her paycheck.

Frick's study sends a clear message regarding the impact of fund fees: In the end, it's the return on your investment that matters. And the return is calculated by subtracting a fund's expenses from its gains. Obviously, the higher the expenses, the lower the returns. In Frick's comparison, over a 25 year period, the fund with the lower expense ratio delivered gains of 50 percent more than the fund with higher expenses. The difference in their returns was only two percent, but oh what a difference that two percent makes when it's compounded.

Never be fooled into thinking that higher fees equal higher performance. Sheldon Jacobs, editor of the *No-load Mutual Fund Investor* newsletter, says that if you invest in a fund with an expense ratio higher than 2 percent, you're twice as likely to be in the lower 20 percent of portfolio performance.[2] And that's because it's practically impossible for a fund to earn gains high enough to offset the damage done by compounding fees over the long term.

The most important message in this book, the mantra that has the most impact on your bottom line is that **over time, fund fees and expenses make a huge difference in your nest egg.** Keeping fees down is one way you have of controlling the performance of your 403(b) portfolio.

Figure 5.1 indicates the impact of a one percent fee on long-term portfolio performance. A fund with an 11 percent return yields $650,000 over 40 years. Subtracting just one percentage point in additional fees lowers that yield to $452,000, showing how painful compounding can be when applied to fees.

### It's Greek to Me

To further complicate matters, the jargon used by the mutual fund industry to explain costs and fees can be very confusing and many investors are completely in the dark about them. One survey found that only about 12 percent of investors knew the difference between "load" and "no-load" funds.

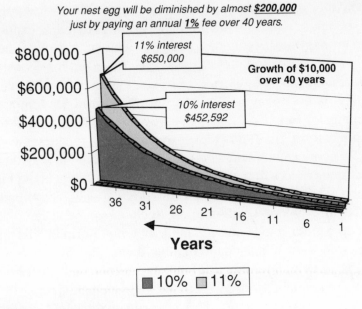

*Your nest egg will be diminished by almost **$200,000** just by paying an annual **1%** fee over 40 years.*

11% interest
$650,000

Growth of $10,000
over 40 years

10% interest
$452,592

$800,000
$600,000
$400,000
$200,000
$0

36  31  26  21  16  11  6  1

**Years**

■10%  □11%

**FIGURE 5.1**  Compounding Pain.
Copyright 1998, *USA TODAY*. Reprinted with permission.

The Securities and Exchange Commission (SEC) has been pushing the mutual fund industry to make expenses easier to understand, but the progress has been slow. In 1999, SEC chairman Arthur Levitt asked the industry if they "really expect investors to understand the alphabet soup of A,B,C,D,I,Y and Z shares—to figure out what combination of front-end loads, contingent deferred sales loads, 12b-1 charges, commissions, and who knows what else they're paying."[3]

## Mutual Fund Advantages

Mutual funds offer several advantages over other types of investments such as individual stocks or bonds. The following are some of them.

### Fund Managers

Mutual fund managers are professionals; I like to think of them as my personal financial advisors who use their expertise to buy and sell equities. Fund managers have access to detailed research information, the analysis of which is their full-time job. Few people who are busy growing a nest egg have the time or resources to do this on their own.

No fund manager can be expected to understand every investment sector, so look for one who has a focus and sticks to it. For example, if a fund invests only in technology, the manager needs to thoroughly understand the perils and pitfalls of that sector. In order to boost the fund's technology-based returns, he or she has to have a handle on which tech is hot today and what's on the horizon for tomorrow. Kevin Landis of Firsthand Funds is a good example of what strong leadership can do. His funds have excellent track records and as a Silicon Valley resident, Landis is strategically situated to stay on top of the latest advances in technology. There are six funds in the First-hand fund family: The Communications Fund, Technology Innovation Fund, Technology Leaders Fund, Technology Value Fund, The e-Commerce Fund, and Global Technology Fund. Kevin Landis takes an active role in the management of all of them.

There is so much investment potential out there and the choices can be overwhelming. How can you find out which company will become the leader in gene mapping? Are you up on the latest in cloning techniques? Do you have a handle on who will launch the next Microsoft? While fund managers may not have crystal balls, I am confident they know a lot more than I do about which companies have the most potential.

## Diversification

When you buy a mutual fund, you're actually buying stock in multiple companies. Most funds own several securities, thereby spreading the risk and distributing investors' eggs in several baskets. To achieve this level of diversification on your own, you'd have to invest a lot more money in multiple securities so that if one plummets, your entire portfolio won't go with it. You can see how diversified a mutual fund is by looking at the companies in which it invests. Fund families list major holdings in the prospectus; that information can also be found on their Web sites or by accessing Morningstar (www.morningstar.com).

## Record Keeping that Won't Strain Your Brain

Keeping track of your mutual fund investments is easy thanks to statements sent out courtesy of your 403(b) vehicle. This "portfolio summary" lists the funds you own and their past and present monetary values. It should also show the total contributions you've made to each.

If you buy multiple funds through a broker such as Charles

Schwab, Jack White, Waterhouse, and the like, your investment results are combined into one statement. Investments made through individual fund families require a separate statement from each, while information on investment activity in your 403(b) comes in one monthly statement from the 403(b) vehicle.

### Sixty Years of Safety

In 1940 Congress passed the Investment Company Act to regulate the mutual fund industry. Since that time, no fund has ever gone under. The same cannot be said for banks and insurance companies. Their demise can and does occur because too many investors decide to cash in their holdings at the same time. Failure of those institutions is often the unfortunate result.

The safety of a mutual fund is further increased by the fact that its investments are held by a custodian from an organization independent of the fund company. Your money is completely protected and can't be used for any purpose other than that for which it was intended.

### Risk Tolerance

While Chapter 8 explains risk tolerance in detail, it's mentioned here as yet another advantage of mutual fund ownership. With their infinite variety of choices, mutual funds offer many different levels of investment risk.

Conservative investors can choose bonds, money markets, or a combination of stocks, bonds, and cash securities. Risk takers, on the other hand, can opt for aggressive growth stock funds that invest in smaller companies with potential but without proven track records. In the mutual fund world, there truly is a fund for everyone.

## Mutual Fund Choices

Mutual funds come in three flavors, based on whether they invest in stocks, bonds, or cash reserves. A fund's investments reflect its goals and objectives. Stock mutual funds, for example, focus primarily on present and future growth. Bond funds concentrate on providing income, and cash investments offer stability to preserve investor assets. Some mutual funds such as "balanced" and "asset allocation" funds attempt to meet all three objectives by combining stock, bond, and cash investments in a single fund. The attributes of each type of mutual fund are discussed below.

### Cash

Mutual fund cash investments are generally referred to as money markets. They carry very little risk, protect your principal, and pay a higher rate of interest than ordinary savings accounts. If held in a taxable nonretirement account, most money markets allow you to write checks against your balance. So what's the downside?

The return on cash investments can be very low—so low, in fact, that it may not even keep pace with inflation. You can effectively preserve your assets, but you will see only minimal growth. Investors may choose to invest in money markets for the following reasons:

*A money market can serve as a "holding tank."*

Suppose the market is bouncing around and you're not sure in which direction it's going. The beginning of the twenty-first century, for example, took investors on a wild see-saw ride; one day the Dow was up; the next day it was trumped by Nasdaq. In times like these, people often park their investment dollars safely in a money market account until the coast is clear and confidence in the market is restored.

*A money market brings balance to a portfolio.*

You won't earn a whole lot in one, but you won't lose either. And if your other investments are risky and include sector, aggressive growth, microcap, or emerging market funds, a money market component protects at least part of your assets.

*A money market offers asset protection during retirement.*

Suppose your working days are over, you're finished growing your nest egg, and now you want to protect it. A money market account is the perfect place to do that.

### Bonds

Bonds can be purchased from the government, government agencies, or through normal investing channels like mutual fund families, brokerage houses, and financial services companies. Essentially, a bond is an IOU. You're loaning money with the promise that you'll get your principal back, plus interest, by a given date. For example, a $1,000 Treasury bond with a 6.25 percent coupon rate will pay $62.50 annual interest.

Bonds usually have higher returns than cash investments and are considered less volatile than stocks. However, bond prices do fluctuate with the rise and fall of interest rates and they offer no guarantee against loss.

Rate of maturity is one way to differentiate between different types of bond funds. *Short-term bonds* will mature in two or three years. Those with a maturity date of seven to ten years are known as *intermediate bonds*, and *long-term bonds*, on average, will reach maturity in ten to twenty years.

Suppose that ten years ago you invested $10,000 in a long-term bond fund with a fixed interest rate of 7 percent. At the time of maturity, ten years later, you would get your original investment—all $10,000 of it—back. Factoring in a 3 percent rate of annual inflation, however, the purchasing capacity of those dollars is greatly diminished. By the time you get your original investment back, its actual worth (buying power) is only $7,374. And as for the 7 percent annual interest you received on your investment, that equates to just 4 percent after subtracting 3 percent inflation.

If bonds sound appealing but becoming a bond expert isn't your goal in life, you might consider no-brainer investing in a total bond market index fund—one fund that represents the performance of all bond fund types. For a list of bond index funds, see www.indexfunds.com.

If you're in the "accumulation phase," the time when growing your nest egg is a top priority, a portfolio of only bonds and/or cash investments isn't advisable. Save those safety nets for the retirement years when you want to hold on to those assets you've worked so hard to accumulate. But even while accruing assets, you need a bond component for balance. When stocks are falling, bonds act as a buffer and continue to pay interest when other investment types are in negative territory.

## Bond Types

*Municipal bonds*   Issued by local governments to fund public projects like parks and roads. Municipal bonds are exempt from federal taxes and also state taxes if you live in the state where the bond is issued.

*Mortgage bonds*   Mortgage-backed bonds issued by GNMA, Government National Mortgage Association (Ginnie Mae) and FNMA, Federal National Mortgage Association (Fannie Mae). These government-sponsored agencies pool home mortgages and sell them to investors. Should a home buyer default on the mortgage, the government protects the bond investor from any loss.

*Government bonds*   U.S. Treasury securities commonly known as savings bonds.

*Corporate bonds*   Issued by corporations to raise capital.

### Stocks

When you buy stock, you're buying part ownership in a company and will be affected by the rise or demise of its profits. Mutual fund managers invest your money in assorted stocks from different companies. If you buy shares in the Bjurman Microcap Growth Fund, for example, you are actually buying stock in 86 companies including Cryolife, Haven Bancorp, and Ameripath, among others.

Stocks offer the greatest potential for high returns; they also offer a higher level of risk. Stock investments move up and down with the whims of Wall Street, whispers of the federal reserve chairperson, or fluctuations in the economy.

### Total Return Funds

When a mutual fund invests in a combination of asset classes, it's called a *hybrid, equity-income, asset allocation,* or *balanced fund.* A typical total return fund might include a combination of any of the following: large, medium, or small growth fund; large, medium, or small value fund; assorted bond funds; index funds; or international funds. Investing in more than one asset class in the same fund appeals to investors seeking to build a balanced portfolio under one umbrella.

The big plus of asset allocation funds is that they're diversified to minimize risk. For example, when the bond component of a portfolio falls, the stock portion often rises, and vice versa. By limiting risk, however, these fund combos also tend to limit returns as well.

## More about Stock Funds

You now know that if you buy mutual funds, you're selecting cash, bonds, stocks, or balanced funds, which are a combination of all three.

The greatest returns, however, can usually be found in mutual funds that invest in stocks. Since a 403(b) portfolio should contain a core of stock funds, it's important to have some knowledge of stock fund categories. Your decision to make a particular fund part of your portfolio will depend, in part, on which of the following categories it belongs to:

## Fund Categories

Growth

A growth fund buys stocks whose earnings are growing at a rapid rate. Growth fund investors generally don't receive dividend checks because the profits are reinvested for further growth. This fund class is particularly sensitive to market highs and lows and is best suited for long-term investments such as 403(b) plans.

*Growth and Income*

These are mutual funds with primary holdings in blue chip stocks from established companies like Coca Cola and General Electric. Growth and income funds work well for investors seeking steady conservative long-term growth.

*Aggressive Growth*

Not for the faint-hearted, aggressive-growth mutual funds invest in companies with the potential for serious growth spurts. This approach, however, leaves aggressive-growth funds open to wide pendulum swings: They can skyrocket in a bull market but fall apart when the bear appears. If you are young and have many investing years remaining, aggressive growth funds can be a good option. Because of their volatility, however, they aren't recommended as core portfolio holdings.

*Equity Income*

Like balanced, hybrid, and asset allocation funds, equity income funds invest in a mixture of stocks and bonds, focusing on companies that pay consistent dividends. Investors often favor these funds because their returns can be much less erratic in a down market. On the other hand, they also don't rise dramatically in a market that's moving up.

*Value*

Stocks become part of a value fund when they're perceived as being bargains. Value funds tend to move in the opposite direction from growth funds: When growth funds rise, value funds often fall.

*International*

These funds consist only of equities outside the United States. They represent exposure to broader, more diversified markets but can be extremely volatile. Like all mutual funds, international funds can also be defined according to their objectives. Consequently, you can invest in an international value fund, an international growth fund, and so forth.

*(Continued)*

*Global*

Unlike international funds, global funds spread their investments over the entire world, including both American and foreign holdings.

*Emerging Market*

An emerging market fund is made up of stocks from companies in developing nations. Countries in the Far East, Asia, South America, and Eastern Europe are often the focus of emerging market funds. These funds can be very volatile; investors can strike it rich, or lose it all.

*Sector*

Sector funds invest in particular segments of the economy such as finance, healthcare, technology, or energy. Because their focus is so concentrated, sector funds can be extremely volatile and depend, to a large extent, on economic cycles. Market timers can lose the most money in sector investing because they tend to jump in when a sector is hot—and expensive—and, unfortunately, on the way out. . . .

*Socially Responsible*

If you're concerned about saving the planet or standing up for your beliefs, you can make socially responsible funds a part of your portfolio. This fund category invests only in companies that avoid tobacco products, prohibit animal testing, and use recycled materials—you get the picture.

Those who want investments that promote Judeo-Christian principles can invest in the Noah Fund (www.noahfund.com), a mutual fund that doesn't support entertainment companies that produce pornography, companies involved in alchoholic beverages, or healthcare corporations that sanction abortion. For animal lovers, there's the Humane Equity Fund (www.humanefund.com), a fund from Salomon Brothers Asset Management that shuns investments in companies that harm animals or their habitats. Few investors, however, are willing to sacrifice fund returns for social responsibility. When considering a fund that reflects your moral fiber, it's still prudent to look at its operating costs before buying.

*Index*

Indexing is yet another way of categorizing mutual funds. Index funds don't have active managers and invest only in stocks that are part of a specific index, such as the S&P 500 or the Russell 2000. Actively-managed funds have managers whose goal is to beat the index. If you invest in an index, whatever that index gains will be your gain, no more and no less. Chapter 7 has extensive coverage of index funds and how they compare to funds that are actively managed.

# Mutual Fund Awareness

While mutual funds have become the investment-of-choice for many—and the only choice for 403(b) holders—they do have some drawbacks.

## Too Big

*Beware of funds with rapid growth spurts.* A fund that takes in too much money too fast can become unmanageable. In their haste to spend dollars that keep pouring in, fund managers may not make the best decisions when buying new equities. That can have a very negative impact on a fund that, when smaller, was performing nicely.

Vanguard Chairman John Bogle cautions that "funds that have created a record of remarkable returns at relatively small asset levels have a pronounced tendency to lose that edge when they get too big."[4]

In mutual fund investing, bigger is definitely not always better. Hard to imagine, but having too much money to invest can be detrimental to a fund's wealth. For example, when the Janus Twenty fund grew too fast, its managers had to move investment dollars quickly. Perhaps they were investing in unfamiliar territory; perhaps they had to make hasty decisions without enough research time. Whatever the reason, the end result was a major decline in the performance of Janus Twenty. When considering purchases for your portfolio, look for fund families that are astute enough to close funds to new investors when they become too big.

## Too Many Choices

The average investor can be overwhelmed by the myriad of mutual fund choices. With so many players on the field, how can you possibly know who's on first? 403(b) plans narrow the choices considerably because investors can only choose from the funds available in their plan.

However, if you're a 403(b) holder who still feels confused by too many choices, there is a way to narrow them down. Beware of slick funds that try to stand out with a gimmick. For instance, the Pauze Tombstone fund's claim to fame is its focus on investing in tombstone companies and coffin makers. Not surprisingly, its returns have been consistently poor. Because your 403(b) is a retirement plan and should be solid, you'll probably be better off if you bypass funky funds and stick with the tried-and-true.

### Moving Managers

Fund performance is often a good indicator of the manager's expertise. If a fund has shown positive returns under the same manager for an extended period of time, then it's a sure sign that the manager is good at his or her job.

Mutual fund managers have been known to jump ship if something better beckons. And that can be your cue to move on too, because a fund is only as good as its manager; he or she makes the decisions about what to buy and sell. A fund's performance is bound to falter if it has a new manager every six months, so try to avoid funds with a high rate of manager turnover.

## Pick of the Litter

Now that you're aware of the pluses and pitfalls of mutual funds, here is a list of suggestions to help you pick the best.

### Fund Selection Suggestions

*Look at long-term performance.* Yesterday's darlings can become tomorrow's duds, so look beyond short-term performance. Examine a fund's three-, five,- or ten-year track record to see how it stacks up over the long term. In 1998/1999, for example, the Munder NetNet fund invested in technology stocks and realized returns of 143 percent. Following that dramatic performance, the fund fell into the minuses the following year—an unfortunate but all too common riches-to-rags investment story.

*Monitor the manager.* Since a fund's performance is closely tied to its manager, never underestimate his or her power. Look for a manager whose fund returns have been consistent over the long term. Every stock, fund, and sector can have down times; that's why you need a fund manager who's in it for the long haul and knows what to do during volatile periods.

*Don't forget the senior citizens.* As a 403(b) investor with retirement assets at stake, the core of your portfolio should be funds that have been around for awhile. Brand-new funds have no long-term performance records to follow, no manager's tenure to track. Rather than taking a risk with the new kid on the block, keep the bulk of your investments with the tried-and-true senior citizens of the mutual fund world.

*Diversify your assets.* Mutual funds used to offer one-stop shopping and investors simply chose a balanced or asset allocation fund. However, the mutual fund market has become as broad as the stock market itself. Its diversity extends to fund choices based on size, sector, and objective and today's risk-conscious portfolios are no longer limited to one fund. A balanced portfolio with diversified assets is still the best formula for successful investing.

*Consider sector funds.* For a stake in the new economy, look at sectors like biotech and financial services. Sector funds focus on small groups of companies and can make trades easily. They also enable fund managers to do what they do best: intense research on one segment of the economy. Just remember that investing in sector funds can be a trade-off. Their limited focus is definitely risky, but they can also deliver high returns if the manager is savvy.

## Summary

When selecting funds to meet the objectives of your 403(b) portfolio, you need to consider the following:

*Your goals*
Are you trying to save enough to retire in twenty years or to buy a home in two?

*Diversity of fund class*
Each new fund you buy should add to the overall balance of your portfolio.

*Manager*
The most stable funds are often those with an experienced manager who's been there for a while.

*Performance*
Look at the fund's performance over the past three, five, or ten years and compare it to similar funds in its category.

*Fund fees*

Keep in mind that a fund's expense ratio, 12b-1 fees, and/or loads can have a major impact on its returns.

Finding good mutual funds shouldn't be an emotional decision. Armed with the right research, you will be able to make objective choices for your 403(b) portfolio. How to create that perfectly balanced portfolio is the topic of Chapter 9.

## Chapter 5 Homework

1. If your 403(b) vehicle choice includes fund families to which you can invest directly, call them to request literature on their 403(b) mutual fund options.

2. Track possible fund choices before deciding which to buy:

   www.morningstar.com

   www.mfmag.com   Click on: Portfolio Tracker

   www.quicken.com   Click on: Fund Finder—This site allows you to specify criteria such as expense ratio, fees, and performance. You tell it what you're looking for, and it will suggest funds that meet your criteria.

3. For general information about bonds and bond mutual funds, go to: www.investinginbonds.com

# Planning and Saving for Retirement

The word "retirement" should be displayed right next to a neon sign flashing "investments." Without investments (or a trust fund) retirement can be pretty bleak. Picture soup kitchens, multiple part-time jobs, subsidized housing. Investments are a sure way to brighten that picture.

Technically speaking, investing means buying assets now that will increase in value and be converted to income later. To some, the concept of investing is synonymous with "sacrifice"—deferring momentary pleasure for the realization of future goals. Investing takes planning, hard work, and a lot of patience. Contributing to your 403(b) plan is a significant piece of the retirement puzzle.

## Setting Goals

The first step in retirement planning is to decide where you're going. Simply wanting a "comfortable" retirement is too vague. You need to have specific goals in order to create a workable plan. Whether you want a retirement home on the beach or a penthouse apartment, a cabin cruiser that sleeps six or a cabin in Vermont, *you* define the terms. How much will you need to make that major purchase? How much will it cost to live that life? And how long will you be living it?

Modern medicine has managed to control or eliminate many life-threatening illnesses. You may already be taking vitamin supplements and/or cholesterol-reducing medication. Hopefully you're doing some form of regular exercise and limiting your fat grams. This focus on health paves the way to a longer life span. If you retire at 65, you can probably expect to live another 20 years or more.

The goals you set, along with an evaluation of your present and projected financial situation, will help determine a savings program that's right for you. Harry Dent, author of *The Roaring 2000s Investor*, maintains that "the most important dimension of your financial plan should not be merely how you can survive through retirement, but how you can create the lifestyle and life work you most desire. Such freedom comes from the security of being able to live off of your financial investments."[1]

## Calculating Your Goals in Dollars

A rich fulfilling retirement is more than just having enough money. It also means time for relationships with family and friends, as well as time for hobbies and interests that enrich your days. Money, however, remains a necessary evil in this equation. Without enough of it, you may have to spend your golden years as a member of the senior work force.

Once you have established your goals, the next step is to decide how much money you'll need to realize them. Many retirement calculators are available on the Internet to help you do just that. I have included some of the best sites in the homework section at the end of this chapter.

Table 6.1 gives a rough estimate of how long you can expect your savings to last. For example, if you have $200,000 in retirement savings, you can withdraw approximately $2,000 a month for 10 years (assuming a 5.5 percent annual yield compounded quarterly). If that money has to last for 20 years, your monthly withdrawal will be about $1300.

Some financial planners believe you'll need approximately 75 percent of your pre-retirement income during retirement. Others calculate it as high as 100 percent. Yes, you may have paid off your mortgage and no longer need to include commuting costs in your

**TABLE 6.1** How Long Will Your Money Last?

Here's how long you can expect your savings to last, making the following monthly withdrawals.

| Starting with this much | You can withdraw this much each month for 10 years | You can withdraw this much each month for 20 years | You can withdraw this much each month forever |
|---|---|---|---|
| $ 50,000 | $ 535 | $ 337 | $ 222 |
| $100,000 | $1,069 | $ 674 | $ 443 |
| $150,000 | $1,604 | $1,011 | $ 665 |
| $200,000 | $2,138 | $1,349 | $ 886 |
| $250,000 | $2,673 | $1,686 | $1,108 |
| $500,000 | $5,345 | $3,372 | $2,216 |
| $750,000 | $8,025 | $5,055 | $3,330 |

Based on 5.5% annual yield compounded quarterly.
*Source:* American Express.

budget, but you may actually spend more money during retirement, especially if you have big dreams such as travel to exotic places or helping your grandchildren through college.

After you retire, your taxes will certainly be less. You won't be paying Social Security or Medicare taxes because those taxes apply only to earned wages, not to distributions from retirement plans. On the other hand, you will probably increase medical and dental expenses. You have to be 65 to qualify for Medicare and if you retire before that, you might be responsible for your own health insurance. This cost varies from state to state; in New York, for example, a monthly health insurance premium can be as high as $350 per person.

Home maintenance and repairs may also require a larger chunk of your budget if you hire others to do the work. And spending more time at home often means an increase in the cost of utilities, including heat and air conditioning. Long distance phone bills can also become more costly when you have extra time to keep in touch.

The good news for late starters is that some financial gurus don't believe you need a million dollars to fund a comfortable retirement. The Employee Benefit Research Institute claims that approximately 80 percent of current retirees have annual incomes under $22,000. Much of that money comes from Social Security and pension plans, but it also could be easily generated with less than $300,000 in savings (i.e., 5 percent interest yields $15,000 annually).

According to Dr. Paul Farrell, personal financial columnist on *CBS Marketwatch*, "Americans are brainwashed into believing that the only way you can protect yourself in this brutal world is to do everything you can to retire with a million bucks. That's the message we hear over and over again from Wall Street, financial planners, the internet, and the financial press."[2]

If you're tired of power lunches, nouvelle cuisine, and sport utility vehicles, and if you look enviously at people who live in the country and grow peaches, you probably aren't a candidate for the millionaire lifestyle anyway. Dr. Farrell claims that there are people "living like millionaires all over America, in Montana, New Mexico, South Dakota, Pennsylvania, Vermont. They know what's important. A question of values, of attitude. Anyone can have it, no matter how small the bank account."[3]

With a minimal amount of retirement income, it's possible to find joy in those aspects of life not related to money. And contrary to what Wall Street would like us to believe, retirement provides the richness of time—wealth that can't be measured in monthly cash flow.

No matter which retirement lifestyle you seek, you still need to save. Lawrence Summers, former Secretary of the Treasury, worries that Americans don't save enough. He thinks we're spending our way through a booming economy. Summers started a national program to make "saving" a household word and hopes to sell the concept of saving to the American public. He also sees automatic enrollment in job-related retirement plans as one way to solve the spending problem.

"Individuals are much more likely to save when saving is made easy," says Summers. "That's one reason why employer-sponsored retirement savings plans have become America's most popular savings vehicles."[4]

The National Partners for Financial Empowerment (NPFE) feel that Americans at all levels of income have problems understanding the basics of personal finance—and that makes them susceptible to poor financial choices such as the abuse of credit cards. "Many low and moderate income families lack access to financial services, and personal debt levels and bankruptcy filing rates are high. The inability of many households to budget, save and invest prevents them from laying the foundation for a secure financial future."[5]

The mission of the NPFE is to help Americans improve their personal financial circumstances through nationwide workshops targeting specific population groups. The organization hopes to bring greater financial awareness to students, young adults, retirees, and immigrant communities. Indeed, there are few among us who wouldn't benefit from increased financial literacy.

## Savings Depend on What You Earn *and* How Much You Keep

As you set your savings goals, you'll need to make many decisions. To have more money later, you may need to spend less now. If, for example, one retirement goal is to pay off your mortgage, moving to a smaller house now may help make this goal more attainable, as the following scenario illustrates.

Assume you retire, pay off your mortgage, and continue to live in your $300,000 home, mortgage-free. If you think you're now on Easy Street, think again. A mortgage-free home can still cost up to $20,000 a year to run, a total of $400,000 for a 20-year retirement.

Instead, suppose you sell that home and scale down to one that costs half as much in a less expensive location. A maintenance-free condominium can be very appealing when you're ready to retire the lawn mower and sell the snow blower. In the condo scenario, you put away $150,000, free of capital gains tax, and also reduce your yearly household expenses. Moreover, being the astute investor that you are, you invest that $150,000 and get a 10 percent return. That can go a long way toward the cost of running your condo throughout retirement.

At the end of this chapter, you'll find a Web site that compares the cost of living among different locations. For example, if you're currently a resident of Darien, Connecticut living on $100,000, you need an annual income of only $55,690 to enjoy that same lifestyle in Santa Fe, New Mexico.

## Creating a Savings Plan

The sooner you start saving and investing, the better. Money that remains invested and untouched has the power of compounding behind it. However, before you can sit back, relax, and watch your money multiply, you have to have a savings plan in place.

### Early Birds (Twenty to Thirty-Somethings)

Lucky you if you're getting a head start on retirement savings. With time on your side, the journey to retirement will be easier and require fewer sacrifices because you're blessed with the gift of compounding. In other words, the earlier you start, the less you'll need to save.

Unfortunately, few under-thirty-somethings learn that valuable lesson. By sacrificing a sun roof, dining out less, or taking a more modest vacation, you can grow a sizeable nest egg. Of course when you're 25, saving for retirement is not a high priority; show me a baby boomer who thought he or she would ever get old.

If you're an early bird investor, you have the advantage of time—time to weather the ups and downs of the stock market, time to create a sensible savings plan that won't impact on your present lifestyle. All you need to do is save regularly, invest wisely, and watch your money grow through the magic of compounding.

Rather than investing a lump sum once in a while, you're far better off if you invest a set amount *regularly*. (This is called "dollar cost averaging.") To do that, you have to think of saving as a fixed expense, like paying your phone bill. And therein lies the beauty of your 403(b) plan.

A 403(b) takes the money right off the top of your paycheck. What you don't see, you don't spend. It's also tax-deferred, enabling compounding to work unencumbered. Your savings dollars can feed on themselves without any tax bites that eat up the profits. Try to contribute the max to your 403(b). Trust me, you'll be glad you did.

No one can deny that being young is a good thing. As a young investor with time on your side, you can have more fun with your investments. You don't have to be too conservative because you've got many investing years still on your horizon. You have time to go in and out of sectors as they go in and out of favor, time to ride the stock market roller coaster and recoup from its plunges.

Being young, however, is no excuse for failing to diversify. Diversification is important for everyone, because no stock or stock fund can perform well *all* of the time. You need to have a balanced portfolio in which your money is distributed among a range of equities, from aggressive growth to bond funds.

### RECOMMENDED MIX FOR EARLY BIRDS

    70 percent stock funds

    20 percent bond funds

    10 percent cash (money market, CD, etc.)

See Chapter 9 for detailed information on how to create a balanced portfolio at any age.

## Late Bloomers

Hello! It's time to play catch-up. According to financial planner Gary Schatsky, "Retirement is not built on play money, but planned money."[6] So if you're getting a late start, start planning *now*. Set some goals. Look at your investment time horizon, and read the "Stashing Cash" section of this chapter.

As a late starter, you don't have time on your side, so you can't afford to let your money languish in underperforming investments. You have to make it work harder and smarter. The main thing to remember is that it's never too late. While you can't get back lost years, you can begin to make every year count from now on. By starting now, you still have choices, but if you never start saving, your retirement may have to be subsidized by the charity of your children. Following are three things you can start doing now to catch up.

### 1. CLIFF NOTES INVESTING

Give yourself a crash course in finance and investing. You can't play any kind of investment game without a basic understanding of the rules.

Charlotte, a teacher in Detroit, enrolled in a 403(b) plan when she was 47. Charlotte had gotten a late start in her teaching career and worried that the small retirement pension she'd get wouldn't be enough. She also had a timid approach to investing, typical of people whose lack of financial knowledge keeps them on the stock market sidelines. But Charlotte wanted to get wiser, so she joined an investment club. She pooled her money with the other members and learned the basics about investing for growth and return.

Charlotte applied her newly-acquired financial knowledge to her 403(b) investments and began to see a significant improvement in her portfolio's performance. By adding a touch of technology and a hint of healthcare to her fund mix, she doubled her money in less than five years. Through hands-on experience with her investment club, Charlotte gained the confidence she needed to expand her 403(b) holdings and broaden her investment outlook.

To find an investment club in your area, contact the National Association of Investors Corporation at www.better-investing.org/clubs/clubs.html. This site offers "just about everything you need to successfully operate an investment club" including "frequently asked questions about investment clubs," articles about family investing, and even some memos from the Beardstown Ladies—a group of financially-savvy senior citizens who took the investing world by storm until some major miscalculations burst their bubble.

## 2. READ AND COMPARE

Don't be afraid to discuss 403(b) returns with co-workers. Ask them what they invest in and how their investments are performing. You can be sure that if their funds are doing well, they'll be glad to share. But remember that you'll still want to track the fund's performance yourself.

It's also important to read something financially-based everyday. If you're not yet ready for prime time and don't consider the *Wall Street Journal* "beach reading," then start small. The Money Section in *USA TODAY*, for example, usually has several articles related to investing. You can read it in hard copy or access *USA TODAY* on the Web (www.usatoday.com). Every article you read, every conversation you have, will broaden your investment knowledge and add to the financial foundation you're building.

## 3. GET ON THE RIGHT TRACK

Late bloomers without enough years in the market may worry about too slow a pace. Trying to make up for lost time, they can be tempted to buy only aggressive funds and abandon the traditional buy and hold philosophy in favor of a "get rich quick" scheme. Unfortunately, no one—not even Warren Buffet—knows when to jump in or when to cash out, when a hot fund has peaked or a downtrodden fund is on the road to recovery.

Because it's virtually impossible to time the market and win, it makes good sense to get back on a track that includes a healthy core of blue-chip stock funds.

## Somewhere in the Middle

So is there something between buy and hold and just plain gambling? I know there is; I've been there. There are many funds with long-term track records that far exceed Granny's Global Growth. If you believe, for example, that technology is the place to be, you can certainly find lots of good no-load funds with a tech focus.

According to NoLoad Fund*X, you should always try to upgrade. They define "upgrading" as "hold funds as long as they do well, then move to the current winners when the original choice falls behind."[7] Remember, one of the advantages of owning a 403(b) is the freedom to switch in and out of funds without paying a penalty. If you're not happy with a choice, it's easy to switch.

My personal upgrading strategy consists of maintaining a "hit list." I follow my least favorite funds for six months or so, give them a fair chance to redeem themselves and then ditch them if they don't. Suppose I bought XYZ Technology two weeks before the market had a major correction with tech funds getting a significant splash of red ink. In this scenario, I'd fasten my seat belt, stay on the roller coaster, and hope for the best. I most certainly wouldn't panic and rush to sell XYZ Technology at a loss.

A minister from Indiana wanted to upgrade, hoping to plump up his meager nest egg. So he consulted a financial advisor who suggested he invest $100,000 in new economy securities like tech, biotech, and telecommunications. The timing was right and six months later his investments had grown to $170,000.

Knowing that the minister had only $110,000 in his retirement account, I would have had a hard time giving him that advice. I probably would have told him to "go for broke" with no more than $30,000 of his savings. And therein lies a major investment conflict.

If you think you've saved too little too late, should you take an all-or-nothing approach to investing? Why not take the chance? It probably won't be enough to retire on anyway. The opposing theory says: Hold on to your assets; the closer you are to retirement, the less you can afford to lose. In the world of investing, there is no one-size-fits-all philosophy. You have to find strategies that work for you. Chapter 10 can help you do that.

## Stashing Cash

Once you have a savings plan in place, the next step is finding the dollars to fund it. In a 403(b), those dollars are automatically deducted before you ever see them. But you may have to do some real number crunching in order to maximize your contributions.

Start by taking a hard look at what you're spending. No financial plan can be implemented without some sort of budget. In addition to calculating your monthly bills, consider keeping a spending journal. For many, this is the moment of truth, the reality check, the I-can't-believe-I-spent-$50-on-gourmet-muffins epiphany.

Carry your journal around for a month or so and write down every cent you spend. You've heard this before: You'll be shocked at the amount of money that gets frittered away. An amazing amount of would-be wealth is spent at the corner drugstore.

And while you're logging your spending, remember that shopping creates needs. You didn't know how much you "needed" that solar alarm clock until you saw it at KMart. Obviously, the less you shop, the more you'll save. A walk in the park or a trip to the library works wonders on the budget.

Financial expert Paul Farrell thinks you should approach saving with nothing less than military discipline. "The way you think about investing better change. Dramatically. Your money's gotta last a long time after you retire. Think survival. Get tough. Be aggressive."[8]

Even if you're presently saving nothing, you can easily sock away between ten and twenty percent of your salary—and I did say "easily." Once you've done the math and figured out how much you're spending, you can begin to map out a plan. Here are a few suggestions to get you started:

## Money Saving Suggestions

*Minimize restaurant meals.* Bag lunches and hearty homemade breakfasts can keep $5 or more a day in your pocket. That's $150 a month, $1800 a year. If you take that tidy sum and compound it at 10 percent a year for 10 years, you'll have $31,317 more in your retirement fund.

*Limit plastic purchases.* Unless you pay your credit cards in full each month, you're paying an exorbitant amount of interest on the unpaid balance. For instance, if you have a credit card interest rate of 16 percent and maintain an unpaid monthly balance of $300, at the end of the year you will have shelled out an extra $48 in fees. Switch to cash and you'll no longer be paying $40 for a $30 sweater. Moreover, using cash instead of plastic may help you conclude that you really didn't need that sweater anyway.

*Lay off loans.* Like credit cards, the interest on loans will wreak havoc on your attempts to stash away cash. Every penny you pay in interest now is that much less for your retirement fund later.

*Pay yourself first.* This isn't new news, but no section on savings suggestions would be complete without it. If you wait until the end of the month to save, you'll end up with nothing. Most people spend their way through a typical month—and we're not even talking December. They *intend* to sock away something at the end; we know all about those good intentions. . . . One way around this is to think of yourself as a bill that must be paid when the first of the month rolls around. Your 403(b) plan does this for you automatically with prearranged deductions from your paycheck.

## Now that You've Found It, Where Do You Put It?

Hopefully, the strategies you implement will free up extra dollars for retirement savings. The next question then becomes: Where can you invest them so they will grow and multiply?

### The ABCs of Retirement Planning

A. Invest in tax-deferred accounts first: 403(b), IRA, or Roth IRA.

B. Invest primarily in stock mutual funds.
   Stocks and stock funds have greater growth potential than bonds during your "accumulation" phase.

C. Invest in no-load funds with low fees.
   Avoid funds that charge fees to buy or sell them. Just say no to funds with loads.
   Compare expense ratios (management fees).

The basic rules of retirement investing haven't changed:

- Save as much as you can.
- Start as early as you can.
- Contribute the max to a tax-deferred retirement account.

However, they can be tweaked a bit . . .

Suppose you're stuck in a 403(b) plan with dismal fund choices. Of course you'll still want to take advantage of its income tax reduction and tax-deferred features by contributing to it. But you might also consider investing outside your 403(b). When you retire and begin making withdrawals from your tax-deferred account, you'll be taxed at ordinary income tax rates. However, non-retirement accounts (investments through a brokerage house with after-tax dollars) are taxed at the lower capital gains rate (20 percent in 2000) and that benefit can have a very positive effect on your returns.

While it's true that your money grows tax-deferred in a 403(b) account, remember that you have to surrender a percentage of those gains to income tax when you start to withdraw.

## Other Sources of Retirement Income

An ideal retirement package includes Social Security, personal savings, a pension plan, and/or a tax-deferred investment program like a 403(b). Figure 6.1 gives approximate percentages of these retirement income sources. The figures will vary depending on your personal circumstances.

### Social Security

During your working years, you pay Social Security taxes that enable you to receive monthly income at retirement. See the homework section at the end of this chapter for a Social Security Web site to help calculate your potential benefits.

Social Security was never intended to be a complete source of retirement income. Rather, it should be thought of as a foundation on which to build. And while it's rumored that Social Security money is drying up, Congress is implementing strategies to assure that Social Security will be there, in some form, when you retire.

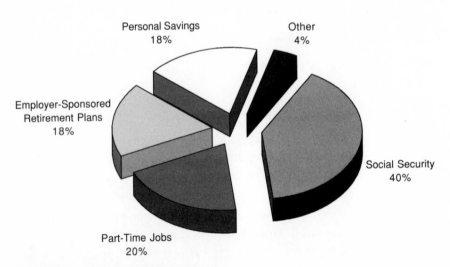

**FIGURE 6.1**   Sources of Retirement Income.
*Source:* U.S. Social Security Administration, 1998.

Table 6.2 gives an estimate of Social Security benefits through 2015. Because exact amounts are based on salary and years of employment, the chart shows only average and maximum benefits. A person retiring at age 65 in 2010, for example, can expect an average of $19,517 annually, up to a maximum of $30,341.

If you are over 25, you will automatically receive an annual statement of your projected future Social Security benefits. The mailing also contains an insert for workers 55 and older with everything you always wanted to know about Social Security but were afraid to ask. It answers questions such as what happens if you begin to take benefits before full retirement age or continue to work while receiving them.

### Personal Savings

This is usually money held in taxable accounts such as money markets, CDs, savings bonds, bank savings accounts, and other investments outside your 403(b) plan.

### 403(b) Plan and/or IRA

Both of these are considered long-term investments in which taxes on the growth are deferred until you begin taking withdrawals.

### Roth IRA

A Roth IRA is a long-term investment, similar to a traditional IRA, with one major difference: You pay the taxes upfront on your yearly contribution but pay no taxes, ever, on the growth. Chapter 2 has detailed information about both IRAs.

**TABLE 6.2** Estimated Annual Social Security Benefits (Single Retiree at Age 65)

| Retirement Year | Average | Maximum |
| --- | --- | --- |
| 2000 | $12,362 | $17,984 |
| 2005 | $15,423 | $23,262 |
| 2010 | $19,517 | $30,341 |
| 2015 | $24,910 | $39,503 |

*Source:* U.S. Social Security Administration.

### Employment

A part-time job is another way to supplement retirement income. Because retirement is no longer viewed as a transition from a swivel chair to a rocking chair, many retirees plan to continue working in some capacity—but they want to do it on *their* terms. They look forward to being productive without the stress, to blending eighteen holes of golf with a part-time job that's personally rewarding.

## Security from Planned Savings

A secure retirement doesn't just happen; it comes from planned dollars. Taking the time to plan ahead will ensure the payoff you expect after many long years as a nine-to-fiver. Set your retirement goals now and make a plan to achieve them. And keep in mind that sometimes the hardest part is sticking to that plan when life gets in the way, when designated savings dollars get diverted to a set of braces, an unexpected illness, or an emergency car repair.

A survey of almost 2000 households found that those who committed their financial plans to paper saved a lot more than those who just talked about them. Goals that are written down tend to be more realistic and more achievable. It also helps to create separate long and short term "wish lists." That way you'll define allocations for immediate needs, as well as projected amounts for future expenses.

Your short term "wish list" might include

- Buying or upgrading a computer
- Taking a trip to visit loved ones
- Replacing an old car with more reliable transportation
- Taking piano lessons and buying the piano to go with them
- Saving for a child's college tuition
- Stashing away some emergency cash

Long term "wishes" may be

- Saving enough for a secure retirement
- Buying a second home
- Contributing to the costs of a grandchild's education

- Making a significant contribution to a favorite charity
- Helping with the down payment on a child's first home
- Accumulating a travel fund for vacations and family visits
- Owning your own business

Today's retirement world is far more complicated than the "good old days" when the end of a career was marked by a gold watch and a guaranteed pension plan. We need to be much more financially informed than our parents' generation; the burden is on us to save for our own retirement.

It's important to remember that retirement planning is just that—a plan—and we all know that plans, like good intentions, are subject to change. There will always be detours on the road to retirement. When you get off track, simply get back on the road as soon as you can and continue the journey.

## Chapter 6 Homework

Consult one of the following Web calculators to help determine how much you'll need to save for the retirement you want.

www.mortgage-calc.com

1. Click on "How Much to Retire"
   With minimum input, you can get a rough estimate of how much money you'll need to provide a certain income during retirement.

2. Click on "IRA/401(k)/403(b) Calculation"
   Calculates how many tax-deferred dollars you'll need to save for a desired stream of income during retirement.

Mutual fund sites with especially good retirement calculation tools:

   www.fidelity.com

   www.troweprice.com

   www.vanguard.com

www.ssa.gov
This site contains an overview of how Social Security works along with several calculators to help you determine projected benefits.

   Click on: Top 10 Services

   Click on: 4. Compute your own benefit estimate.

*(Continued)*

You can also call 1-800-772-1213 and ask for Form SSA-7004: *Request for Earnings and Benefits Statement*.

To find an affordable place to retire, compare the cost of living among cities:

www.money.com

1. Scroll down to "Retirement"

2. Click on: "Best places to retire"

3. Click on: "Cost of living calculator"

# Managed versus Index Funds

**M**ost mutual funds have the common denominator of being actively managed by a fund manager. Active managers use research, market forecasts, and their own judgment when selecting investments for the funds they head. Index funds, on the other hand, are a different breed; their holdings mirror the holdings in a particular index like the S&P 500, and, as such, don't need monitoring by a manager.

The objective of an index fund is to simply match the performance of its target market index. Unlike managed funds, index funds don't attempt to *outperform* any segment of the market; rather, they simply *represent* it. Their goal is to *match* the performance of some piece of the stock market, not to exceed it.

## An Index Fund Is . . .

An index fund is designed to deliver, with only minor deviations, the same returns as the index it tracks, minus annual expenses.

Actively-managed funds, on the other hand, are run by managers who try to beat the returns of a particular index. They buy and sell funds in a particular category and strive for maximum performance with the highest returns. In a charging bull market, astute managers are often able to surpass index fund performance. Bear markets, however, are a different story. When many segments of the economy are faltering, an actively-managed fund tends to go down with the sinking index.

Hopping aboard an index ship can be a pleasant, predictable ride. Your index fund won't provide the heart-stopping thrill of a tech stock gone wild, but you'll be able to sleep at night and won't have to spend your days worrying about fund performance. You'll simply do as well as the market does, based on the market sector your index fund represents.

Index funds are the brainchild of Vanguard funds founder, John Bogle. Wanting to give investors a break, Bogle created the passively-managed, low-cost index fund. Bogle believes that because investors can't predict market returns, they should focus on what they *can* control: fees and risk factors, both of which are minimal in an index fund.

According to Vanguard, "an actively managed fund's performance is less predictable than an index fund's. The active fund has the opportunity to be among the best-performing funds, but it can also post disappointing results when compared with market averages."[1]

## An Index Fund for Everyone

There's a place for Index funds in every portfolio, so it's important to understand how they work. The stock market contains a variety of indices that track different segments of the market. Standard & Poor's 500 index (S&P 500) replicates the performance of 500 established blue-chip corporations. These are large-growth stocks with high valuations. For tracking the performance of small companies, many rely on the Russell 2000 index, while the progress of the entire stock market can be tracked using the Wilshire 5000 index. Technology investors find the Nasdaq 100 a reliable index for tracking "new economy" stocks.

Table 7.1 gives the performance of six major indices. During the

**TABLE 7.1** Index Returns

|                          | 3 Years  | 5 Years  | 10 Years | 15 Years |
| ------------------------ | -------- | -------- | -------- | -------- |
| Index Name               | '97–'99  | '95–'99  | '90–'99  | '85–'99  |
| Standard & Poor's 500    | 27.55    | 28.54    | 18.20    | 18.92    |
| Wilshire 5000            | 26.13    | 27.11    | 17.61    | 18.12    |
| Barra Large-Cap Growth   | 35.52    | 33.64    | 20.60    | 20.38    |
| Barra Large-Cap Value    | 18.88    | 22.94    | 15.37    | 16.96    |
| Russell 2000             | 13.08    | 16.70    | 13.40    | 13.23    |
| NASDAQ Composite         | 46.62    | 40.17    | 24.50    | N/A      |

time periods shown, the Nasdaq Composite outperformed the S&P 500 and the Wilshire 5000, and large cap growth has outperformed large cap value. However, it must be emphasized that these relationships can and do vary from year to year, and it's important to remember that past performance is no guarantee of future returns.

More ways to invest in an index are springing up every day. Unit investment trusts (UIT) are the newest form of index investing. A UIT is like a mutual fund in that it invests in a variety of equities. Unlike a mutual fund, however, a UIT trades like a stock. UIT investors control when and what they want to buy or sell. The advantage over mutual funds is that capital gains taxes are triggered by the investor, not by the fund manager. For example, when a fund manager sells a profitable holding, that creates a taxable event and the burden of those taxes is passed on to you. With a UIT, however, the decision of whether to sell an investment and incur a capital gains tax is up to you.

You can often tell a UIT investment product by its strange name. Technology buffs can buy "Qubes" (QQQ) that invest in the Nasdaq 100. People interested in tracking the S&P 500 index through a UIT can look for "Spiders" (SPDR), and those with rich taste can buy "Diamonds" (DIA), a UIT that invests in the 30 companies making up the Dow Jones Industrial Average.

The average 403(b) investor doesn't need to complicate life with Qubes, Spiders, or Diamonds. These exotic index trackers aren't usually among 403(b) options, and their freedom from capital gains tax benefit doesn't apply to 403(b) investors anyway. All 403(b) contributions are tax-deferred until they are withdrawn, at which time they're taxed at ordinary income tax rates.

## To Buy or Not to Buy (Index Funds), That Is the Question

According to John Bogle, "People are investing very heavily in the S&P 500 because they are always looking for the hot fund, but where index funds find their finest fruition is in the total stock market (Wilshire 5000 index). That is the theory of indexing: Own the market and by the time we take out our tiny costs, you will beat most participants."[2]

Figure 7.1 compares the performance of general stock funds with the S&P 500 index from 1981 to 1999. In 1985, for example, almost 80 percent of general stock funds underperformed the S&P 500 index. Conversely, just 20 percent of actively-managed funds outperformed this index. Similar claims can be made for the periods from 1984 to

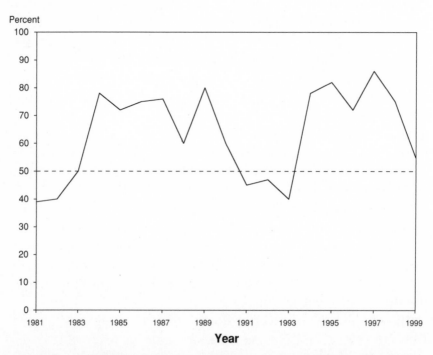

**FIGURE 7.1**   Percentage of General Stock Funds that Underperformed the S&P 500 Index 1981–1999.
*Source:* Lipper.

1989 and from 1994 to 1998. There was only one period in which the S&P 500 index underperformed most stock funds.

### Diversity

Index funds enable you to participate in a large segment of the stock market. No one ever really knows where the market is heading, which stocks will stay hot or end up in a deep freeze, so the diversification aspect of index funds can be quite appealing.

*BusinessWeek* magazine says, "How you divide your portfolio among stocks, bonds, and other assets is the main determinant of its long-term performance. With an index fund you make a commitment to a whole market or sector, rather than to individual securities or a money manager who may or may not remain true to an advertised goal of sticking to growth, value, or big or small cap stocks."[3]

It's easy to become confused by the concept of diversity. Indexing doesn't mean you automatically have a diversified portfolio. Yes, index funds do hold many different stocks, but their holdings are quite specific. The Nasdaq 100, for example, is heavily weighted in tech stocks (81 percent). The S&P 500 is also heavily weighted in technology. Tech stocks currently represent one third of that index. Because of their volatility, index fund investors may not want their dollars tracking so much tech.

All categories of the market move in and out of favor, so it won't be technology and financials forever. Even with index funds, you can't diversify unless you hold an assortment of them or buy one fund that replicates the Wilshire 5000 index of the entire stock market. The theory is that if some equities in an index tank, there are still enough good ones to keep the ship afloat. Sometimes this philosophy works; sometimes it doesn't. The following section explains why.

### Performance

Performance plays a major part in people's passion for index funds. Over the past two decades, both the S&P 500 and the Wilshire 5000 performed better than the average actively-managed mutual fund investing in stocks. In 1995, for example, growth stocks returned 25 percent, while the S&P 500 index climbed to 37 percent.

Keep in mind that the investing game has winners and losers and they're seldom consistent. Index funds can certainly have down periods in which they're outpaced by the picks of astute fund managers. On the other hand, the performance of index funds over the years has been quite respectable. Also, they don't generate the heart-stopping, indigestion-inducing effect of many of their actively-managed, volatile brothers.

Table 7.2 compares the down market performance of the S&P 500 index and the average general equity fund during various time periods. The chart indicates that index funds can clearly hold their own, even in a down market. In the market dip of January 1973 to September 1974, for example, the S&P 500 index was –42.5 percent while the average equity fund was –47.9 percent.

## Low Cost

Low fees and expenses are index funds' claim to fame and one reason so many investors favor them. For the most part, index funds are managed by computers. Unlike human managers, computers don't demand six-figure salaries, an office with a view, or three-martini lunches.

Index funds also keep expenses down with their low rate of turnover; they hold a collection of stocks, thus avoiding the buy and sell frenzy of managed funds. Infrequent trading makes them extremely tax-efficient; they don't have excessive capital gains that become the investor's liability. Their holdings only change when the stocks in the index itself change.

Index funds generally have very low expense ratios. Table 7.3 shows the performance of a low-cost index fund (expense ratio

**TABLE 7.2** Indexing versus the Average Equity Fund

| Period | S&P 500 Index (%) | Average Equity Fund (%) |
|---|---|---|
| January 1973–September 1974 | –42.5 | –47.9 |
| October 1974–September 1975 | 38.1 | 35.4 |
| September 1987–November 1987 | –32.1 | –28.7 |
| December 1987–November 1988 | 25.4 | 22.0 |

*Source:* Lipper.

**TABLE 7.3** How Expense Ratios Affect Returns

| Year | .28% Expense Ratio | 1.75% Expense Ratio |
|------|-------------------|---------------------|
| 1 | $11,472 | $11,325 |
| 2 | $13,161 | $12,825 |
| 3 | $15,098 | $14,525 |
| 4 | $17,320 | $16,450 |
| 5 | $19,870 | $18,629 |
| 6 | $22,795 | $21,097 |
| 7 | $26,150 | $23,893 |
| 8 | $29,999 | $27,059 |
| 9 | $34,415 | $30,644 |
| 10 | $39,481 | $34,704 |
| 11 | $45,293 | $39,303 |
| 12 | $51,960 | $44,510 |
| 13 | $59,609 | $50,408 |
| 14 | $68,383 | $57,087 |
| 15 | $78,449 | $64,651 |
| Added savings with lower expense ratio = $13,798 | | |

.28 percent) and an actively-managed mutual fund with much higher costs (expense ratio 1.75 percent). Assuming a 15 percent rate of return for both funds and an equal initial investment of $10,000, after 15 years you would be $14,000 richer had you invested in the index fund.

## 403(b) Plans and Index Funds

The absence of dividends in an index fund, combined with infrequent trading and few tax consequences, make index funds a good choice for both retirement and nonretirement accounts.

When an active mutual fund manager sells an equity and realizes a gain, the fund investors get hit with a tax. Fortunately, 403(b) investors don't face this taxing problem. Their returns are totally tax-deferred until withdrawal, so the tax advantage of index funds doesn't mean much to them. Keep in mind, however, that tax-deferred doesn't mean "tax free." Some way, some day, Uncle Sam will get his share—even from a 403(b).

If your 403(b) is in an annuity, you have even more reason to consider index funds. Chapter 4 called attention to the extra fees charged by annuities, so including index funds in an annuity portfolio may offset some of those fees. Unfortunately, not all annuities offer index fund options, so you may not have that choice.

## The Other Side of Index Funds

Like many good things in life, index funds have a downside. If they were the perfect investment, we wouldn't need managed funds and unemployment lines would be overrun with jobless mutual fund managers.

### Safety

The strong performance of index funds in recent years has led some investors to believe that indexing is a no-lose proposition. Not true. Like their managed brothers, index funds are still subject to market risk. They're comprised of stocks, and stocks move up and down whether or not they're indexed.

The market can be very fickle. For example, if growth stocks fall out of favor, the index funds that mirror them will also take a nose dive. An index fund, by nature, can't diversify its holdings or get rid of losers in a down market. If an index falls, so do the funds that replicate it. On the other hand, in a down market active managers have an advantage. They can buy or sell some of their holdings or convert them to cash. This approach, while not entirely avoiding a market correction, can at least cushion the blow.

The overall performance of index funds, however, is impressive. Vanguard Mutual Funds maintains that "during the worst bear market in recent history (1973–1974), the average general equity fund fared worse than the S&P 500 Index. And when the market eventually recovered, the index outperformed the average equity fund in the subsequent 12-month period."[4]

If you decide to place your hard-earned dollars in the hands of fund managers with solid reputations, remember that even the best fund managers don't have crystal balls. However, they may not need one if they're managing a small cap fund. Actively-managed small cap funds have a history of beating comparable index funds because astute managers find it easier to sniff out small companies with a potential for profit.

What about a traditional bank-on-the-corner savings account? It's definitely safer than any mutual fund because the Federal Deposit Insurance Corporation (FDIC) protects up to $100,000 of assets held in it. But once again inflation rears its ugly head. If your savings account is earning 5 percent interest, but the rate of inflation is 3 percent, you're only earning 2 percent on your $100,000 investment—an example of how playing it safe can stunt your growth.

### Fees

Usually the expense ratio of an index fund is substantially less than that of a managed fund, but not always. Some S&P 500 index funds have fees as low as .10 percent, while other funds mirroring the S&P can be as high as 1.60 percent.

An index itself simply tracks specific benchmarks, the performance of major players in specified market segments. For example, the S&P 500 index holds primarily blue-chip stocks like Proctor & Gamble or Motorola; these companies and others like them represent approximately 75 percent of the stock market's total value.

An index *fund*, however, is a spin-off of an index with the added variable of expense ratios and transaction costs (fees to buy or sell them). So beware of index funds bearing high fees.

### The Bottom Line

Indexing is simply a method of capturing the stock market by diversifying your holdings. Because you don't know which segment of the market will perform better at any given time, index funds give you the broadest exposure to all sectors. With index funds, you won't have to watch returns as closely and you won't waste valuable time trying to time the market.

"The whole point behind buying an index fund is to own a large part of the market—for better or worse—and ride it over a long period of time, at least 10 years,"[5] says Dagen McDowell, a reporter from TheStreet.com.

But be careful what you choose to index. The broader the index, the less risk you take. For many investors, even the S&P 500 doesn't cover enough territory. If you want a well-cushioned index with a wide spread, consider index funds that mirror the following:

- Wilshire 5000 (all U.S. stock funds)
- Lehman Brothers Aggregate (all bond types)
- Morgan Stanley Capital International EAFE (stocks from Europe, Asia, and the Far East)

"Indexing is changing the way Americans invest," says an article by Anne Tergesen and Peter Coy in *BusinessWeek* magazine. "It's cheap, it's easy, and it makes sense to investors who care about long-term gains, not playing the latest hot tip. A citizenry that demands discounts on everything from cars to computers is increasingly dissatisfied with paying stockbrokers and mutual fund managers to pick stocks and bonds—especially when their choices often don't work out."[6]

Because of their low cost, index funds are the core holdings in many portfolios. However, a portfolio of only index funds is like ordering a hot fudge sundae and telling the waitress to hold the fudge, whipped cream, and cherry. There is a certain drama in stock market gyrations, a euphoric feeling that comes from having picked a winner. That thrill is gone if you're invested in nothing but plain vanilla index funds. On the other hand, if you want to fire your fund manager whenever the market plunges, then perhaps you're really a closet indexer at heart.

## Chapter 7 Homework

1. Contact your 403(b) vehicle to find out if index funds are available through your plan.

2. If you have index fund choices, track them in the Sunday edition of a major newspaper (i.e., the *New York Times*) or on the Internet (i.e., morningstar.com).

3. Compare your index fund options to index funds in the same category. For example, if your 403(b) plan offers an S&P 500 index fund, compare its

performance to an S&P 500 index from different fund families (i.e., Vanguard, Fidelity).

4. If it measures up to similar index funds, consider adding it to your portfolio.

NOTE: If you want technology without too much exposure, try an index fund that mirrors the Nasdaq Composite (Nasdaq 100).

For additional information on a particular index or more details about an index fund, go to www.indexfunds.com on the Internet.

# Buy and Hold or Go for the Gold? Investing in Bull and Bear Markets

## The New Economy

We're living in what's been termed the "new economy" with liberty and technology for all. It's also called the "creative economy" because it's being driven more by ideas than by sweat. In 1994, three million people had access to the Internet and in just four years that figure increased to 147 million. By 2005, it's estimated there will be 740 million people logging on. The world is shrinking in bits and bytes, rapidly becoming one giant global community.

Crossing the country by covered wagon is no longer an option and the gold rush is over. Or is it? The "prospectors" of the new economy are still trying to strike it rich. Lottery tickets, sector funds, a stash of Microsoft—people are looking for new ways to cash in. But just as there was no map to the nearest gold vein, there is also no sure way to spot the next Microsoft.

Day trading is the newest version of "get rich quick." Staring into a computer screen, cup of Starbucks by their side, day traders buy and sell stocks with a frenzy, hoping to make a killing by day's end. 403(b) investors fortunately can't get caught up in the computerized game of "Dialing for Dollars" because a 403(b) is restricted to mutual funds and tracking the stocks in them is the fund manager's job.

A few 403(b) investors, however, seem to have found the retirement plan equivalent to day trading. Market turbulence, combined with confusion about whether to hold new or old economy stocks, have led to increased buying and selling within retirement accounts. According to Lawrence Cunningham, author of *How to Think Like Benjamin Graham and Invest Like Warren Buffet*, "When the market is soaring, people think they're living in a special time."[1] That leads to what Cunningham calls "Q" (Quote) Fever" where people confuse the price of a stock with its actual ability to produce profits. Indeed, investors were throwing money at a company called Razorfish when it was selling for $57 a share. A year later the price dropped drastically to less than $2 a share. Typical of Q fever, many investors bought Razorfish at its highest point, just as they devoured anything remotely related to dot-coms. Safe investing for maximum returns, however, falls somewhere between buy and hold and frequent trading.

### Old Age and the New Economy

"The aging population, equipped with high disposable incomes and additional wealth from inheritances, should provide attractive opportunities for many markets," says the Invesco mutual fund family. "Upscale retirement communities, healthcare delivery systems, financial advisory firms, and the travel industry all stand to benefit from this trend."[2]

The graying of America has already had a significant impact on the biotech and healthcare sectors. According to Ron Gillespie, manager of the Rydex biotechnology fund, "Not only will people be buying drugs to alleviate the pains of aging and to keep the fountain of youth going, but investors are aware of this and are buying those stocks."[3]

Aging baby boomers, for example, are impacting the economy in a big way. It's predicted that by 2005, there will be an unprecedented amount of senior citizens in the United States. This huge elderly population will need healthcare—lots of it—and thanks to advances in biotechnology, they'll need it longer.

Extended life spans also mean that retirement savings will have to be substantial. But saving for retirement can be a real challenge when money has to stretch between you, your spouse, parents, and children. The problem for many baby boomers may be how to find the money to invest rather than where to invest it.

Harry Dent, author of *The Roaring 2000s Investor*, believes "baby boomers will drive stellar performance in industries like financial services, healthcare, home furnishings, and travel and leisure. The technology revolution will favor those stocks, especially the software and Internet-oriented companies."[4]

### FINANCIAL SERVICES

There's a definite correlation between wealth and the need for help to manage it. Banks, insurance companies, stock brokers, and mutual fund families are all eager to provide this money management service.

### HEALTHCARE

Baby boomers tend to spend more on healthcare and related vanity services like plastic surgery, hair loss treatments, personal trainers, teeth restoration, and even sexual dysfunction.

### LEISURE ACTIVITIES

A lot of boomer prosperity can be attributed to the hard work of their parents. Combine this with a tendency to self indulge and you have zillions of disposable dollars directed toward entertainment: movies, theater, lavish vacations, and "play equipment" like hot tubs and backyard waterfalls.

According to the Federal Reserve, real disposable income in 2000, after deducting taxes and inflation, was up 452 percent since 1960. And a large portion of that is being spent on leisure time goods and services. So if you're thinking about sector investing, don't overlook funds that invest in financial services, healthcare, and leisure time facilities and products.

On the other hand, some analysts fear that the boomer retirement years could have a negative impact on the market. For example, moving large sums of money out of stocks and into less risky bonds could significantly increase the volatility of the market.

### *Investing in the New Economy*

Financial columnist Paul Farrell thinks it's now possible for the "average Joe" to become a millionaire in the stock market. Farrell interviewed one such Joe who managed to accumulate a million dollar nest egg in just ten years. He credits his success to tech funds and says he's "betting on what he believes in—technology, the new economy, Nasdaq, and America's future."[5] Joe waited until his fifties to begin investing and can now retire as a millionaire. He's an inspiration to late bloomers who put off saving for retirement. The message is clear: It's never too late to begin.

The new economy presents investment opportunities that didn't exist when the average American bought and held blue chips like General Electric and Hewlett Packard. And while many of those tried and true companies have always been good investments, the same cannot be said for many of their newest competitors. Of 34 top-of-the-chart tech stocks in 1980, only one—Intel—has stayed on top. Twenty-two of those once upon a time hotshots aren't even trading any more, and the other 11 have consistently lagged behind the S&P 500 Index.

The hardest part of investing in new economy stocks is deciding which ones to buy. Unlike old established corporations, companies in the new economy are just that—new. They haven't been around long enough to have a track record or performance history. Most 403(b) plans allow changing choices, so don't be afraid to switch to a tech fund offered by your plan. But be prepared to exit if the fund plunges and your gut tells you it's time to get out.

Gary Lewis of Van Kampen Emerging Growth holds the track record for the best performing mutual fund over a ten year period and credits his success to "knowing when to hold them and when to fold them."[6] Lewis also believes that investors shouldn't be scared off by periods of extreme volatility and that the sustainability of the growth rate in technology is higher than ever.

### Technology in the New Economy

Technology stocks have played a major part in the evolution of the new economy; but they do have a downside. Tech investments can rise dramatically and then crash with alarming severity. However, their place in the new economy—and in every portfolio—can't be ignored. Robert Turner, manager of Turner Technology, says "the nice thing about technology is that it's continually innovative. Technology reduces costs and increases productivity. People will always pay for that."[7]

Technology contributes almost two trillion dollars to the economy and that figure has been increasing at the rate of 20 percent a year.

The good news is that you don't have to understand technology to invest in it. As a 403(b) investor in mutual funds, it's not necessary to know a bit from a gigabyte. Hopefully your 403(b) holdings are with a fund manager who is gigabyte-enlightened like Kevin Landis, manager of Firsthand Funds. Kevin cautions investors to keep the faith and hold on to the belief that tech companies will continue to grow. "Take the growth out of tech stocks and there's little reason to own them,"[8] he says.

In 1998, Federal Reserve Chairman Alan Greenspan, controller of the economy, gave two thumbs up to technology. "The rapid acceleration of computer and telecommunications technology is a major reason for the appreciable increase in our productivity and is likely to continue to be a significant force in expanding the standard of living into the twenty-first century,"[9] said Greenspan.

Lest you have any doubt about the future of technology, Dorothy, the wizard has spoken. The new economy is new because of tech. Not only does technology drive the new economy, it also propels the Proctor & Gambles of the old economy into becoming part of it.

It's not news that technology is cyclical. Consequently, you're better off buying on a downturn when prices are lower. That old market-timing dilemma again—how can you tell when they're the lowest? How do you know when they'll start to go back up? With dollar cost averaging built into your 403(b) plan, you don't have to play those mind games; you're investing regularly without having to worry about stock prices being high or low.

If you're like most 403(b) investors who don't have the luxury of unlimited funds from which to pick, look at the funds available in your own plan. Successful funds can often be found in established fund families, so if you're already investing in one, check out their tech offerings. Fund families with solid track records often have excellent research staffs to sniff out hot stock prospects.

Some been-around-for-awhile tech funds to consider:

- Invesco Technology
- T. Rowe Price Science & Technology
- Firsthand Technology Value
- Northern Technology
- White Oak

Because technology travels in unchartered waters, it will always be volatile and subject to everchanging economic cycles. A typical tech cycle can run the gamut from bull to bear markets and goes something like this:

1. A tech-based market soars. The Nasdaq creates trillions of dollars in paper wealth. Investors are euphoric and Silicon Valley is synonymous with Utopia. A full-fledged bull market is helping investors do the happy dance.

2. The bear stirs. Company earnings fall short of projections. Price to earnings ratios (P/E ratios) suddenly matter.

3. Large companies pull back and spend less on technology. Budgets suddenly matter.

4. Spending, in general, is postponed and product orders are cancelled. Belts are tightened and fewer new toys are bought.

5. Technology stock prices continue to fall; the bear's roar can be heard across the land.

### What the Experts Say

It's hard to be an expert in technology when that sector changes daily. Just when you thought it was safe to invest in Big Broadband along comes Bigger Broadband. Overnight your hundred shares of Big Broadband become wallpaper. However, there are some tried-and-true investment strategies that can be applied to technology. This section looks at some "expert" opinions on what to buy and when to buy it.

In his book *Irrational Exuberance*, Robert Shiller urges us to save more. He fears that stock market hype has led to a belief that the market, alone, will make you rich. Shiller reminds us that corrections happen all the time and that you have to diversify your holdings. A portfolio of pure tech funds is no way to protect your life savings.[10]

Sir John Templeton of the Franklin-Templeton fund family tells us to "buy when pessimism is at its maximum; sell when optimism is at its maximum. Therefore, buy what most investors are selling."[11] Easier said than done, Sir John.

William Keithler, senior vice-president of Invesco funds, believes "most investors can justify investing in technology simply because the long-term growth opportunity is so strong. But individuals must decide how much of their portfolio they want to devote to technology, understanding that it is a high-risk sector. Volatility is characteristic of technology investing, and if you can't stand the heat, you don't want to be in this particular kitchen."[12]

Financial columnist Paul Farrell feels that tech investors should "focus especially on no-load funds with low expenses, low risk, low turnover rates, and low taxes. You can build a solid, well-diversified portfolio without brokers and without investing in high-risk loaded funds run by gun-slinging managers with high turnover and high expense ratios."[13]

For timid tech investors who just want to get their feet wet, financial planner Mark Bass says he keeps his conservative clients' tech holdings under 25 percent and steers them toward blue-chip companies like automakers whose products depend on technology. Mark thinks "people focus too much on technology, as opposed to companies themselves that are taking advantage of technology."[14]

*The Wall Street Journal* echoes Bass's philosophy. "The successful tech funds were the ones buying companies serving blue-chip giants that are aggressively moving out of the Jurrasic industrial age into the new economy."[15]

Robert Markman, a financial advisor in Minneapolis, also believes in the value of both old and new economy stocks. "I feel confident that the only way old economy companies will survive is to write big checks to Oracle, Cisco, and Sun," says Markman. "If you're bullish on technology, stick with it. But don't forget that people still buy cars from Ford, borrow money from Citibank, and eat Campbell's soup. There might be a pot of gold there, too."[16]

Vern Hayden, financial columnist and promoter of "safe sector investing," gives advice on how to invest in the tech sector without getting burned. "There are three ways to allocate money to the tech sector or any other sector. One is to find a highly focused fund with limited sector diversification, but not a pure sector fund. The second way is to buy a pure sector fund. The third way is a combination of the two. Keep in mind, the purpose is to manage risk while achieving gains and not get killed during a correction,"[17] says Hayden.

Michigan financial advisor Rick Bloom also sits prominently in the let's-hear-it-for-tech cheering section. "Our economy is now one based on technology and services; the change you see in the stock market is reflecting this. As an investor, technology is where it's at. Yes, the ride will be volatile and there will be many winners and losers. But I believe technology-based companies will continue to lead the economy."[18]

If worry about a possible bear market has made you tech-phobic, consider this commentary by William O'Neill, publisher of *Investors Business Daily*. "Did you know that in the last 100 years we have had more than 25 bear market slumps and *every single time* the market recovered and ultimately soared into new high ground. That's fantastic. It's one of the greatest success stories in the world."[19] O'Neill's message is that whether you buy and hold or go for the gold, you're bound to win as long as you stay invested.

## Surviving a Bear Market

In the 1990s, triple-digit returns in tech stocks created a false sense of exuberance. Billions of investment dollars poured into Internet companies like E-Bay and Amazon. The historical stock market average returns of 10 percent and 12 percent began to seem like small potatoes. It was hard to be happy with double-digit returns when triple-digit returns were so easy to come by.

Mutual fund managers, eager to boost fund returns, were buying anything remotely related to the World Wide Web. Ultimately, a shakedown occurred in techland. Word got out that technology was trading at unrealistic, outrageous prices and suddenly the emperor had no clothes. Tech-hungry investors had been buying up tech stocks without any substance, pouring money into flimsy ideas until they finally realized it's hard to generate a profit without a product. The bear had found his window of opportunity. . . .

### Three Stages of a Bear Market

When the market takes a downward turn it looks like this:

1. A major market index plunges 20 percent from its high. Investors' mindsets shift from confidence to denial and then to doubt.

2. The stock market see-saws between dramatic highs and devastating lows. Hope gives way to confusion and even despair.

3. Mass panic and major sell-offs take place. Painful losses trigger a flight response; investors take what's left of their money and run.

On a cold day in February, 2001, the headlines said it all.

"Sun Microsystems Give Gloomy Outlook"

"1999 Nasdaq Gains Nearly Wiped Out"

"Dow Jones Industrials Plunged 204.30 points"

*USA TODAY* journalists Adam Shell and Matt Krantz wrote "The Nasdaq composite, which a year ago was a can't miss money-making machine is now a money pit. The Nasdaq bear market that began in March 2000 refuses to go away."[20]

Stock market exuberance had been replaced by gloom and doom. The wealth effect that fostered a spending frenzy in the 1990s was a distant memory, and worries about the failing tech sector fueled the fire. No new breakthrough technology products were on the horizon. Small and mid-sized companies began to burn out because of lower than expected earnings, too much inventory, and not enough cash. "The burnouts spread like wildfire," said Jim Paulsen, Chief Information Officer at Wells Capital Management "because small companies have been top customers of giants like Cisco, Dell, and Microsoft."[21]

Anxiety and confusion rippled from Wall Street to Main Street. People who believed in the stock market as a predictor of the economy had no idea where to invest because they had no clue where the economy was going. "There is a new mood in the marketplace, a keen desire to return to investing in value stocks, a willingness to accept a dull 14 percent return on your money from companies that don't have swashbuckling names like Cisco and Lucent,"[22] said Henry Pearson in an article that appeared in *USA TODAY*.

Bear markets are almost always accompanied by prolonged pauses in spending, saving, and investing. Layoffs aren't unusual in companies where supply exceeds demand. Fortunately, 403(b) investors work for non-profits and aren't usually affected by unemployment consequences occurring in the private sector.

Not to say that negative economic cycles don't affect everyone in some way. Employees of charitable organizations have to dig deeper for donations. School systems slash budgets in a "downsizing" of sorts. On a personal level, life can get very mean and lean if a two-income household suddenly has to survive on one salary. However, there are some things you can do to prepare for a worst case scenario.

1. Set aside an emergency fund now. Try to stash away six months of basic expenses such as mortgage, utility, car, and insurance payments.

2. Sacrifice some spending today for peace of mind tomorrow. Once you've reached your six months' worth of expenses goal, you can begin to enjoy that occasional movie or restaurant meal.

3. Temporarily defer contributions to your 403(b) plan and put them into your emergency fund instead. Deposit those dollars in short-term CDs, U.S. savings bonds, or money market accounts—someplace slightly inaccessible.

4. Consolidate credit cards. Transfer the unpaid balance to a card with a lower rate of interest and *don't* use it. Your goals are to be free of credit card debt and build up an emergency fund. And until you get that stash of cash securely sequestered, consider paying the minimum on your credit card balance.

### Bear Market Upside

Even a recession can have a silver lining—and even a bear market can offer some relief from the charging bull. Job, housing, and other markets can actually benefit from the bear. During the booming bull years, the price of homes in desirable areas skyrocketed. A tiny one-story home in Silicon Valley could easily sell for $700,000, with people beating a path to the door to bid on it. They were willing to pay astronomical prices for almost anything with indoor plumbing.

One home buyer from Michigan was pleasantly surprised when he went in search of a home in Mountain View, California. The bear market had begun and he became the proud owner of a home in Silicon Valley for less than the asking price. Just weeks earlier, he would have stood in line to bid thousands of dollars above it.

A bear market can offer some wiggle room in a previously tight economy. Hotels have empty rooms that may be negotiable. Car dealerships will bargain and even throw in a few incentives to clinch the deal. Home remodeling becomes possible without picking a number and waiting months for a contractor's quote.

The labor force also experiences a return to sanity in a bear market. Workers' expectations are lower. There's less emphasis on making that first million before age thirty, and a measly five-figure salary seems better than none at all. The grass is no longer greener at the company down the street, and employers find it easier to hire and hold onto the best and brightest.

And with an emergency fund set aside for security, temporary unemployment can even be a good thing—a chance to sit out a dance and contemplate your next partner. It can be difficult to assess a high-powered career when you're in the throes of it, so a short time out can be cathartic; it can help you decide if the track you're on is indeed the right one.

An amazing thing happened on the way to the unemployment line. Many of the newly jobless saw this as an opportunity to upgrade their skills in a slowing economy. In the bear market of 2001, colleges and universities reported record applications. Georgetown University, for example, reported a 10 percent increase in applications for their MBA program, as did the University of Washington in Seattle.

The effects of a bear market can also be quite sobering. Where would-be students were once lured away from college to join the dot-com world, the tide suddenly turned, and they began to realize that success in life may depend more on education and less on finding the pot of gold at the end of the Internet spectrum.

## Summary

It would be hard to find a portfolio without at least a few new economy holdings. Hidden in most growth and index funds is sure to be a tech stock or two. However, if you think you want to add more, consider the following before you do:

## Seven New Economy Investing Strategies

1. Rethink your new economy investments. If too much tech makes you queasy, scale down the amount you already hold.

2. Be honest about your own tolerance for risk; how much tech can you handle without the possibility of loss keeping you awake at night?

3. Consider tech funds that reflect the needs of an aging population: healthcare, biotechnology, and leisure time products and services.

4. Stay invested and don't panic at market plunges. Investors who try to time the market by jumping in and out always lose.

5. Don't invest money you'll need soon. The tech sector is very volatile, so you need a long-term time horizon to weather its peaks and valleys.

6. Diversify within technology funds. Consider investing in a combination of large, medium, and small caps.

7. Look for an experienced fund manager with a successful track record. Good managers can assess a tech company's financial position as well as its potential for burn-out.

The bottom line: A balanced portfolio with new and old economy holdings is the key to successful investing in both bull and bear markets.

## Chapter 8 Homework

How to evaluate a portfolio in any market

Make sure your portfolio contains a mixture of stock, bond, and money market funds.

- Go to a fund tracking Web site like Morningstar and look at the asset allocation percentage of each fund.
- Calculate the total percentage of stocks and bonds.
- See how that calculation compares to your original asset allocation plan and rebalance if necessary.

How to evaluate a portfolio in a bear market

Make sure your current asset allocation fits your risk tolerance profile.

- It's easy to think your risk tolerance is high in a bull market, but when your assets are dwindling in a bear market, you might find it's lower than you think.

Looking at "losers" in a new light

- If your losers were good solid funds when you bought them, don't sell them when they're way down. They can and most likely will rebound but if you sell them now, you're turning paper losses into real losses.

- If your losers were questionable high fliers when you bought them and you need portfolio diversification, consider selling them to cut your losses.

But whatever you do, don't try to time the market. Instead, follow the advice of Maxfunds.com:

> Don't sell everything when you think times are bad and don't buy everything when you think times are good. Just let the wheels turn, tweak your portfolio now and then, and keep contributing to your 403(b). You and your money will be fine.

# Creating a Balanced Portfolio

**N**ow that visions of new economy funds are dancing in your head, it's time to talk balance. As appealing as biotechnology may be, tech funds alone do not a balanced portfolio make. A portfolio consisting solely of blue chips won't do it either.

There are several factors that enter into the balance equation and they're not all mathematical.' This chapter explains how personal portfolio balance is affected by both emotional and practical considerations. It also contains information about diversifying in asset categories, as well as sample portfolios for different risk tolerances and time horizons.

The purpose of balancing a portfolio, of allocating assets to a variety of funds, is so that if one fund falters, the others can cushion the blow. Stock sectors move in and out of favor, and yesterday's winners can quickly become tomorrow's losers.

Market gyrations at the turn of the last century are proof positive that no sector is safe forever. In 1999, technology was the place to be for triple-digit returns. But in 2000, tech tanked to the tune of a 33 percent loss for that year. And telecommunications, another hot sector in 1999, also fell 35 percent in 2000. That's why you need to protect yourself with a balanced portfolio containing a mix of stock, bond, and balanced funds.

### Stock funds

Funds that invest in actively-managed growth and value stocks, as well as index funds that track a particular market segment.

### Bond funds

Funds that invest in short, intermediate, or long-term corporate or government bonds. Index bond funds are also available.

### Balanced funds

Actively-managed funds containing a mixture of stocks, bonds, and cash investments. Sometimes referred to as asset allocation or hybrid, balanced funds offer diversification in a single package.

### Money market

Funds that invest in money market instruments such as cash and cash equivalents.

The performance of your portfolio also depends on how the assets are distributed in it. That distribution is referred to as "weighting" and is influenced by your:

- Risk tolerance
- Time horizon
- Fund options in your plan

If you're a 403(b) investor who's getting a late start (less than ten years until retirement), it makes sense to invest somewhat conservatively. The market rises and falls over big chunks of time. A late starter with limited chunks has to be more cautious and keep an eye on protecting assets as well as growing them.

For the unsure among us, there is a wealth of Web sites to help you calculate your personal asset allocation. (See the homework section at the end of this chapter.) Once you've determined the best asset allocation for you, stay with it. Whenever you abandon a classic strategy of diversification, you're drifting out of balance and assuming more risk; no one market segment can stay on top forever. Sometimes the stock gods favor value; other times they're big on growth. Your job is to please them all by keeping some money invested in each.

## Gut Level Investing

There are two unrelated parts to successful portfolio building. The first is based on your emotions—the side of you that says it's time to have a little fun, time to ditch the rabbit ears for a satellite dish. However, investing in the new economy is not the same as buying its toys. Your gut will tell you if the prospect of owning new economy mutual funds feels right. Only you can decide when you're ready to exit security blanket funds that invest in stocks like General Electric. Remember that if you never take any risk at all, you will be incurring the "risk of safe investments."

Safe investments such as CDs, money markets, and bank savings accounts are popular with conservative investors who want to avoid risk at all cost. However, the real risk with "safe" investments is that you can actually lose money. After factoring in the effects of inflation, the return on a safe investment may be no return at all. Stock investments have more risk but, over the long term, offer the best defense against inflation.

The key here is *long term*. Investors who have held stocks and stock mutual funds for a long period of time have been rewarded. Over time, stocks have historically outperformed bonds and money market funds. With enough time in the market and adherence to tried-and-true investment strategies, your retirement nest egg should grow substantially.

Harry Dent, author of *The Roaring 2000's Investor*, believes that "too many people play it safe by choosing low risk money market or bond funds when a prudent equity portfolio could produce much higher returns at similar or slightly higher risk levels."[1] It's common knowledge that ultra-conservative funds like bank savings accounts and money markets produce the lowest returns—especially after inflation does its damage.

Figure 9.1 shows how inflation eats into the returns of so-called "safe investments." This graph assumes a consistent 3.1 percent rate of inflation. Taking the total return of a cash investment at 3.9 percent and subtracting the 3.1 percent inflation rate produces a net

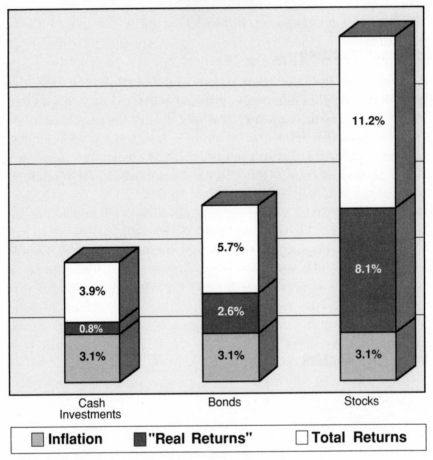

## Average Annual Total Returns: 1926–1998

FIGURE 9.1 Inflation's Impact on Investment Returns.

return of .8 percent. At that rate, it could take two lifetimes to grow a retirement nest egg of any significance.

We know 403(b) investing is long-term and that long investment timelines enable investors to ride out short-term market volatility. But *it's your own tolerance for risk* that really determines how you balance your portfolio. No matter what statistics and historical averages say, you have to adopt an investment style that makes *you* comfortable. If Nasdaq's neon lights are dimming and a voice inside your head is screaming for help, you may be a biotech holder in a blue-chip body.

It's easy to get caught up in day-to-day market volatility and to want to beat a hasty retreat to blue-chip territory. However, if you don't succumb to the daily market crazies and can see the whole picture, you will be pleasantly surprised. From 1987 to 2000, the Nasdaq composite index varied from a 48 percent gain to a 33 percent loss. Nasdaq represents technology; technology is volatile. But that volatility has produced excellent overall returns. So stay focused on long-term performance and then decide how much risk you'll actually be taking over time; it's probably not as much as you think.

Even the most aggressive investor with little fear of risk should have a base of core funds with only a small portion invested in sector funds like energy, healthcare, and technology. He or she will still have plenty of tech exposure because many core funds invest in companies whose performance depends on the technology that runs them.

## Other Risk Factors

Once you've determined your own personal tolerance for investment risk, you then need to look at risk factors that are beyond your control: economic risk, market risk, and political risk.

### Economic Risk

This is the risk that when the economy slows down, a negative cycle begins. People buy less; factories lay off workers; companies can't meet earnings projections; and stocks fall, taking mutual funds with them. The only companies that prosper are those that make antacids.

### Market Risk

Market risk is simply there, like sunrise and after-Christmas sales. Sometimes a mere hiccup from a financial analyst can set the market spinning. A tiny little whisper of doom can cause the market to crash just before the closing bell. Market performance is often irrational and there's no way to predict its volatility. However, focusing on long-term performance can help dilute the gut-wrenching effect of market swings.

### Political Risk

Suppose every Republican decided to become a vegetarian; say farewell to the meat packing industry and hello to the Jolly Green Giant. The rise and fall of stocks often depends on what's in or out of favor, politically or otherwise.

Americans can be confused and indecisive. When electing a new president takes weeks instead of the customary day, the stock market goes berserk. There's nothing the market hates more than indecisiveness. Thus, political risk has to be included on the list of factors beyond our control. We can only wait patiently while politicians work on solving the crisis of the day, knowing that this, too, shall pass.

The bottom line is that without risk there can be no reward. Mutual funds minimize risk by investing in several companies so returns aren't riding on the performance of only one. Moreover, a small commitment to risk can add pizzazz to your portfolio. Sector funds can boost returns, or they can lower them. Usually, it's a little of both. But if the sector percentage of your portfolio is safely limited, you can sit back and relax.

## The Practical Side of Portfolio Building

The other side of portfolio balancing involves information gathering rather than wishful thinking. ("I wish I had bought Apple stock in Steve Jobs' garage.") And while "past performance is no guarantee of future results," market history can be a valuable source of information on which to base investment decisions.

### Long-Term Lessons

In 1996, the Dow Jones Industrial Average had a growth rate of 26 percent. Based on that information, one might have been tempted to take out a second mortgage and run to the nearest brokerage house.

But if a market correction came (and they always do), you could have diluted a major retirement asset—your home.

A more rational approach is to survey a chunk of history. Taking any 20 year period (excluding the Great Depression), the market's average rate of return has been between 10 and 12 percent. That return won't help you "get rich quick," but with compounding, it can build a substantial nest egg.

History also reminds us to keep our eye on the balance ball. Past statistics show that you can't rely on any one sector to stay in favor forever. While technology has had a long, lucrative run, no one knows which segment of tech will stay on top. Consequently, it's wise to spread your money among different sectors and maintain diversity in fund size and objectives.

You can cash in on the market's average performance over time, but only if you subscribe to the potpourri theory. No historical average was ever achieved by a one-fund portfolio.

### Market Cap Matters

Mutual funds invest in companies of all sizes. The term "market capitalization" (market cap) refers to the market value of a particular company.

**Small-cap funds** invest in the stock of companies with a market value of two billion dollars or less. Because small cap companies are still in a growing phase, buyers can get in on the ground floor. Obviously there's more risk; the company can grow and prosper or the opposite can occur. Fortunately, as 403(b) investors, we don't have to research hundreds of new, emerging companies. We can leave that time-consuming job to the managers of our mutual funds.

**Mid-cap funds** buy stock in companies with market values between two and fifteen billion dollars. More mature than small caps, mid-caps are also less risky because they've been around longer and are more established than their smaller siblings.

**Large-cap funds** invest in large companies with market values over fifteen billion dollars. The big boys like Coca Cola,

General Electric, and IBM have established themselves as dominant players in their respective industries. They're usually more stable (and considerably more costly) than small- or mid-caps and can usually be counted on to provide a steady stream of income for their stockholders.

Market cap matters because it's one more way to diversify and balance your portfolio. Small-, mid-, and large-cap stocks will perform differently during different time periods as Figure 9.2 clearly illustrates. From 1980 to 1984 small-, mid-, and large-caps grew at similar rates. However, from 1995 to 1997 large-caps took the lead. Because they are less risky, large-cap giants are a good choice for core portfolio holdings.

### Time Horizon

Age is another factor that needs to be considered in the balance equation. How your portfolio holdings are weighted depends in part on your time horizon: the number of years remaining until retirement. If you're young and have a time horizon of 15 or more years, your goal is to grow assets rather than preserve them. With time on

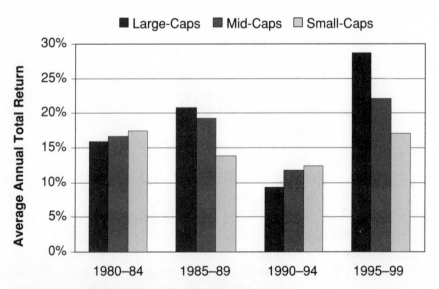

**FIGURE 9.2** 20 Years of Market-Cap Performance.
*Source:* Invesco Funds and Standard & Poor's COMPUSTAT™ Data.

your side, you can afford to take more risk; you have many years to recover from the bumps along the way.

Charles, a stock market-savvy 18-year-old has an automatic investment plan and contributes $500 monthly to aggressive funds like science and technology. With 40 years to weather the ups and down of the market, his portfolio may be volatile, but he has lots of time to fine tune it. And he can also use that time to gain valuable hands-on financial experience.

### Fire!

When building your portfolio, don't jump into hot fund fires. Never forget the fickle nature of the market. Funds go in and out of favor as fast as fashion fads. (Think leisure suits.) That doesn't mean you should assume that yesterday's losers will be tomorrow's winners. No one can time the market. We have no way of knowing where it's going; we only know where it's been.

There are plenty of good, long-term performers with solid track records. Buy 'em, hold 'em, and add a sector fund for some sex appeal. As long as your portfolio has a core of trustworthy funds, you can have a small percentage in sector funds without threatening your entire life savings.

If you're still unsure about where you stand on the risk issue, look back at the bottoming out of the market at the end of 2000. The Nasdaq had fallen 50 percent from its high, the growth of the economy was alarmingly slow, and consumer confidence was falling fast. Internet stocks had become "internots," two candidates for president were slugging it out, and investors wore an I-just-lost-my-best-friend look. Then, on December 5, after weeks of negative returns, the Nasdaq had its highest one-day gain, up 274 points (10.5 percent). If you were a market timer who decided to throw in the towel and sell all on December 4, you'd be beating yourself up big time.

A full-fledged bear market can change your attitude toward risk in a hurry. That's when emotions run rampant and the voices of doom are loudest. The mood is dark; panic ensues, and people start cursing their fund managers. So what's a 403(b) investor to do when the bear roars?

The answer is simple: Diversify. Diversify. Diversify. And continue to save regularly using the dollar cost averaging that's built into your 403(b) plan. Your investment dollars buy more shares in a bear market and those additional shares turn into more dollars for your retirement nest egg.

### Diversifying Funds

Along with diversifying the asset allocation mix in your portfolio, you also need to vary the funds you put into them. In general, there are four important factors to consider before giving any fund a place in your portfolio:

- Diversification
- Fund Manager
- Cost
- Performance and Risk Ratings

Fortunately, fund choices are limited to those offered by the provider you've chosen as your 403(b) vehicle. Without some process of elimination, you would have to wade through the thousands of funds for sale in the mutual fund marketplace—a daunting, if not impossible, task.

Most mutual fund families offer funds in the following broad categories:

- Large growth
- Growth and income
- Bonds
- Hybrid (Balanced, Asset Allocation)
- Money market
- Index
- International
- Sector

A hypothetical 403(b) portfolio might hold some of the following:

**Large Growth**—Funds investing in large companies that have been the backbone of American industry. The S&P 500 index contains large blue-chip companies that, from 1990 to 2000, grew at an average annual rate of 18.2 percent, making large growth funds an excellent choice for core investments in a 403(b) portfolio.

**Small Growth**—Funds that invest in infant companies who hope to grow up and become blue chips. They tend to be unpredictable but have the potential for big returns if they survive their childhood. Small growth funds can be part of a 403(b) portfolio but not a major player (core holding) because of their volatility.

**Index Funds**—Index funds simply track the performance of a particular market index so their returns aren't diminished by a high rate of turnover or excessive expenses. The owner of an index fund can expect to do as well as the index it tracks.

**Bond Funds**—Bond funds contain short-, intermediate-, or long-term corporate or government bonds. For safety's sake, bonds should have a place in every portfolio; their weighting depends on your age and risk tolerance.

**Hybrid Funds**—Also called "balanced" or "asset allocation," hybrid funds contain a mixture of stocks, bonds, and money market instruments. These can be excellent core holdings in a retirement portfolio.

**International Funds**—International or global funds enable you to invest in foreign markets. A portfolio can certainly be balanced without foreign funds, and some people feel uncomfortable investing in markets they don't know much about. If you decide to go global, it's safer to select funds that invest in both U.S. and international stocks.

**Sector Funds**—Sector funds invest in market segments such as healthcare, technology, energy, and communications. They are the most volatile fund category and require monitoring. So if your goal is to buy and hold, stay away from sector funds.

Other fund categories invest in a variety of stocks, so you can own technology without having to buy a pure sector fund. Large growth funds, for example, are sure to have some tech holdings. You can have exposure to several market segments without owning a single sector fund.

### Fund Manager

The manager is the "expert," the guru that stands between you and those thousands of stocks that can make or break your fortune. Manager expertise is what you rely on, so it's important to look at their track record before entrusting them with your retirement dollars.

Performance and manager tenure go hand-in-hand. Look for a manager who's been managing the same fund for a number of years, then look at the fund's performance during that period. According to Vern Hayden from TheStreet.com, "The manager has to be exceptional with a consistent track record of excellence for at least five years."[2]

### Cost

By now you know the impact of even a small one percent fee on your bottom line. Over time, those fees compound and rob your nest egg of thousands of potential dollars.

The lower the expense ratio (cost to operate the fund), the more money that remains in your pocket. With the exception of passively-managed index funds, an expense ratio of one percent or less is about as good as it gets. And loads are another expense that you don't need. If you see a fund with A, B, and C shares, you know that fund is loaded. With so many great no-load funds out there, just say no to loaded funds.

### Performance Rating

The star rating system used by Morningstar has long been a respected tool for evaluating fund performance. The rating is sometimes reflected by stars and sometimes numerically, as in the *New York Times* mutual fund section where you'll see two numbers separated by a slash (i.e., 5/5). The first number indicates a fund's performance compared to the stock market overall. The second number compares that fund to others in the same category. Isabel Energy, for example, has a 4/3 rating. That means that in the total market, Isabel Energy has four out of a possible five stars. Compared to other energy funds, Isabel, with three stars, is in the middle.

### Risk Rating

There has to be some balance between risk and reward. The more risk a fund assumes, the more potential it has for high returns. On the other hand, more risk means greater volatility and the possibility of devastating dips. Somewhere in the middle is the best place to be when seeking a balanced portfolio.

The Web site www.morningstar.com is a good place to find the risk rating of individual funds. Simply type in your fund's five letter abbreviation, hit "go" and a Morningstar Quicktake appears with that fund's risk rating in its category as well as its risk-versus-reward ranking. For example, typing VHCOX for Vanguard Capital Opportunity fund shows that this fund has a risk rating of five, the best in its category of mid-cap growth funds. The report also indicates that Vanguard Capital Opportunity has the potential for high returns with low risk. See Figure 9.3 for a sample Quicktake report and Appendix E for how to read it.

## The Rebalancing Act

Investors generally rebalance their portfolios for two reasons:

Asset allocation

Upgrading

Because stock and bond prices fluctuate, your asset allocations may drift from your original intentions. Suppose, for example, you held a mix of 50 percent stocks and 50 percent bonds and were investing $100 a month in each. In a bull market, the price of stocks would most likely rise while the price of bonds would fall. Consequently, your combined monthly investment of $200 will buy more shares of bonds than stocks, and your portfolio is no longer a 50/50 split between stocks and bonds. To maintain your original allocation, it becomes necessary to sell some bonds and re-invest that money into stocks.

Upgrading refers to the strategy of selling losers to buy winners. The trick here is to make sure you buy and sell within the same category so your portfolio retains its balance among asset classes.

Some investors rebalance yearly; others pay no attention to this "annual mandate" preferring, instead, to let their winners ride. The theory behind this is that in a long-riding bull market, you're cutting performance potential by selling winners to stay balanced. A bear

**FIGURE 9.3** Morningstar Quicktake® Report.

*Source:* www.morningstar.com. Reprinted with permission.

market, however, is a different story. Anyone who has been an investor during a bear market knows that huge gains from hot funds can be erased in a matter of weeks.

The best approach to rebalancing is usually compromise. Some rebalancing is necessary, but not as often as financial pros would like us to believe. Keep in mind that each time you rebalance, a buy and sell situation occurs and generates more revenue for brokers. Fortunately for 403(b) investors, rebalancing is not a taxable event. You can change allocations within your plan without the sting of trading costs or taxes.

Figure 9.4 indicates the performance of two identical portfolios in a study on portfolio balancing done by *USA TODAY*. A $10,000 portfolio established in 1976 and rebalanced annually would have yielded $146,557 by 1998. However, if it was rebalanced less frequently (seven times in that 22-year period), your portfolio would be worth $150,286 in 1998. While the approximately $4,000 difference isn't much, the fact that you're further ahead and didn't have to hassle with those investment scales every year is worth a lot.

### The Bottom Line on Balancing

It's easy to become side-tracked by the prospect of becoming a millionaire in a sustained bull market. The phenomenal returns of tech funds in the 1990's were quite seductive, and no one wanted to get left behind. The Internet Fund is a prime example of how that thinking can get you into trouble.

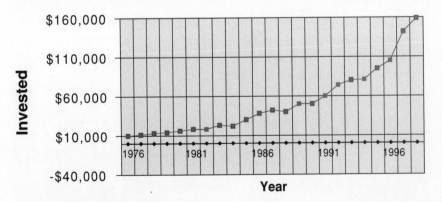

**FIGURE 9.4**   Rebalancing Result.

At the end of the 1990's, Ryan Jacob, then manager of the Internet Fund, could do no wrong. People poured money into his fund and were rewarded by triple-digit returns. Did they take their money and run to the nearest balanced fund? Not a chance.

In 1999, Jacob left the Internet Fund (renamed the Kinetics Internet Fund) to start his own Jacob Internet Fund. His devotees followed their piper, only to watch in disbelief as Jacob Internet Fund sank to the bottom of the dot-com barrel. Those whose portfolios had remained in balance were dismayed, but not as devastated as others who had had a disproportionate amount in Jacob. They had to pay the piper for an investment decision based on greed.

The long-term success of a 403(b) portfolio depends as much on *how* you allocate your assets as *where* you put them. Of course you want to pick the best funds for each of your asset categories, but, above all, you need to stay balanced. Balancing is a lot like buying insurance. You're insuring the success of your portfolio by spreading the risk and by accepting the fact that, in the stock market, there's a definite trade-off between risk and return.

## Chapter 9 Homework

There are a variety of excellent calculators on the Internet to help you construct a balanced portfolio. Your assignment is to visit the following sites and develop your own investment portfolio focused on your retirement goals.

www.apps.com
The calculator king. Every conceivable way to crunch all kinds of numbers. You can even calculate your percentage of body fat! Apps has a particularly useful asset allocation worksheet from which you can create an investment portfolio based on goals, tax bracket, and risk tolerance.

www.scudder.com
Take their three-minute retirement planning quiz. Up comes a pie chart with asset allocation recommendations.

www.fidelity.com
Fidelity also has an excellent portfolio planning tool. After completing their quiz, the calculator uses your input regarding time horizon, risk tolerance, current financial situation, and investment experience and creates a graph showing a portfolio that should work for you. The recommendations are

specific. A growth portfolio, for example, might suggest that you invest in 70 percent stocks (50 percent large cap, 10 percent mid and small cap, 10 percent international), 25 percent bonds (15 percent investment grade, 10 percent high yield, or 25 percent municipal), and 5 percent money market.

www.americanexpress.com
You build your own portfolio based on answers to the questionnaire. Your investment profile is then calculated, along with a recommended portfolio for that profile. For example, if your response to the questionnaire indicates that you are an aggressive investor with assets of $50,000, a tax bracket of 28 percent, and 8–12 years remaining until retirement, your suggested portfolio will contain the following funds:

- 30 percent large cap
- 25 percent mid cap
- 20 percent small cap
- 25 percent international

# Tried-and-True Investment Strategies

The importance of using investment strategies cannot be overemphasized. Without strategies, you might as well be throwing darts at a board or coins into a slot machine. While the market's movements will always be mysterious, there are several strategies that can give you some control over your investments.

Strategies are tools to use when you don't know the outcome. They're not predictors. Even day traders who buy and sell stocks on an hourly basis can't predict market changes. How can we, as long-term 403(b) investors, know which funds to hold onto and which to sell? Once again, just because a particular fund or sector is hot today is no guarantee of future performance.

This chapter will explain several possible strategies to consider when making investment decisions in both bull and bear markets. Successful portfolios don't just happen; they're almost always the result of selecting sound strategies and sticking to them.

How frustrating it can be to live with a losing fund for too long, finally make the decision to dump it, and then watch it return to the winner's circle. The reality of mutual fund performance is that funds go up and down faster than hemlines. If you jump into a fund at its peak, Murphy's law says it will start a downhill spiral very soon thereafter. The tendency then is to wait until it's back to break-even, breathe a sigh of relief, and trade it for the next hot commodity. And so on and so on until you finally come to the conclusion that chasing your tail is a strategy that produces more angst than positive returns.

John Rekenthaler, research director for Morningstar, summarizes the tail-chaser's lament by saying, "In terms of trading less, most trades occur after the fact. I find most people selling a mutual fund after it's gone through a prolonged period where its investment style has been unpopular. In general, that's a good time to buy. If you accept the fact that most trades go in the wrong direction, you'll improve your odds simply by fighting off temptation, realizing that the trade you want to make is probably the wrong trade."[1]

## Dollar Cost Averaging

Dollar cost averaging is the strategy of investing the same amount at regular intervals so you will automatically benefit from market fluctuations. When the price of a fund drops, your 403(b) dollars buy more shares; conversely, when the price rises, you then own more shares and can reap the benefits.

Dollar cost averaging provides some protection from the pitfalls of market timing where investors jump in and out of the market, trying to profit from its highs and lows. The market will always be unpredictable and there's no way of knowing the best time to buy or sell.

Some investors think dollar cost averaging works best with high risk funds. Actually the opposite is true. Suppose you buy two funds at the same time; Fund A boasts high returns while Fund B is mediocre. According to Jonathan Clements, financial columnist for the *Wall Street Journal*, "You will fare better with the fund that does poorest early on because your initial investment will buy more shares. As your lagging fund catches up, those shares earn handsome gains, leading to better results."[2]

Perhaps the biggest benefit of dollar cost averaging is the cushion it provides against major losses in sudden market drops. Suppose you invested a large sum of money in funds outside your 403(b) plan and the price of your purchases dropped significantly the next day. Your investment portfolio would be in the red at its inception. This won't be the case when you're using a slow and steady investment strategy like dollar cost averaging. Best of all, it's a strategy that's already built into 403(b) plans.

Table 10.1 illustrates how dollar cost averaging works in different market cycles.

Asset allocation—how you diversify your portfolio—was discussed in Chapter 8 and is one of the defining characteristics of a successful portfolio. Putting all your eggs in one basket and expecting them to arrive safely at grandma's house may work in fairy tales, but it doesn't work in the stock market. Faster than you can say Little Red Riding Hood, fund sectors fall from grace. However, if your investments are diversified, you have some protection against market pitfalls. One caveat: your portfolio may not be as balanced as you think.

Catherine Daniels has a portfolio containing the Berger New Generation, Janus Enterprise, and the Red Oak fund. Unbeknownst to Catherine, all three funds are heavily weighted in technology. But she didn't know that because she never looked at their primary holdings. Consequently, Catherine has to hope that large growth technology will continue to be a top-performing sector although throughout stock market history, no asset class has stayed in favor forever. So she's betting against the odds, and she's unlikely to win.

Instead, Catherine should diversify her assets into small-cap, large-cap, index, and international funds. For additional balance, she might even consider adding a sector other than technology. Diversification can't be accomplished with a portfolio of funds that all do the same thing.

**TABLE 10.1** Dollar Cost Averaging in a 403(b)

|  | Monthly investment amount | Shares bought | Share price |
|---|---|---|---|
| January | $200 | 20 | $10 |
| February | $200 | 25 | $8 |
| March | $200 | 10 | $20 |
| April | $200 | 40 | $5 |
| Total shares bought = | | 95 | $8.44 Average share price ($800 divided by 95) |

With dollar cost averaging the *average* dollar amount you pay for each share will be lower than the *average* market price per share.

According to *In the Vanguard*, a publication of Vanguard mutual funds, "Diversification is not designed to produce the highest possible returns, but to balance a portfolio's return potential with its risk. The overall return of a diversified portfolio will always be lower than the return of its best performing asset. However, it will also always be higher than the return of the worst performing asset."[3]

### Diversifying with One Fund Only

If Catherine prefers beach reading to asset allocation research, she can simply invest in an asset allocation fund—one fund that does it all. An asset allocation fund is a combination of stocks, bonds, and money markets that varies its holdings based on market performance. Essentially, it provides diversification and portfolio balance in one neat package. Most major mutual fund families offer asset allocation funds and they can be worth their weight in gold in a market gone mad.

During and after the presidential election in 2000, for example, the stock market played serious mind games with investors. The Dow Jones Industrial Average shot up one day, only to be crushed by Nasdaq the next. In times like that, it's difficult to know where to place your assets; a good asset allocation fund can relieve you of that guesswork. In 1999, for example, the Vanguard Asset Allocation fund was 40 percent stocks, 60 percent bonds. A year later the reverse was true; the fund reacted to market changes and reallocated to 60 percent stocks and 40 percent bonds.

It's very hard for the average investor to know when to buy what. Our tendency is to sell low and buy high. Hoping to cash in on technology, we buy it at its peak and then watch with horror as our assets dwindle. While the pros tell us to buy on the dips (when stock prices are falling), that's easier said than done. It takes more courage than most mere mortals have to continue throwing money at a fund that's on a downhill spiral.

To believe in the strategy of portfolio diversity is to be aware of sector rotation. One quarter may find financial stocks climbing, while healthcare is the place to be in the next quarter. Soon after that, energy becomes the sector du jour. The market is elusive. No one can ever be sure of being in the *right* place at the *right* time. Diversification, however, can help ensure that you're not in the *wrong* place at the *wrong* time.

## Low Fees

The importance of keeping costs down and paying as little as possible to own a fund is a strategy that can be applied to all situations. Whether buying a car, a camera, or a cabin in Vermont, Americans are bargain hunters. We like to compare prices and will go to great lengths to get a good deal. When it comes to portfolio purchases, the penny-pinching rule also applies. Given enough time, the principle of compounding will turn your pennies into dollars. So the fewer pennies you pay in fees, the more dollars you can keep for yourself. You can't control market gyrations, but you can control the fees you pay for a ride on the stock market roller coaster.

All mutual funds have management costs. Those costs are passed on to you, the investor, in the form of fees. There are, however, vast differences in fund costs, and paying higher fees by no means guarantees higher returns. The Investment Company Institute maintains that "a fund with lower expenses may perform better than a fund with higher expenses. And the opposite may be true. It is important to remember that neither higher nor lower expenses guarantees better performance."[4]

It's difficult for the average investor to calculate fees, especially when they're a combo of a fund's expense ratio, 12b-1 fees, and loads. Only a careful study of the fund's prospectus will reveal this information. Keep in mind that the total return of a fund is calculated *after* expenses are deducted, so it's not necessary for the investor to subtract fund costs in order to determine actual performance; the costs have already been factored into the final figures.

Figure 10.1 considers a $20,000 investment in two hypothetical funds with equal returns of 8 percent, both in tax-deferred accounts. Fund A has an expense ratio of .30 percent, while the expense ratio of Fund B is 1.20 percent. That seemingly small difference of .90 percent translates to a loss of more than $14,000 over 20 years.

## Just for Fun—The Rule of 72

The Rule of 72 is a method of determining how long it will take to double an investment. While its scientific validity is questionable, stock market returns are anything but scientific. Here's how the Rule of 72 works:

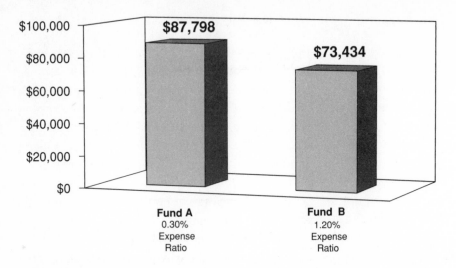

**FIGURE 10.1** How Costs Affect Returns.
©2000 The Vanguard Group, Inc. Reprinted with permission from the PlainTalk® brochure, *Mutual Fund Basics*. All rights reserved. Vanguard Marketing Corporation, Distributor.

1. Find your fund's annual rate of return.
2. Divide the annual rate by 72.
3. The result will show, theoretically, how many years it will take to double your investment.

For example, if you are holding a fund that earns a 6 percent annual rate of return, your investment will double in 12 years. If your investment yields 8 percent annually, you can expect it to double in 9 years. (See Table 10.2.)

## Approximate the Stock Market Average

A reasonable goal—and a strategy practiced by many—is to set an investment goal that mimics the performance of the stock market, in other words, to make sure your investments are doing at least as well as the overall market. On average, the stock market has been benevolent to its investors. Looking at the results cumulatively over 20-year segments, the median average return of stocks has been 11.5 percent since 1945.

One way to potentially achieve this outcome is through index funds. Index funds, discussed in Chapter 6, simply mirror the performance of a particular benchmark. The Standard & Poors (S&P) 500 is an index of large blue-chip stocks. If you own an S&P 500 index

**TABLE 10.2** Rule of 72 Table

| Annual return (%) | Years to double |
|:---:|:---:|
| 12 | 6 |
| 9 | 8 |
| 8 | 9 |
| 6 | 12 |
| 4 | 18 |
| 3 | 24 |

fund, you're guaranteed that the fund's performance will be as good as the S&P 500 index itself. Your returns will be neither higher nor lower than the index it mirrors.

In a surging bull market, investors often think the performance of an index fund is small potatoes. How boring to settle for 12 percent when an actively-managed tech fund is sporting triple digit returns. But when the bear comes, paper wealth can quickly become paper loss and so-called "average" returns of 10 or 12 percent start to look good again. Index funds are one way to get average returns and the peace of mind that comes with them. If "moderation in all things" is your motto, look no further than index funds.

Bill Schultheis, author of *The Coffeehouse Investor*, believes that fund managers rarely beat an index anyhow, so it makes sense to simply invest in index funds that will approximate the stock market average. He believes that "by trying to beat the stock market average, it's easy for investors to ignore the fact that the stock market average itself has historically provided an excellent investment return. And by trying to beat an already good thing, you are virtually guaranteed to end up below it."[5]

Simplification is another reason to approximate the stock market average with index funds. By owning an assortment of them, you own a share in many markets and your selection process is simplified. Indexing means choosing from a few good funds instead of confusing yourself with the 8,000 mutual funds out there.

Indexing also provides diversity at low cost, no managers' salaries to pay, less thrills but fewer spills. The Vanguard 500 Index fund, for example, offers an assortment of diversified stocks at an extremely low expense ratio of .18 percent. If hands-on, manager-directed investing makes you squeamish, consider mimicking the market average with index funds.

Two approaches to portfolio diversification using index funds:

| AGGRESSIVE | CONSERVATIVE |
|---|---|
| International—25% | International—10% |
| Large Company—50% | Large Company—70% |
| Small Company—25% | Small Company—20% |

## Emotional Investing

Dear Abigail,

I couldn't stand hearing my brother-in-law brag about high returns from his Extra-Terrestrial tech fund, so I took a second mortgage on my house and bought 200 shares of Extra-Terrestrial. The day after I bought it, the fund tanked and it's gone downhill ever since. Now my house is in foreclosure and my wife left me. She took the dog. Can I sue my brother-in-law?

Devastated Donald

Dear Donald,

Emotional investment decisions are almost always doomed to failure. Portfolio purchases should be based on hard facts, not on whims, moods, or a recommendation from your brother-in-law. Beware the four deadly sins of emotional investing for they have undermined a lot of good intentions and wreaked havoc on many a retirement portfolio. They are:

- Envy
- Greed
- Pride
- Denial

### Envy

The fictitious Dear Abigail letter is an example of how devastating envy can be to your portfolio—and your life. How many times have we heard tales of mutual funds making millions for a lucky investor? With so much money to be made, it's hard to hang onto last year's losing growth and income fund. So we buy our brother-in-law's fund and pay a high price to join the party. Unfortunately, the party is often winding down by the time we get there. The fund may already have peaked and is on a downhill spiral. An investment decision based on envy can be worse than no decision at all.

## Greed

Greed gets in the way of many rational investors and gives the stock market a Las Vegas-like quality. When Internet funds stunned the market with unheard of returns, investors went on a buying frenzy. Unfortunately, there is no shortcut to sticking with a sound asset allocation strategy.

When the greed mentality takes over, investors lose their sense of balance, both emotionally and financially. They often fail to heed market corrections and other warning signs until it's too late. In March of 2000, the Nasdaq Composite was at its peak. Nine months later it had lost 48 percent. All the hindsight in the world won't make up for the fact that greed kept people in too much tech for too long. By the time they're saying "could've, should've, would've," it's too late; the damage has already been done.

## Pride

Pride is another emotion that threatens portfolio performance. Unwilling to acknowledge mistakes, many investors buy and hold . . . and hold . . . and hold. The buy-and-hold approach has proven its worth in conservative investments such as growth and income or balanced funds. However, if you happen to be a fan of sector funds, it's important to know when to bail out.

Many people let pride get in the way of good investing strategies. They don't want to let go of a losing fund because they're sure the fund will bounce back. When it doesn't, they've lost not only their pride but real, hard-earned dollars as well.

## Denial

Like pride, denial stops many investors from sensible decision making and keeps bad mutual funds from going broke. Rather than cut their losses and get out, some investors prefer to play ostrich. They may claim to be buy-and-holders, but that theme song simply becomes an excuse for hanging on too long. It's as if the losses aren't real if they don't confront them. But losing principal, along with years of potential growth, demands a wake-up call.

Upgrading is a strategy I've referred to throughout the book and can be helpful to investors who are stuck in losing funds. Upgrading means selling losers to buy winners, a philosophy that can add a measure of success to portfolios drowning in denial.

## Start Early

Diversification, dollar cost averaging, staying balanced—important strategies for successful investing to be sure, but nothing beats getting an early start. The magic of compounding feeds on time. Short-term compounding is better than none at all, but there's no substitute for long-term compounding benefits.

An investment that compounds at 10 percent a year for 15 years will quadruple in value. Add another 35 years to the equation and each initial investment dollar is compounded 117 times.

*15-year plan*

A one-time investment of $10,000 for 15 years at 10% interest = $40,000

*50-year plan*

A one-time investment of $10,000 for 50 years at 10% = $170,000

Unfortunately, few learn this financial formula until it's too late. Many baby boomers, for example, didn't begin to take investing seriously until confronted with approaching retirement. Better late than never, but too late to recoup many lost years of potential compounding.

The secret to saving early is to live within your means. How many young people leave the nest only to bury themselves in credit card debt and hefty car payments? The only good thing is that they have time on their side and can afford to make a few mistakes, learn from them, and move on.

One way to become a saver is through automatic payroll deductions; there's far less temptation to spend what you don't see. A 403(b) plan does just that. Contributions to it are taken directly from your gross pay, hidden from view, and tucked away until retirement. Your 403(b) plan provides a healthy dose of financial discipline and an easy way to get a head start on investing.

## Stay Focused

If there was ever a doubt in your mind about the need to protect your assets while growing them, consider the following scenario:

It's December 2000. You're planning to retire in five years. The bulk of your portfolio is still in stock funds and most of those are technology. Even though you knew you should, you didn't convert any stocks into bonds. The market was booming and you wanted to ride that bull just a little bit longer.

Suddenly the market roller coaster plunges straight down and takes your retirement savings with it. Yes, it will go up again; historically it always has. But in the meantime, you're five years from retirement and have just lost 50 percent of your nest egg.

And therein lies the danger of not sticking to a plan in the later years that includes protecting your assets while continuing to grow them. Every portfolio needs some protection in the form of bond and money market funds. When the market plunges, it can wipe away years of high returns. By not adhering to an asset plan, you're placing yourself in a danger zone, and you may not have enough earning years left to recover from those losses.

Mike and Lilly are the proud owners of a two million dollar home in Silicon Valley that they bought in 1999. To "win" their prize home, they had to bid $300,000 over the asking price. Like many Silicon Valley residents, Mike worked for a major tech company and was counting on stock options to pay the mortgage and fund his retirement. But by the end of 2000, the price per share of his company's stock had fallen dramatically and Mike could no longer afford to exercise his options.

"We're thinking about selling our home," Mike says, "but it's a catch-22 situation. I can't afford the mortgage payments anymore, but I don't want to sell my house for less than I paid for it."

Like Mike, others who got carried away with the "wealth effect" and thought the market would always go up are in bad shape when the bubble bursts. Research from Salomon Smith Barney found that some market "bubbles" take years to overcome. In the early sixties, for example, computer stocks like IBM peaked in the fourth quarter of 1961; they fell drastically soon after and didn't recover until 1964. Nothing lasts forever, least of all triple-digit stock market returns. And that's a hard lesson for many novice investors to learn.

As a 403(b) investor, you're in it for the long term. Falling returns in a retirement account shouldn't threaten your monthly mortgage payment. However, if you fail to shift some assets to safer harbors like bond and money market funds, you're playing Russian roulette with your nest egg. You can't control the stock market; you can't predict or outsmart it. But you can protect your assets by switching to investments with less risk as you approach retirement.

## Strategies for Surviving a Bear Market

A bear market means that the stock market has plunged 20 percent or more. It's calculated by declines in the major indices: Wilshire 5000, S&P 500, Dow Jones Industrial Average, and the Nasdaq Composite. There have been a total of three bear markets since 1978. On average, the market fell 27 percent during a seven-month period and took eleven months to recover. The shortest bear market occurred in 1990 when the market plunged 21.2 percent in less than three months and recovered in six.

Bear markets have a snowball effect in which investors:

- Sell more of their losing investments for tax deductions.
- Sell on rallies, rather than buying on dips.
- Lose confidence in the economy, so they buy less and companies scale back to cope with falling demand.

There are several strategies you can use to ease your mind during bear market days.

### Cut Back on Spending

Buy only what you need for survival. This does not include a high-definition TV or that trip to Alaska. Postpone extravagant spending until the bear goes back into hibernation. Alaska will still be there.

### Stick to Your Goals

Keep your portfolio in balance by revisiting your original goals. If part of your portfolio is invested in technology, be sure you're holding solid tech funds like T. Rowe Price Science & Technology, Fidelity Select Technology, and Firsthand Technology Value. Limit your exposure to any one sector, including technology, so you'll be sure to stay on track.

### Continue to Make Regular Contributions to Your 403(b)

Always remember that you're a long-term investor so you shouldn't sweat daily, or even monthly, market fluctuations. Bear markets are usually short, so tough it out and don't sell yourself—or your investments—short. Above all, don't give in to the temptation of cutting back 403(b) contributions. Your assets may look like they're disappearing, but it's only temporary. They will come back. However, if you sell during a bear market, you'll lock in real losses that can't be easily recovered.

### Buy Old Reliables

A bear market goes hand-in-hand with economic slow down. And when the economy slows, business profits are greatly reduced. That's when you want to own funds that invest in "old reliables" with proven track records. A simple way to track consistency is by looking at dividends: cash disbursements to shareholders based on a company's profit. An increase in dividends usually signals higher earnings, while a reduction in dividend payments is a sign of weakness. If you own mutual funds, however, you needn't be concerned with tracking the profit/loss of individual companies; that's why you have a fund manager.

### Look on the Bright Side

A PricewaterhouseCoopers study found that 140 Internet companies went under in 1999, but a total of 1700 were funded that year. So a large number of companies managed to stay afloat. Internet growth wasn't slowing; it was simply going through a weeding-out process. Those with substance and solid infrastructures survived. The bottom line is that as technology continues to develop, bull or bear market, you want to be there.

## Strategic Words of Wisdom

Strategies don't mean that you can have it all or that your investments will go nowhere but up. However, strategies can give you the best chance at a respectable retirement nest egg. So pay less attention to the "experts" and trust yourself more. If you follow your goals and use your favorite strategies, you can stop worrying (about the stock market) and start living. And the winning strategies are:

### Do What It Takes to Keep as Much as You Can

1. Use dollar cost averaging to stay invested in both bull and bear markets.
2. Avoid funds with loads and high expense ratios.
3. Save more; trade less. The greatest threat to your savings dollars are taxes and inflation, not short-term market fluctuations.

### Don't Chase Rainbows—Trust Me, There's No Pot of Gold

1. Forget about timing the market. Jumping in and out doesn't work.
2. Remember that compounding takes time. There's no shortcut to wealth.
3. Don't count on Social Security or an inheritance for retirement income. Count only on yourself.

### Stick to Your Asset Allocation Plan

1. Hang onto those boring bonds. Don't be led into temptation by Tommy's triple-digit tech fund.
2. Don't deviate from your plan by trading a core fund for this year's prom queen.
3. Upgrade by selling losers to buy winners. Just make sure they're in the same asset allocation category.
4. Keep your diversification style and your portfolio balanced at all times.

### Be Realistic about Returns

1. You're doing well if you can approximate the stock market average.
2. Trust compounding to pump up your investment dollars, not someone's get-rich-quick scheme.

### Don't Put off 'til Tomorrow What You Can Do Today

1. Start saving early.
2. Invest consistently. Even small amounts of money add up.
3. Just do it!

## Beware of Sales Pitches

1. Don't follow the advice of a "professional" who works on commission.

2. Don't succumb to high pressure from annuity salespeople.

3. Do use the expertise of fund managers with proven track records.

## Avoid Information Overload

1. Don't let media hype influence your selected strategies.

2. Don't believe everything you read, see on TV, or find on the Internet.

3. Be selective about your information sources. If they're reputable, you only need a few.

The bottom line: Invest as much as you can, as often as you can, for as long as you can.

## Chapter 10 Homework

How many of the following strategies are you using in your 403(b) plan?

Diversification—Are you spreading your wealth?

Are your assets spread among funds that include stocks, bonds, and money markets? Are you tech-heavy? You are if you have more than 30 percent of your investments in technology.

Dollar Cost Averaging—Are you averaging your dollars?

If you're a 403(b) investor, dollar cost averaging is a given. Your 403(b) contributions are constant and invested at regular intervals.

Low fees—How low can you go?

Use a source like Morningstar.com or Maxfunds.com to look at the expense ratio of each fund you own. Consider eliminating from your portfolio underperforming funds with high expense ratios.

Balance—How's your portfolio karma?

Is it in balance or have you strayed from your original investment plan? Examine your fund holdings to see if you have the proper balance of yin and yang.

Realistic Goals—Do you equate investing with buying lottery tickets?

Be realistic about your expectations. There's no shortcut to long-term investing. People who get greedy almost always get burned.

# CHAPTER 11

# Hired Help

## DO YOU NEED IT?

Whether or not you need help from a financial planner depends on many factors and is a decision that only you can make. Keep in mind that you will pay for expert advice in one form or another and that charge will be reflected on your bottom line. This chapter will help you decide if you need outside financial advice. If you think you do, it will show you where and how to find it. If you want to go it alone and be your own financial planner, it will help you do that, too.

There is no one-plan-fits-all philosophy. Some people enjoy the challenge of tracking their own investments; others are appalled at the idea of Wall Street watching. Whichever route you choose, it's important to make an informed decision based on knowing the different types of financial assistance available. You have to determine how much financial advice is worth to you and who is competent to give it.

### Financial Planner Fees

Financial planners come in assorted flavors according to their credentials and the way in which they're paid for their services. Independent planners, annuity sales representatives, and reps from financial companies or brokerage houses all have one thing in common: They receive compensation from any one of the following:

1. Annual fee.
2. Transaction fee (on each investment bought or sold).
3. Commission (from loaded funds that carry a sales charge).
4. Hourly fee.

Of primary concern to you is how those fees affect your 403(b) account. Remember, these fees are deducted from your total return before you even see them, and they can be difficult to calculate.

### Financial Advice from a Financial Company Representative

Suppose you're investing in Mutual Discovery A shares fund through a financial company or brokerage house. Profits from that investment are calculated *only after the following expenses are deducted*:

1. Mutual Discovery A shares carry a load (sales charge) of 5.75 percent each time you buy them. That means that whenever you make a 403(b) contribution to that fund, 5.75 percent is taken off the top.
2. The financial representative who sold the fund to you also receives a commission on each transaction—typically one percent.
3. An additional deduction of 1.38 percent is levied for Mutual Discovery's expense ratio (cost to manage the fund).

That translates to an automatic reduction of 8.13 percent before you begin to realize a profit. For example, if the manager of Mutual Discovery makes investments within the fund that add up to a 15 percent total return, *your* return will be only 6.87 percent after deductions. And chances are you will have received little financial advice from the representative who manages your 403(b) account to justify those fees.

### Financial Advice from an Annuity Salesman

Now let's look at the scenario of a 403(b) held in an annuity. The account is handled by an annuity salesperson who gives limited financial advice pertaining only to the mutual funds within that annuity.

To call that salesperson a "financial advisor," in my opinion, is using the term very loosely.

When my 403(b) plan was in an annuity, the "advice" given to me was based on the two questions the salesman asked: "Do you consider yourself a conservative or aggressive investor?" and "When do you plan to retire?" This twenty second interview determined my asset allocations within the annuity. For this dubious financial service, the following fees were deducted from my return:

1. Salesman's commission

2. Administrative charge

3. Mortality and expense charge

4. Expense ratio of mutual funds within the annuity

### Financial Advice from a Fee-Only Planner

If you're seeking financial recommendations that aren't tied to sales commissions, kick-backs, or loads, look for an independent, fee-only financial planner. On average, fee-only planners charge an hourly rate somewhere between $100 and $150 for personal consultation and may have lower rates for research hours. In addition to objective advice, they offer peace of mind that comes from financial planning without any conflict of interest. Because they have no hidden agenda, fee-only planners make unbiased suggestions that are in your best interest.

The information you need is limited to the choices available through your 403(b) plan, so a minimal amount of advice can point you in the right direction. Also, if your financial questions are strictly 403(b)-related, you probably won't require more than one or two hours of consultation.

### How to Find a Fee-Only Planner

According to a 1997 survey conducted by the National Endowment for Financial Education, "seven out of ten financial planners accept commissions for investments and insurance."[1] Steer clear of those seven because their recommendations are based, in part, on what's in it for them. The National Association of Personal Financial Advisors has simplified the search for fee-only planners with an "FO" designation, indicating that their compensation comes from the client only; they receive no commission on any investments recommended by them.

**NAPFA (National Association of Personal Financial Advisors) www.napfa.org** can help you find a fee-only financial planner in your area.

NAPFA is the largest organization of fee-only financial planners. Members must have extensive financial planning experience, industry certification, and, most importantly, "compensation untainted by any type of fee received by vendors of financial products, investment funds, insurance companies, and estate attorneys."

NAPFA's Web site is easy to navigate and has a prominent icon: "Find a Fee-only Planner Near You." Click on it for local financial planner information.

### Those All-Important Credentials

In the 1990s, a booming stock market gave rise to an increase in the number of people calling themselves financial planners. Because financial planning is basically an unregulated industry, those who made a few good stock picks could hang up a financial planning shingle. The most professional financial planners, however, are those with a designation of CFP (Certified Financial Planner) or CFA (Chartered Financial Analyst) next to their name.

A CFP must complete a course on finances and investing and then pass a ten-hour exam. This procedure is regulated by the Certified Financial Planner Board of Standards, which says that only about 55 percent of applicants pass the test. In addition, a CFP has to have at least three years of experience in the field of finance and must agree to abide by a code of ethics. To find a CFP in your area, call the Institute of Certified Financial Planners at 800-282-7526 or visit their Web site at www.fpanet.org.

The Certified Financial Planner Board of Standards can also verify your potential planner's credibility and tell you if there's been any disciplinary action taken against him or her. They are a non-profit organization and can be contacted at 888-237-6275 or on the Web at www.cfp-board.org. The CFP Board of Standards has a search window on their home page allowing you to "check the status of a CFP certificant" by entering his or her name.

If the financial planner you're considering is also a stock broker, you can access information about him or her through the National Association of Securities Dealers by calling 800-289-9999 or by going to the Web site (www.nasdr.com.) This is a particularly helpful site for fact-finding about individual brokers and to view or register complaints about them. Their "Customer Complaint Program" investigates all complaints for potential violations of securities laws and regulations. An investor might go to this site to register a complaint if:

- their advisor/broker has represented or omitted material facts relating to the investment.

- they were given investment recommendations that were unsuitable for their objectives and profile.

- they were solicited by a broker/advisor using high-pressure, persistent tactics and/or unwanted phone calls.

Chartered Financial Analyst (CFA) is another financial planner designation that requires more extensive education, financial experience, and testing than a CFP. Applicants have to complete a program that includes passing a three-part examination, only one part of which can be taken in a given year. In the year 2000, approximately half of the candidates passed the Level I and II exams, while 65 percent of the 9,684 applicants passed the Level III exam.

## Financial Planner Pros and Cons

Isabel Baker was determined to do retirement right. Well aware of the need to plan ahead, Isabel was willing to do her homework. She read the *Wall Street Journal*, subscribed to *Mutual Fund* magazine, and requested literature from all the mutual fund families in her 403(b) plan.

Isabel soon found herself on information overload. Her investment library was growing, but her free time was shrinking and her moods changed with the movements of the stock market. When the Nasdaq soared, Isabel was sure she didn't own enough technology. When it fell, she wanted nothing more than to trade her tech for blue chips. Isabel's emotional state varied from euphoria to depression. But most of the time she just felt confused.

The remedy for Isabel's malaise was easy. She enlisted the help of a fee-only financial planner, met with him for an hour at a cost of

$150, and concluded that it was money well-spent. For $150, Isabel reviewed her portfolio and became confident that it would serve her well in retirement.

Most 403(b) investors aren't financial experts and can find it very overwhelming to sift through the endless amount of material available. By the time they finish a typical day of work-related stress and errand running, there's little energy left for hard-core investment research. That's when paying a planner can feel like getting a financial massage at the end of a long day.

### The Balancing Act

All the data in the world won't help if you can't put together a portfolio that's balanced for risk and for your ability to tolerate it. It's easy to build a portfolio in a bull market when just about every fund is on an upswing, but it may take a financial expert to help select investments that will hold up in a bear market as well. While we know that a balanced portfolio contains cash investments, bonds, and stocks, filling in those blanks with the right funds can be complicated. What's the difference between aggressive growth, growth and income, and large growth? How much should you invest in each category?

Good financial planners use historical data to show how different types of investments move in relation to each other. They can also give concrete examples that put you in touch with your inner risk tolerance. When technology funds are booming and you're tempted to throw caution to the winds and all your savings at tech funds— that's when you need a financial advisor over your shoulder saying, "Would you really feel okay if that $12,000 you invested turned out to be $8,000 at the end of the year?"

That advisor can pull you back to reality and help develop an asset allocation plan you can live with. He or she can recommend a balanced portfolio with staying power and the percentages you need for successful long-term investing in each segment of the market.

### Diversification

Easier said than done. Your mutual funds may have different names, but chances are they have similar holdings. Assume that your 403(b) account contains a growth fund, a growth and income fund, a value fund, and a balanced fund. "How balanced am I," you say, patting yourself on the back. But take a closer look.

As Isabel Baker discovered, even if you have different investment categories spread among several fund families, you're probably not as diversified as you think. However, if your 403(b) is directly invested with one fund family, diversification is easier. You need only track different funds within that family to determine their holdings. And that information is easily accessed by phoning the family or going to its Web site.

## Other Reasons for Using Hired Help

There are other reasons to seek financial help. Many of them are emotionally-based and may include the following:

- Overloaded Circuits
- Annuity Angst
- A Second Opinion
- One-Stop Shopping
- Research-Impaired

### Overloaded Circuits

You're drowning in a sea of mutual funds. You own too many but aren't sure which ones should go. A professional planner can help you decide, based on that all-important principle of balance.

### Annuity Angst

You're stuck in an annuity and don't know how to get out. There are ways to transfer some annuity assets without paying exit penalties. (See Chapter 3.) If you don't want to tackle this yourself, a financial planner can walk you through the process.

### A Second Opinion

You need some direction to make sure your portfolio is on track. Consider paying for an hour's worth of time with a fee-only planner. He or she can give your portfolio a little tweaking and reassure you that you're on the right path.

### One-Stop Shopping

You want one financial package that puts your mind at ease about your 403(b) plan, insurance requirements, estate planning, and short-term obligations such as college tuition. In that case, you might need a full-service fee-only planner who can address all your financial needs.

### Research-Impaired

You have no time or desire to do investment research, but you'd like to know that your money is working its hardest for you. A professional financial planner has easy access to financial information and can apply that information to your particular portfolio needs.

## Questions You Should Ask

Many people do extensive research before buying a car or a new home, yet they will entrust their portfolio to the first planner that comes along. An investment portfolio is a precious asset and requires some serious sleuthing before giving control of it to someone else. It's important to interview more than one planner and ask the following questions before deciding whom to hire.

### What Are Your Credentials?

As previously discussed, many unqualified advisors are calling themselves "financial planners." Experienced and well-educated planners will have either a CFP (certified financial planner) or CFA (chartered financial analyst) designation. In addition, financial advisors, regardless of their credentials, are now required to take what's known as the Series 65 exam. At the very least, any planner you're considering should have passed this test. There won't be any letters after his or her name to indicate this; you have to ask.

### How Do You Get Paid?

This crucial question determines whether they are paid by you and you alone or if they get additional compensation (commission) from investments they recommend. For truly unbiased advice, you must be absolutely sure they are working independently and have no affiliation with any type of investment product.

This is also the time to ask about the fees. If he or she is a fee-only planner, is it an hourly or an annual fee? Is it based on the amount of your investments? If so, you need to find out if it's a percentage that will compound over time. A percentage-based scenario is unlikely in a 403(b) account but just to be safe, you need to ask.

### How Long Have You Been Practicing?

The longer the better. Your planner should have many years of experience under his or her belt with exposure to both bull and bear markets. You also want someone who is knowledgeable about retirement investing and 403(b) plans, in particular. And don't hesitate to ask for references; personal recommendations are often the most reliable and can reveal a lot more about planners than the letters next to their name. If possible, look for a planner who has experience with clients in financial circumstances similar to your own.

### What Types of Services Do You Offer?

Find out if he or she is a full-service advisor who can handle investments, taxes, insurance, and so forth. Ask about phone availability. How frequently can you call with questions and is there an additional charge for that? Reputable planners don't usually charge for phone calls unless you call them too often and talk for too long. Also ask whether you'll be dealing with the advisor only, or with others in the firm.

## Questions *They* Should Ask

In addition to quizzing prospective planners on their credentials and experience, it's also important to pay attention to the questions *they* ask *you*. Their queries to you can reveal a lot. Beware of questions that are too general and don't address your personal needs. Following are a few examples of inquiries a qualified financial planner should make.

### What Are Your Goals?

Before a financial planner can begin to do his or her job, he needs to know the basic financial goals and objectives your investment program has to meet. The planner will want to know if you're saving for retirement, college tuition, care of an elderly family member, and so on.

### When Do You Plan to Reach Your Goals?

Here's where that all-important timeline comes in. You need to have a handle on just how much time you have to amass the money you'll need. Have you already taken steps to reach those goals?

A financial planner has to know any investment programs you already participate in so that he or she can develop an all-encompassing financial plan.

### What Is Your Feeling about Risk versus Reward?

Your personal risk tolerance is an important factor in creating a financial plan. The financial planner you're considering should take your comfort level into account and structure an investment plan that lets you sleep at night.

### How Involved Do You Want to be with the Investment Process?

This question will be a determining factor in how extensive a plan you require, how much time needs to be devoted to creating it, and what your participation level will be. Realize that how you answer this question will have a definite bearing on the fees that you'll pay. Clearly, a complete financial planning package will cost a lot more than one or two hours of consultation.

## Do-It-Yourself Financial Planning

John Rekenthaler, research director of Morningstar, believes that the average investor doesn't need professional help. "If you use common sense—focus on costs, taxes, and other fundamental issues, as opposed to going performance chasing, you can pretty readily pick mutual funds and put together a portfolio that's as reasonable as what a financial pro would do. Very sensible, diversified portfolios can easily be constructed if you've educated yourself in the marketplace."[2]

Rekenthaler advocates investing with one fund family, an option available in most 403(b) plans. He believes that cost is a major factor when evaluating a fund and that you can stack the deck in your favor by picking from a pool of low-cost funds. His criteria for a reputable fund family is:

- Stability in both management and personnel; in other words, companies whose employees want to stay there.

- Shareholder-friendly policies such as a willingness to offer help and information whenever needed.

- Honest, open communication that goes the extra mile to educate shareholders and keep them current on fund happenings.

In a raging bull market, investors often don't pay much attention to the loss of a few percentage points in the name of financial advice. After all, with triple-digit returns, who cares? But at the end of 2000 when the tech bubble burst, one or two percent suddenly mattered.

Remember, the long-term norm for yearly gains in the stock market has historically been between 10 and 12 percent. You want to pay out as little as possible so there's more left for you and the retirement lifestyle you envisioned. A strong selling point for being your own financial advisor is that the market always reverts back to the norm. And if your 403(b) is invested with a good fund family, they can provide enough information to help you make your own decisions. As you learned in Chapter 3, investing through a financial planner—even with a fee as low as one percent—can diminish your nest egg by as much as $200,000 over 40 years because of compounding fees.

Few financial planners are astute enough to actually earn that one percent. You can do just as well for yourself—often better—by building your own balanced portfolio of low-cost funds. Again, a 403(b) plan has limited choices, and no paid financial planner can pull rabbits out of a hat to make you a millionaire.

So even if you hire a full-service planner for your other financial needs, you're better off going it alone with your 403(b). You might get lucky and receive free 403(b) advice if you pay a planner for everything else. But if he or she says "show me the money" and wants a percentage of your 403(b) investments, run, don't walk, to the nearest low-cost, no-load mutual fund family. There should be one on your 403(b) provider list, and they'll be happy to supply all the information you need to become your own financial planner.

### Know Thyself

Suppose you're not sure if you can—or even want—to be your own financial planner. Remember the old adage "you won't know until you try?" Here are some questions you can ask yourself to get a reading of your own financial planning barometer. If you can answer yes to most of them, chances are you're ready to take on that job.

#### DO YOU LIKE TO BE IN CONTROL?

Are you a follower or a leader? It's possible to be both. For example, you may take a strong stand on certain issues and refuse to follow the pack, while preferring to stay on the sidelines on others.

I straddled the fence on financial issues for years. "Math and money just aren't my thing," I told myself. But another voice in my head constantly interrupted. Because, deep down, I really didn't like the feeling of being in a tunnel when it came to finances. I was plagued with nagging doubts that my investments could be better, but I didn't know how to make that happen. When I finally took control, I saw the proverbial light at the end of the tunnel. And if you've gotten this far in my book, I know you're seeing it, too.

### CAN YOU ACCEPT RESPONSIBILITY FOR YOUR OWN ACTIONS?

There's no investment guru alive who hasn't made mistakes. The stock market's unpredictability can turn yesterday's investment decision into tomorrow's ulcer. Decisions to buy or sell are based on a lot of factors beyond your control. You may have made a wrong choice by following the advice of a friend or acting on a hot tip from a broker. Even the press can lead you astray with a fund-you-must-own article. But you're only human. Accept the responsibility (and loss) that comes from making a bad investment decision and move on. A few poor choices are simply part of the learning curve as you travel that long winding road to retirement.

Of course it's important to take financial responsibility seriously—not just for you, but also for your loved ones and your community. Your budget, portfolio, and overall spending and saving habits have a lasting impact; without sufficient assets, you could easily become a burden on both family and society in your retirement years.

### ARE YOU DISCIPLINED?

Exercising discipline in finances means that you've set goals, both short- and long-term, and you're determined to do whatever it takes to achieve them. We all have a few unforeseen financial crunches, but they probably won't have a major impact on your investment plan; you've set realistic goals and have the discipline to make them work.

The good news for 403(b) investors is that built-in dollar cost averaging keeps you on track. This forced pay-yourself-first plan makes disciplined saving for retirement relatively painless.

### ARE YOU A TEAM PLAYER?

You may already have a financial team in place that includes an accountant, banker, and tax advisor. You may even have a financial

planner on board. Just remember that it's your money they're dealing with and *you* are the coach. Like it or not, you need to be somewhat financially literate unless you're willing to give them carte
blanche with your dollars.

When you become financially savvy, you then have what it takes to
be your own financial planner. You may not know enough to be your
own accountant or tax advisor, so keep those players on your team.
But you can probably do without the services of a financial planner
to manage your 403(b).

### WHAT PRINCIPLES DO YOU LIVE BY?

Throughout your life, you have had experiences that shaped your
values. Maybe you've been a scout, a member of the military, a
teacher, or a mentor. Each role you play helps develop your own personal code of ethics, and that code of ethics becomes integrated into
your relationships with family, friends, co-workers, and even money.

If you've always been frugal and have had a healthy respect for
money and the discipline to save it, you're perfectly capable of becoming your own financial planner.

## Financial Planning When You're the Pro

In *Making the Most of Your Money*, Jane Bryant Quinn says, "Most
of us don't need professional planners. Conservative money management isn't hard. To be your own guru, you need only a list of objectives, a few simple financial products, a time frame that gives your
investments time to work out, and a well-tempered humbug detector
to keep you from falling for rascally sales pitches."[3]

Quinn's philosophy echoes the strategies explored throughout this
book. To be your own planner, you need:

### A List of Objectives

The importance of setting goals and objectives was discussed in
Chapter 6, "Planning and Saving for Retirement." Articulating your
goals and developing a plan to implement them is the first step toward becoming your own financial planner.

### A Few Simple Financial Products

Chapters 2 and 5 showed you how to select a 403(b) vehicle and how
to choose the funds in it. That's the second step in do-it-yourself

financial planning; it's not difficult because 403(b) plans offer only a few possible vehicles, and the vehicle you choose determines the choice of funds within it. If, for example, you've chosen to invest with a fund family like Vanguard, your investment selection is limited to the funds Vanguard offers. No need for doctoral thesis research; it's much easier to choose when the pickings are slim.

### A Time Frame that Gives Your Investments Time to Work Out

This book emphasizes over and over again the importance of starting early. Chapter 6, "Planning and Saving for Retirement," emphasizes that it's never too soon. The more years you give your money to compound, the less you need to save. It's that simple. With compounding, $10,000 invested in your twenties will grow to hundreds of thousands by the time you reach retirement age.

It can't be stressed enough—waiting until the age of 40 to start a savings/investment program can be very painful. With less years left until retirement, you'll feel the pinch of having to save a lot in a short time frame. The pressure is on in more ways than one. If you make a poor investment decision in your twenties, so what? You have time to recoup your losses. However, if poor investing judgment coincides with a prolonged bear market when you're 50, you could be in trouble. At that stage of the game, recovering lost investment dollars is much harder. Remember, it's not market timing but time in the market that matters.

### A Well-Tempered Humbug Detector

Hopefully your humbug detector will have been fully-charged after reading Chapter 4, "Choosing the Best 403(b) Vehicle," and learning the difference between an annuity salesperson, a middleman, and direct investing with a mutual fund family. That detector should be filtering out the false claims from commission-based "advisors." The annuity sales rep isn't going to emphasize the excessive fees in his or her financial product and the middleman won't readily reveal the commissions and/or kickbacks he or she receives. It's up to you to read between the lines, do the math, and fully understand the true cost of owning a particular investment.

John Waggoner, financial columnist for *USA TODAY*, sums it up nicely. "About 88 million people own mutual fund shares. An increase of just one percentage point in fund fees can slash investors' returns by 18% over 20 years."[4] The advantage is obvious: pay yourself that one percent to be your own financial planner.

## Chapter 11 Homework

If you want to find a financial planner, here's a quick reference list:

Financial Planning Association—certified financial planners in your area (800) 282-7526. www.fpanet.org

National Association of Personal Financial Advisors—fee-only planners (888) 333-6659. www.napfa.org

National Association of Securities Dealers—verify credentials of planners who are also brokers and/or register a complaint about one in their "customer complaint program" (800) 289-9999. www.nasdr.com

Certified Financial Board of Standards—verify a financial planner's records and credentials (888) 237-6275. www.cfp-board.org

Keep in mind that doing the job yourself means more dollars left to compound for you. Also, look for an independent fee-only planner with a Certified Financial Planner (CFP) or Certified Financial Analyst (CFA) designation who receives no compensation from investment companies.

CFP

- Takes an extensive course on finances
- Passes a 10 hour exam
- Has at least three years of financial experience
- Agrees to abide by a code of ethics

CFA

- More extensive financial experience and education than a CFP
- More rigorous testing than a CFP—passes a three part exam given once a year for three years
- Agrees to abide by a code of ethics

# Changing Choices Changing Jobs

**C**hange is part of today's daily life. As 403(b) investors become more educated, they're changing their minds too. They want 403(b) vehicles that aren't annuity-based. They want access to funds without loads and high fees. They want better investment choices than those available inside the 403(b) box.

"It's ironic that schools do little to educate teachers," says Morningstar analyst Hap Bryant. "Hospitals show scant concern for their employees' well-being, and not-for-profit organizations don't seem to care much about fairness."[1] So 403(b) investors have resorted to educating themselves in bits and pieces.

As discussed earlier, employers of non-profits take little or no responsibility for managing 403(b) plans. Their role is simply to deduct employee contributions and send them on their way. So off they go to one of the 403(b) providers on *their* list, a list that often limits participants' choices to the best of the worst.

It's the twenty-first century, but many 403(b) plans remain stuck in the past, when the government required all 403(b) accounts to be held in annuities. Insurance companies who sell those annuities grabbed hold of the lucrative 403(b) market and haven't let go.

## Changing Choices

When they finally saw the light, many investors wanted out—out of the old plan and into something new and improved. They wanted to be free of the annuity hold with its excessive fees, less than stellar subaccounts, and exit penalties that go on for years. It wasn't easy, but some managed to find an escape hatch.

### Unlocking the Annuity Gate

"I am not at all impressed with the performance of the subaccounts in my annuity and I see that it has a 5% surrender fee if I try to leave. I feel like a captive and think my broker should have told me that variable annuities are not the instrument of choice for a 403(b). I would like to know what recourse I have to get my funds out without losing a bunch of money."[2]

This letter, written by a 403(b) investor to a financial advisor, exemplifies the frustration felt by many annuity owners. They didn't read the fine print, and the annuity sales representative didn't inform them. Now they feel betrayed. But there are ways to unlock the annuity gate and liberate their money.

If you have passed the annuity penalty phase for early exits, you're free to move the money into a 403(b)7 without any fees. The "7" simply means your 403(b) contributions go directly to a mutual fund family. Check with your annuity company to find out where you are in the penalty phase. An early departure can cost as much as 7 percent in surrender fees, so it's wise to know before you go.

Many annuity companies allow an annual fee-free transfer, up to 10 percent of your account, to another 403(b) plan. Call your company to verify this option. Then use your employer's list to pick a new provider and contact them for any paperwork necessary to implement the transfer.

You also have the option of directing all further 403(b) contributions to the new provider and "freezing" the annuity until the penalty years have passed and you can make your final escape. Remember, you can have multiple 403(b) accounts but can actively contribute to only one at a time. Although the annuity account is essentially inactive, it's still open. That means that you can move funds around in it without incurring fees.

If you're near the end of your annuity "sentence," you might consider paying off the guards to let you out. The cost of exit fees declines over time, and it may be worth paying one or two percent to get out. After weighing the loss of potential returns against those high annuity charges, you may decide to bid your annuity farewell forever.

### Lobbying for Better Choices

An article in the *New York Times* described one woman's reaction to her husband's 403(b) choices "limited to annuities with high fees and funds that carry hefty sales charges."[3] Refusing to accept lower returns on their retirement savings, she became an activist and lobbied his employer for better choices. The following steps show how you can do that too.

- Decide on new 403(b) providers you'd like to see added to the list. Focus on no-load mutual fund families with low operating expenses and a large selection of funds.

---

### Sample Letter

My colleagues and I are requesting 403(b) choices other than or in addition to those that are currently offered. We want to include mutual fund families in which we can invest directly. We are unhappy with the fact that our current 403(b) options are limited to annuities only, for the following reasons:

1. Annuities charge unnecessary fees. Those fees compound and subtract thousands of dollars from our retirement savings.

2. At one point, 403(b) plans, by law, had to be in annuities. A new law has removed this limitation and we'd like to take advantage of that.

3. 403(b) plans are already tax-deferred. We don't want to pay extra annuity fees for tax deferral that's built into the plan.

After extensive research, we found that the following mutual fund companies charge lower fees, which lead to higher returns. Please consider adding them to our list of 403(b) providers.

1. Fund A

2. Fund B

3. Fund C

- Share your findings with co-workers and ask them to sign a petition documenting your requests.

- Submit the petition to your employer, along with a letter of explanation. (See sample letter.)

- Present the current list of available options along with your letter so that you can point out the unsatisfactory choices.

### Send in the Suits

Contact a law firm that specializes in class action lawsuits. This may seem like a drastic move, but it's being done more and more all the time. One group of attorneys filed suits against four insurance companies that sell annuities, maintaining that "the practice of marketing annuities for retirement plans is abusive."[4] And three lawsuits in Texas contended that "one company's relationship with a school district led teachers to invest in lower-performing products, such as annuities."[5] In that particular school district, visits from annuity company reps were actually announced over the loudspeaker.

Indeed, there are all kinds of laws in place to protect consumers from misrepresentation and the omission of relevant facts. Before you signed up for an annuity, were you told that

- you are locked into the plan for several years? There are high exit penalties if you try to leave early?

- you will be paying annuity fees on top of mutual fund fees for tax-deferral that you already have in your 403(b) plan?

It's unlikely that annuity companies will admit to any wrongdoing or that they'll willingly agree to pay compensation to the plaintiffs. If nothing else, however, these lawsuits will succeed in bringing attention to this problem, and awareness has to happen before change can occur.

### Out of the Box Transfers

You're not retiring; you're not changing jobs; you just want to put the 403(b) funds you've accumulated in a different place. Many investors don't realize that you can take your 403(b) assets and move them anywhere that handles 403(b) accounts. You don't have to go to a provider from your employer's list. And you can do it more than once.

The catch is that you can only transfer *old* money; you're not opening an account to which you can make new contributions. And if your old money is in an annuity with the penalty phase still in effect, you'll have to pay exit fees. But if your 403(b) account has no strings attached and you've always wanted to put it elsewhere, here are the steps to do that:

1. Decide where you want the money to go. Keep in mind that you don't have to stay with your employer's options. No-loads and low fees—all that can be yours if you choose wisely.

2. Call your 403(b) vehicle of choice and ask for account transfer forms. You also have to contact your current provider for their required paperwork.

3. Be sure to designate beneficiaries for your new account. Forgetting this important step can lead to unpleasant tax consequences for your heirs.

That's all there is to it. So if you're holding funds that you secretly hate, it's now safe to come out of the closet and take advantage of the transfer option to give your old money a new home.

## Changing Jobs

If you're moving to a new job, you need to decide what to do with the money in your 403(b) plan. The Employment Benefit Research Institute (EBRI) says that "25% of job changers don't know they have choices about what to do with the money in their retirement plans, and 60% elect to take a cash distribution."[6] Don't be one of them.

### Cashing out

If you decide to take the money in a lump-sum payment—even if it's only a small amount—you'll be making a definite dent in your retirement nest egg. Fred is a 403(b) investor who takes a new job and cashes out his old 403(b) plan. After all, Fred's only thirty; he has plenty of investing years left before retirement. So Fred takes his

$12,000 and uses it for a down payment on a new car. Down the road, that car will have actually cost Fred approximately $325,000. Had he kept the $12,000 invested and earning compounded interest at the rate of 10 percent annually, it could have grown to $337,229 by the time Fred turned 65. Oh the decisions we make when we're young and foolish.

Many years ago I was a young and foolish teacher in Detroit. After a short-lived teaching career of only three years, I moved to California, taking the money from my pension plan with me. I didn't have a 403(b) plan, but at that time they were virtually unknown. I also knew absolutely nothing about retirement plans and not much more about the stock market.

Granted, I had the option to leave my pension funds untouched. While I didn't have any say in where it was invested, it *was* invested and quietly accruing interest. I should have let it sleep. Had I done that, I would have had quite a bundle 40 years later.

I found a teaching position in California, also short-lived due to the birth of my first child. Of course there was money in my pension plan that could have stayed there when I left. Of course it didn't. After all, I had a new baby coming and was sure I needed every penny I could get my hands on.

Depleting my pension plans cost me many years of potential compounding. When I returned to the workforce several years later, I had lost time in the market that no amount of diligent saving could replace. My retirement nest egg would be forever diminished because of the foolish choices I made.

So listen up all you twenty- and thirty-somethings. A booming stock market has made people of every age more investment conscious. Youth is no longer an excuse to delay investing. In fact, it's the only time you have time on your side. If you waste those years, you can't get them back. Trust me, retirement comes around sooner than you think.

If you're changing jobs and have a pension plan and/or a 403(b), don't even think about withdrawing the money. Keep it right where it is or roll it over to another tax-deferred retirement account. It doesn't matter whether the rollover is to an IRA, a 401(k), or a 403(b). Resolve to keep that money invested *somewhere* and forget about it for the next 40 years.

### Keep Your Money in the Old Plan

Leaving your money in the old plan is one of the easiest choices. Simply let it stay right where it is, continuing to accrue tax-free dollars. If you're happy with the present performance of your 403(b) plan, there's no good reason to switch. You can continue to move money around in it; you just can't make any new contributions. Those will be directed to the retirement plan available at your new place of employment.

### Roll It over into a New Plan

If you like your new employer's options, rolling your old 403(b) money into one of them is another good choice. The asset transfer is tax-free and by consolidating your plans into one, you'll have more ease of management and a lot less record keeping.

### Roll It into an IRA

Rolling over to an IRA is a mixed bag. There are pros and cons if you're changing jobs and choose the IRA option. Many investors, however, feel that the positives outweigh the negatives.

*Pro*: You have practically unlimited investment options with an IRA. Unlike the 403(b) box, IRAs have few investment restrictions. You can put your money into stock, bond, or money market funds, and you can even mix and match. Your IRA account can be in a bank, brokerage house, or mutual fund family. And if you choose the fund family option, your IRA investment isn't limited to their funds.

An IRA is do-it-yourself investing at its best. You're not limited to an employer's list; you don't have to pay commissions to a middleman. The IRA holder you select takes care of the paperwork and you get to make the decisions.

You can also take advantage of the "substantially equal payments" rule. Normally you have to pay a 10 percent penalty if you tap into your retirement plan before age $59\frac{1}{2}$, but the "substantially equal payments" clause gives you early access to your money if you need it. You simply agree to withdraw a specific amount of money for five years or until you turn $59\frac{1}{2}$, whichever comes first.

Your beneficiaries will benefit from inheriting an IRA. The law allows them to spread payments over *their* lifetimes, substantially reducing the tax burden. Money inherited from a 403(b) plan, however, can have serious tax consequences for anyone but your spouse.

*Con*: Maybe you're unsure about your new job and the income it will provide. In an emergency, you can borrow from your 403(b) plan, but you can't borrow from an IRA. And if you get into a real financial bind, creditors can tap into your IRA because it's regulated by state law.

### A Word of Caution

You have to do a direct transfer from your old 403(b) plan to the newly-established IRA. If you don't and a check from your 403(b) comes made out to you, you will immediately lose money—lots of it—because your employer is required by law to withhold 20 percent for taxes.

There is a grace period if your 403(b) money should inadvertently appear in your mailbox. You have 60 days to roll it over and avoid the tax penalty. Pay attention to that ticking clock. If you miss the 60-day deadline, you may have to pay the tax, plus an additional 10 percent early withdrawal penalty depending on your age. And the IRS shows no mercy. If the 60 days have passed, you can't plead that you lost your calendar.

### Roll It over to a Roth IRA

You can't do this directly. Because a Roth IRA is paid for with after-tax dollars, you can't roll before-tax dollars into it. You first have to convert your 403(b) to a traditional IRA. If you decide to go to a Roth later, you'll have to pay taxes on your original pre-tax dollar investments. The cost may be worth it, however. Once you're in a Roth, you'll reap the benefits of tax-free compounding forever. Unlike a 403(b) or traditional IRA, your investment growth isn't tax-deferred, it's tax-free. When those dollars compound, you get to keep them all as long as you wait until you're 59$\frac{1}{2}$ and your Roth is at least five years old.

## Borrowing from Your 403(b)

Relocating and changing jobs can be costly. The costs involved in buying a new home, along with the move itself, can leave you strapped for cash. At a time like this, a loan from your 403(b) may seem quite tempting. Before you take this step, however, you need to consider the pitfalls.

Even though it's your money, the law requires that you pay yourself back, and a funny thing happens to those tax-deferred dollars you're borrowing. You have to pay them back with interest, whatever the going rate is at the time. And while you're paying yourself an interest rate of, say, 8 percent, you could be losing money. Suppose the money you borrowed had been in a fund earning 16 percent returns. Essentially you're losing half of what you might have earned if your money had remained invested.

You're also paying pre-tax dollars back with after-tax dollars. Then when you retire and start making withdrawals, you'll pay tax on the same money again. So a double tax hit is one of the major negatives of borrowing from a 403(b). You're better off taking a home equity loan because the interest on that loan is tax deductible; the interest you pay on a 403(b) loan is not.

Suppose you decide not to pay the loan back. Unfortunately, the IRS says the minute you take money out of a retirement account, some of it belongs to the government. The IRS will leave you alone if you pay it back. Here are the consequences if you don't: income tax due on the amount you've withdrawn and a 10 percent penalty besides. If, for example, you borrowed $5,000 and didn't pay it back, you would owe a $500 penalty and $1400 in taxes (in the 28 percent tax bracket). In other words, it's costing you almost two thousand dollars to borrow five.

## Summary

If you change your mind, there are ways to move 403(b) money. Being forced to invest inside the box doesn't mean you can't be creative. You can:

- Move annuity money out; if not all at once, then in bits and pieces.

- Enlist the help of co-workers and lobby for change together.
- Use the power of the pen to request specific changes from your employer.
- Transfer accumulated 403(b) assets.
- Take legal action if you're convinced of wrongdoing.

If you change jobs, you can leave 403(b) assets in your old plan or:

- Roll them over into your new employer's plan.
- Roll them into an IRA, giving you unlimited mutual fund choices.

Avoid borrowing from your 403(b) because:

- You'll be paying back pre-tax dollars with post-tax dollars.
- You have to pay interest that's not tax-deductible.
- Double taxation hurts your nest egg. You're repaying the loan with after-tax dollars and must pay tax again on those same dollars when you take retirement withdrawals.
- If you don't pay yourself back, you'll owe taxes and penalties on the amount you borrowed.

## Chapter 12 Homework

If you're unhappy with the 403(b) choices offered by your employer, the outline below identifies the steps you can take to implement change.

I. Get a copy of your employer's list of current 403(b) providers.

  A. Divide the list into three categories.

    1. Annuity companies (often have the word "insurance" as part of their company name).

    2. Mutual fund companies (usually have that designation in their name, i.e., Vanguard Mutual Funds).

    3. Financial services companies (anything that doesn't fit into the first two categories—commission-based salespeople).

  B. Check to see how many mutual fund families are on the list.

    If there are none or the choices are poor, decide which mutual fund families you'd like to see added.

II. Draft a letter to your employer and union representative requesting the additions and documenting the reasons why you'd like to see these changes made. Some suggestions:

A. Because the only way to eliminate unnecessary fees and commissions is by direct investing with a no-load mutual fund company.

B. Unnecessary fees, commissions, and loads compound over time and detract from retirement savings.

C. Because tax deferral is built into a 403(b). An annuity-based plan is not needed to get that benefit.

III. Follow through on your request and verify that someone is actively working toward implementing it.

IV. Ask co-workers for support; when employees join forces to lobby for change, the impact is much greater than trying to do it alone.

# The Retirement Years

You've worked hard, saved diligently, and made regular contributions to your 403(b) plan. Retirement is approaching and you're ready to take on a laid-back lifestyle. Or are you?

This chapter looks at two aspects of retirement: emotional and financial. If your financial house is in order, chances are the emotional adjustment to retirement will be easier—but it's still an adjustment. I'll help you look at some of the psychological issues as well as provide information on more practical retirement considerations such as the following:

- Retirement income—how to ensure a steady stream
- Retirement outgo—expected expenses during retirement
- Internet resources to help calculate how much you'll need
- Managing your 403(b) with an emphasis on taxes
- Investing for growth while protecting your assets

## New Beginnings

The key to a fulfilling retirement is to retire *to* something, not from it. The idea of endless weekends fills some soon-to-be retirees with dread. After years of productivity and structure, most people can't envision spending their golden years on one long vacation. For some, suddenly sixty is a big question mark. Who am I now that I'm not who I used to be? As a 403(b) investor, chances are you worked in a helping profession, perhaps as a teacher, nurse, or member of the clergy. If you spent 40 or more hours per week giving to others, it won't be easy to refocus all that nurturing. Every retiree needs activities that are diverse and rewarding, and people who worked as caregivers may feel that need even more.

The psychological implications of retirement can be just as daunting as the financial considerations. You're on your own to develop a new life and that life requires as much balance as the old one. Free time can't be treasured if that's all there is. Fortunately, today's retirees are younger, healthier, and plan to remain more productive. The big difference is that that productivity need no longer be tied to a paycheck.

With a steady stream of income based on years of hard work and astute investing, retirement should mark the beginning of a new life rather than the end of an old one. You're now in control of the rest of your life and you get to choose what you want to do on your own terms. The possibilities are endless.

We all have deferred dreams. Retirement gives us the time to pursue them. It doesn't matter whether they lead to a second career with monetary rewards or to self-satisfaction from doing volunteer work. What does matter is viewing retirement as an opportunity for self-exploration.

The reality of retirement, however, is that your free time and what you do with it often depends on your financial circumstances. Retiring as a millionaire is no longer what it used to be. According to some financial experts, a 40-year-old who wants to have a $35,000 annual income from age 65 to age 90 would need to have saved $1.7 million. To generate that same level of income at retirement, a 25 year old needs to have $3 million. So does that mean only multi-millionaires can afford to retire?

Not saving enough often means that many retirees don't abandon their jobs; they simply find new ones. And the good news is they're happier now than they ever were in their stress-filled pre-retirement days. A second career often means a part-time job doing something you really like. And because you have other income sources like Social Security, a pension, and distributions from your 403(b) (see Figure 13.1), the pressure is off; you can relax and enjoy your new career without worrying about that climb to the top of the corporate ladder. Moreover, you now have more time to monitor and fine tune your portfolio.

Your income during retirement will probably be a combination of Social Security, a pension, and 403(b) distributions (see Figure 13.2). Additional sources could include an IRA, Roth IRA, and other non-403(b) taxable investments.

### Social Security

Social Security is an allowance from the government; and the amount you're entitled to depends on how many years you've worked and how much you've contributed to the Social Security system through payroll deductions. Some educators, however, are missing the Social Security piece of the pie. Connecticut, for example, is a state that doesn't withdraw Social Security payments from teachers' salaries. Instead, those states increase the amount deducted for pensions, and those pensions are considerably higher to compensate.

If you've ever worked in the private sector, you can collect Social

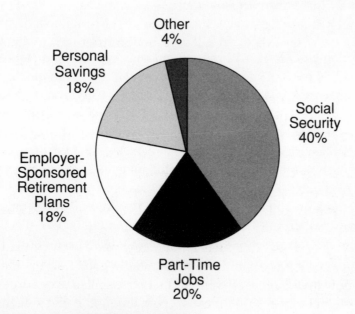

**FIGURE 13.1** Sources of Retirement Income.
*Source:* U.S. Social Security Administration.

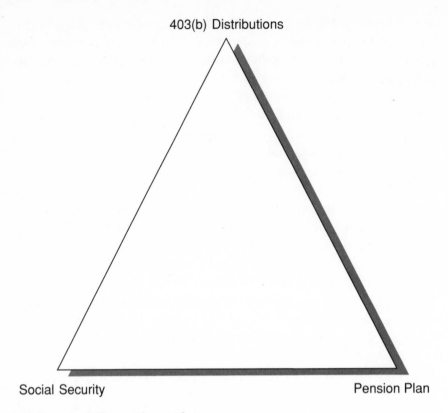

403(b) Distributions

Social Security                    Pension Plan

**FIGURE 13.2** Retirement Income Sources.

Security benefits along with your pension. And if you're married, you're eligible for half of your spouse's benefit. For example, if your spouse receives $1000 monthly from Social Security, you're entitled to a separate $500 payment of your own that won't affect the money he or she receives. However, you can't have both; the amount of your Social Security benefit will be the higher of the two.

Under current law, you can receive full benefits at age 65 or partial benefits from ages 62 to 64. In 2000, for example, taking early benefits at 62 meant a 20 percent reduction in the amount you would receive if you waited until 65. However, waiting until 65 to collect the maximum isn't always the best choice. Although the monthly payments will be larger, it can take up to 13 years to recoup the payments you missed by delaying them.

Suppose you opted to receive Social Security benefits starting at age 62 for a total of $650 a month. If you postpone the benefits until age 65, however, your monthly payment will be $800. That's $150 more in your pocket every month. Now here's the other side of that coin: By taking benefits between ages 62 and 65, you will have collected a total of $23,400. If you take nothing *until* age 65, you will get $150 more each month but at that rate, it will take 13 years to catch up. ($23,400 divided by $150 = 156 months = 13 years)

Before taking a part-time job during retirement, it pays to do the math and find out how that paycheck will affect your Social Security payments. If you're between the ages of 62 and 64 and continue to work while receiving Social Security, your benefits will be reduced by $1 for every $2 you earn over $10,080. But if you're over 65, a change in the law allows you to collect full Social Security benefits regardless of any income from another job.

Most financial experts calculate that you'll need 70 percent to 80 percent of your pre-retirement income during retirement. Social Security provides only a small portion of that. Figure 13.3 indicates how much of your previous earnings you can expect Social Security to replace. The more you earned, the greater the gap between your

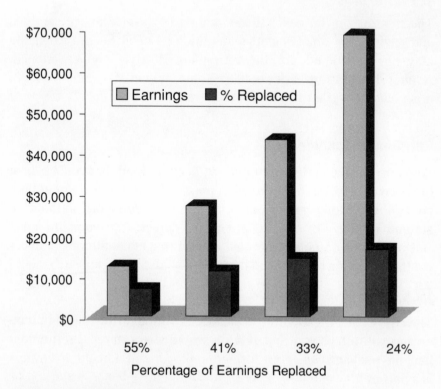

**FIGURE 13.3**   Estimated Percent of Income Replaced by Social Security in 1998.
*Source:* U.S. Social Security Administration.

Social Security benefits and the amount you'll probably need to maintain your pre-retirement lifestyle.

### Pension Plan

Many 403(b) investors will receive a pension in addition to Social Security benefits. Employees of non-profits usually have mandatory deductions taken from their salaries; that money is then invested and becomes part of their retirement pension plan. While employees have no choice of investments, pension funds are still an important part of the retirement income equation.

The amount of income your pension provides depends on your salary and years of employment. Those who haven't worked long enough to qualify for life-long pension benefits will receive their pension money, with interest, in one lump sum. If you're leaving a job but not retiring, you can elect to leave the money in your pension plan where it will continue to earn interest.

### The 403(b) Bonus

The frosting on the cake! Here's where all those years of sacrifice and saving pay off. Pension plans and/or Social Security benefits may not be enough for the retirement lifestyle you envisioned. Adding distributions from a 403(b) plan, however, means that you don't have to settle for "plain vanilla" retirement.

## Retirement Spending

When preparing a retirement budget, keep in mind that you'll probably need approximately 70 to 80 percent of your pre-retirement budget annually. However, it's impossible to put a price tag on the total amount because, of course, that figure depends on your life span. But you can get an idea of projected monthly expenditures by keeping the following expenses in mind:

### Healthcare

The cost of healthcare often escalates as you age. How much that increase will affect you depends on whether you have a retirement benefits package from your former employer and if health insurance is a part of it.

You become eligible for Medicare at age 65; however, Medicare is far from full-coverage health insurance; you pay monthly premiums for minimal coverage that doesn't include prescriptions or nursing home care, so some people buy supplemental insurance to cover the Medicare gap.

### Housing

By the time retirement approaches, you may have very low mortgage payments or none at all. However, if you own a home, you need to consider the cost of hired help for things like lawn care, snow removal, painting, cleaning, and so forth. Some retirees choose condo living because they're tired of home repair hassles. In that case, it's necessary to add condo fees to the financial picture.

### Utilities

When 9 to 5 is no longer part of your daily routine, you may find yourself spending a lot more of those hours at home. And be it ever so humble, heavy duty dollars need to be dedicated to heat and utilities (such as telephone and electricity).

### Travel and Recreation

You've waited a lifetime to play golf on Tuesday or take vacations that aren't connected to school breaks. Now it's time to factor those perks into your budget. Even if you qualify for a senior citizen discount, travel and recreation don't come cheap. And if you're a long-distance grandparent, frequent visits to grandchildren can take a big bite out of your travel budget.

### Inflation

The cost of products and services increases steadily: Inflation, eats away at the buying power of your dollars. The rate of inflation in the United States has been at a relatively mild 4.5 percent per year from 1960 to 1988 and 3.5 percent annually since then. Nevertheless, inflation is there and has to be accounted for in any retirement budget. See Table 13.1, which shows how inflation erodes your purchasing power.

### Nursing Home Care

Although you may not want to think about nursing home care, you may need it someday. And if you require an extensive stay in a nursing home, your entire nest egg could be wiped out; neither Medicare nor private health insurance pay for long-term nursing home care.

**TABLE 13.1** How Inflation Erodes Your Purchasing Power

| | Cost of item purchased in 2000 | Cost in 20 Years (4.5% average annual inflation rate) | Cost in 20 Years (3.5% average annual inflation rate) |
|---|---|---|---|
| Movie ticket | $7 | $16.88 | $13.93 |
| Tank of gas | $20 | $48.23 | $39.80 |
| Airline ticket | $500 | $1,205.86 | $994.89 |

However, for as little as $25 a month (policies vary), you can buy long-term care insurance so that if you have to spend time in a nursing home, all of your assets won't go with you. To many retirees, long-term healthcare insurance is a necessity.

## Calculating the Bottom Line

As stated previously, there are several good retirement expense calculators on the Web to help you find out how much you need to save. If you don't own a computer, borrow a friend's; these Web sites are worth the effort. Some charge for their services, while others are totally free.

### www.vanguard.com

Go directly to Vanguard's retirement section and fill out the questionnaire; out comes feedback about assets needed for the retirement lifestyle you're planning.

### www.fidelity.com

For a quick summary of projected retirement expenses, Fidelity has an excellent Web site. It takes only a few minutes to answer 15 questions, and the site even helps if you're stuck. For example, if you don't have a clue about annual income requirements in retirement, up pops the recommended average of 60 to 80 percent of your current annual salary.

If the figures show that you saved less than you'll need for the 80 percent lifestyle, see what happens when you do the calculations based on 60 percent. At that rate, you'll probably find that you have enough. Consider any excess as a cushion and resolve to scale back your projected lifestyle to stay within the 60 percent range.

When asked to fill in the annual return you expect to get from your investments, a natural tendency is to use the 12 percent average returned by the stock market over the past 40 years. But the stock market isn't consistent. If the market has a bad year, as it often does, your returns for that year could easily be less than 12 percent. With enough bad years, you may find that you're depleting your assets too quickly and they may not last through retirement. Financial planners recommend withdrawals ranging from 4 percent to 7 percent a year. Don't expect your nest egg to last if you feed unrealistic annual returns of 12 percent into the retirement calculator.

## Your 403(b) during Retirement

Let's assume you've decided to stop working, retire, and spend some of that cash you have stashed away in your 403(b) plan. Exactly how do you get your hands on it? There are three ways to access your money and they're not all created equal.

### Take the Money and Run—All of It

Don't think for one minute that you really can have it all! If you opt for a lump sum payment, you'll have to pay income tax on whatever you withdraw, as much as 39.6 percent, depending on your tax bracket. And don't forget state taxes; you have to pay those too. The final whammy: If you're under age $59^1/_2$, you'll be hit with a 10 percent early withdrawal penalty. Combined taxes and penalties can be as much as 50 percent, negating all those tax-deferred benefits. Bye-bye nest egg. Obviously, it makes little sense to cash out of your 403(b) with a lump sum payment.

### Direct Roll over into an IRA

Do not pass go; do not touch the money. Roll it over into an IRA and have the check made out directly to a bank, brokerage house, or mutual fund family. If you send it to yourself, you'll be liable for tax on the entire amount.

By converting your 403(b) to an IRA, you'll continue to reap the benefits of tax-deferral on all but the amount you're required to withdraw. They're called Required Minimum Distributions and you can read more about them later in this chapter.

Your IRA can be in a bank, brokerage house, or mutual fund family. If you choose a mutual fund family, you're not limited to the funds in that family only. Unlike a 403(b) plan that restricts you to funds in your selected vehicle, an IRA lets you choose from thousands of funds that weren't available in your 403(b). You can build your own IRA portfolio of funds and move your assets around in it without paying fees.

Wherever you decide to house your IRA, rest assured that there are in-house experts who will give you the necessary forms, handle the paperwork, and work with you to design a personalized retirement portfolio.

If you already own an IRA outside your 403(b), it's recommended that you roll over your 403(b) into a separate IRA for record keeping and tax purposes. Non-403(b) contributions to an IRA are made with after-tax dollars, while 403(b) contributions came from pre-tax dollars; the original amount (principal) wasn't taxed, so taxes on principal and interest have to be paid on each withdrawal. If you have an IRA outside your 403(b), you've probably already paid taxes on the *principal*, so future taxes are based only on the *growth*. To avoid any possibility of double taxes, it's important to keep your IRAs separate.

There is no limit on the amount of IRAs you can own, and they don't all have to be kept in the same place. You are, however, limited to a $2000 total contribution annually—even if you have five IRA accounts, your combined annual total investment can't be more than $2000. And keep in mind that when you retire, you can no longer contribute to your 403(b) or the IRA that you rolled it into: those contributions have to be made with earned income only. However, if you decide to take a part-time job during retirement, you're entitled to contribute $2000 of that earned income to the IRA of your choice.

Taxation on IRAs can be complicated. Even though these investment instruments grow tax-deferred, they're not immune from taxes forever. In a traditional IRA, those after-tax contributions may or may not have been tax deductible, depending on your tax bracket. Even if you've paid taxes on the principal, you still have to pay tax on the earnings when you begin taking withdrawals. And there are additional penalties for early withdrawals, excessive contributions (over $2000 annually), or failure to begin taking the required minimum distribution by age 70½.

### The Other IRA

If you have a Roth IRA, you've already paid taxes on the principal and aren't required to pay any taxes on the growth. When taking withdrawals from a Roth, your account must have been established for at least five years and you have to be at least age 59½. Failure to comply with the rules can cost you a 10 percent penalty.

Unlike a traditional IRA, there are never any minimum distribution requirements on a Roth IRA. You can leave your Roth untouched and pass it on to your heirs intact.

### Both IRAs

Remember when you were socking away pre-tax dollars in your 403(b)? Those days are gone, but the tax deferral remains. Even if your 403(b) has been rolled over into an IRA, you only pay taxes on withdrawals. Just remember that you can't contribute to an IRA of any kind if you don't get a paycheck.

For many, retirement can mean no more work—ever—unless it's voluntary. So it's important to understand the tax implications of tapping into your 403(b) or the vehicle to which it was transferred. You don't have to pay any taxes on it until you begin taking distributions, and the IRS gives you until age 70½ to start.

### Roll over into an Annuity and Annuitize

The key word here is "annuitize." While the premise of this book has been "just say no to annuities," they can have a place in your financial life *after* you retire. The annuitization option guarantees you a steady stream of income for the rest of your life and the peace of mind that comes with knowing you won't outlive your money.

However, annuities are insurance products, so the gamble here is that you may outlive your savings and the payments will keep coming, or you may die before your annuity assets are depleted. In that case, the remaining money goes back to the annuity company and your heirs get nothing.

Annuitization does offer a plan to protect your spouse. By taking out a survivor or joint annuity, the payments will be less, but the two of you will be guaranteed a monthly annuity check for as long as you both live.

Keep in mind that there is no benefit to an annuity *without annu-itization* and converting to an annuity in retirement can limit invest-ment growth because of excessive fees. According to Ken Deptula, annuity specialist at Vanguard, "It only makes sense to convert to an annuity if you plan to annuitize. Otherwise you're paying for two lay-ers of tax-deferral that you don't need, along with unnecessary fees (mortality & expense, administrative charges) that you don't need."[1]

### Some Taxing Questions

The math goes on. Not only do you have to calculate retirement in-come and expenses, you also need to crunch some numbers to find out how much you get to keep. Remember those two sure things: death and taxes. Uncle Sam has waited patiently for his share of your tax-deferred dollars. He'll be there when you retire, with out-stretched hands. The object of the game is to give him as little as you can.

Your Social Security benefits, 403(b) distributions, IRA with-drawals, and pension income are all taxed at your normal income tax rate. At age 65, you are entitled to the standard income tax de-duction plus an additional deduction of $1,050 for singles and $850 each for couples.

### Required Minimum Distribution (RMD)

As for how much you have to take and how often, your 403(b) vehi-cle has the formula for calculating withdrawals. If, for example, your 403(b) was with Fidelity, a retirement specialist from Fidelity will help you arrive at your personal required minimum distribution.

There's no getting around this; the IRS levies stiff penalties on those who fail to comply with their RMD. If you miss the deadline or take out too little, you'll be faced with a 50 percent penalty on the difference between the amount you withdrew and what you should have taken out.

Your RMD is determined by dividing the assets in your retirement account by a life expectancy factor calculated either as a single or joint life expectancy projection (based on yours and that of your old-est primary beneficiary). For example, if you are 71, your retirement account balance is $100,000 and you divide that amount by a life ex-pectancy of 15.3 years, your RMD will be $6,536 annually (approxi-mately $545 monthly). If, however, you've chosen the joint life expectancy plan and your beneficiary is 68, then your joint life expectancy becomes 21.2 years, and your withdrawal decreases to $4,717 per year. Keep in mind that your beneficiary can't be more than ten years younger than you are.

But before you panic and enroll in a calculus course remember that your 403(b) holder will do the math for you. Just don't wait until you're 70¼ to designate a beneficiary or calculate your minimum distributions. The plan you choose is permanent; once you begin to make withdrawals, there are no options to change, no second chances. So allow plenty of time to make a careful decision.

While you must take your first RMD by age 70½, you can start making withdrawals from your 403(b) as early as age 55 without penalty. Before age 55, however, you'll pay a penalty of 10 percent on early withdrawals. So if you withdraw too much too soon or too little too late, you'll have to pay the piper.

## Proposed Legislation to Benefit Retirees

In 2000, Congress proposed legislation that would sweeten the retirement pie. When this book went to press in 2001, the new laws had not yet been passed. Here are some of the proposed changes:

- Raise the yearly limit on IRA contributions from $2,000 to $5,000 in stages over a three-year period.
- Gradually increase limits on 403(b), 401(k), and 457 retirement plans to $15,000 annually.
- Increase pension flexibility by allowing rollovers among different plan types. For example, a 401(k) plan could be rolled directly into a 403(b) without major hassles or reams of paperwork.
- Loosen income restrictions to allow more people to make Roth IRA contributions and tax-deductible traditional IRA contributions.

## Investing during Retirement

You've just retired and you've got a lot of living to do. However, you still have to pay attention to your investments, and retirement investing can be tricky. Your assets need to continue to grow, but you also need to protect them by taking less risk. On the plus side, now that you're retired you'll have more time to manage your money.

When choosing an investment mix for your retirement portfolio, it's wise to use some caution. At this stage of the game, your assets have grown and matured. Leave those hot new tech funds alone and confine your portfolio to the old-timers who've demonstrated staying power. Common sense dictates that your retirement portfolio take a more conservative track.

So what exactly should you be looking for? Pretty much the same criteria you used to pick investments in your pre-retirement days: funds that invest in quality companies and have low expense ratios, skilled managers, and evidence of consistent respectable long-term performance.

No retirement portfolio can afford to hold only equity (stock) funds. A good balance is made up of cash investments, income products like bond funds, and stock funds. "With an all-equity portfolio, you should be prepared for occasional losses (once every ten years) of up to 40% of your portfolio. That's too much risk,"[2] maintains mutual fund expert Paul Merriman. And if those losses do indeed occur, you don't have enough earning years left to replace them. That's why you can't take a break from portfolio balance during retirement.

The sample retirement portfolios shown in Figure 13.4 give suggested asset allocations for retirement portfolios from ages 45 to 60 and from 60+. In both models, "conservative" refers to income products such as bonds and money markets that have limited risk but also generate little growth, "growth and income" refers to stocks that generate a modest income with minimal risk, and "maximum growth" refers to stocks of both emerging and established companies with the possibility of greater growth and volatility.

Note that the term "aggressive growth" no longer applies. Because you're seeking more protection and less volatility, it's wise to avoid aggressive investing in high-risk sector funds. On the other hand, there are lots of retirement years ahead, so going too conservative with a total bond and cash investment portfolio isn't advisable either. For example, if you have $400,000 invested conservatively, earning 5 percent a year, and you withdraw your assets at the rate of 10 percent annually, your money will be gone in just 14 years. And that doesn't even take inflation into account.

Looking at a hypothetical 3 percent growth in the rate of inflation, a 5 percent gain on your investment becomes an actual gain of only 2 percent. Moreover, at 3 percent inflation, the 10 percent you

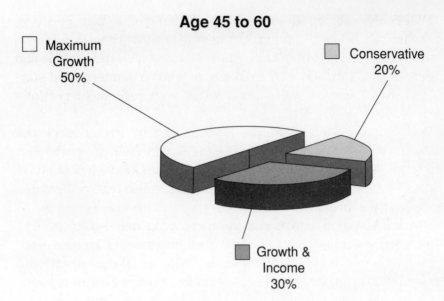

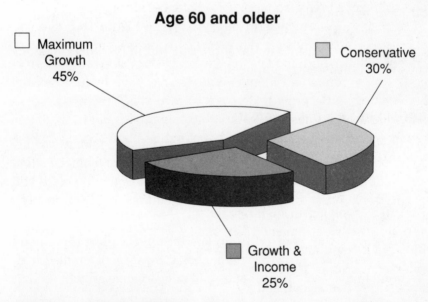

**FIGURE 13.4** Retirement Portfolio.
*Source:* Mutual Fund Education Alliance.

## Retirement Money Outside Your 403(b)

When you begin taking withdrawals from your assets, consider tapping into the taxable accounts first. Here's why:

Your tax-sheltered money should remain tax sheltered as long as possible to continue reaping the benefits of interest compounding on a tax-deferred basis.

Money that's withdrawn from a retirement plan such as your 403(b), regular IRA, or IRA roll over is taxed as ordinary income. The rate could be as much as 39.6 percent, depending on your tax bracket.

Taxable investments are taxed at a long-term capital gains rate of only 20 percent. That can add up to considerable savings, depending on the tax bracket you're in.

withdraw from your investments will have only 7 percent buying power compared to today's dollars. The reality of economics is that you have to continue to grow your money during retirement by keeping some of it invested in equity growth funds. These funds may have more volatility in the short run, but in the long run stock funds have consistently outpaced inflation.

## Retirement Strategy Summary

1. Review your retirement portfolio periodically, taking into account any change in goals, lifestyle, or personal financial situations. A frequent assessment will help determine if you're still on track, based on your original projections, or if you need to make modifications.

2. Make sure that your portfolio is adjusted for protection along with continued growth. That means it must be diversified with bond funds, cash instruments, and conservative growth funds.

3. In case of emergency, keep cash reserves that can be immediately liquidated such as bank savings accounts, money market accounts, or short-term CDs. Having a separate supply of cash means you won't have to tap into retirement money and thereby threaten the balance of your current asset allocation plan.

## Chapter 13 Homework

Follow these four steps to calculate your retirement needs:

1. Contact the Social Security Administration for an estimate of your future benefits.

   800-772-1213

   www.ssa.gov

   The Social Security Administration Web site also has a calculator to help you do your own rough estimate of expected benefits.

2. Eighty percent of current income is the projected goal for many retirees. Calculate how much 80 percent of your present salary will be.

3. Contact your personnel department for a statement of expected pension benefits, if any.

4. Use a Web calculator to help you:

   • Factor in inflation

   • Determine how much you need to save in addition to Social Security and pension benefits to reach your goal. Calculators to check out include:

     www.financiallearning.com

     www.asec.org

     www.kiplinger.com

# Profile of a Successful 403(b) Investor

**S**uccess is often about balance. In conversations I had with 403(b) investors at workshops, all of them said they believed a balanced portfolio is the key to successful investing. This balance seems to be part of every aspect of their lives. Most of them based expenditures on a balanced budget. None were workaholics; all seemed to have good balance between work and play. There were no extremes in the bunch. And they all denounced a get-rich-quick philosophy in favor of conservative investing for the long term.

One investor in particular seemed especially financially-savvy. Meet Dave Kolkebeck, a 48 year old Vermont educator, who displays all the characteristics of a successful 403(b) investor. This chapter explores these characteristics, as they relate to Dave's personal investing philosophy. Dave is confident, knowledgeable about finance, has a healthy respect for money, and uses a variety of strategies to keep his portfolio balanced. He has realistic expectations for his investment holdings and the retirement lifestyle they'll support. Like other seasoned 403(b) investors, Dave has a plan that includes goals and objectives and the perseverance to make them happen.

## A Successful 403(b) Investor Has . . .

- Balance
- Knowledge
- Confidence
- Respect for money
- Strategies
- Realistic expectations

## Emotional Balance

A balanced portfolio is important, but it's not the be-all and end-all of successful investing. While it's wise to build a portfolio of bonds, equities, and cash investments, it's also essential to have a balanced attitude. That means you don't panic when the market drops, nor do you chase the hottest sector by making constant trades. An investor who's in control doesn't let emotions determine what he or she buys or sells. And that's easier said than done. Market performance, combined with volatility, can create a climate of anxiety that's hard to ignore.

Dr. James Gottenfurcht, president of the Psychology of Money Consultants, talks about two personality types related to money issues. Gottenfurcht claims that "prosperity thinkers" and "poverty thinkers" are the two extremes. Prosperity thinkers have an optimistic, balanced attitude toward money while poverty thinkers focus on negativity and loss.[1] Either the glass is half empty or half full. Those with the half-full glass are able to take market fluctuations in stride. The half-empty glass holders, however, are easily influenced by market hype and tend to overreact to market volatility. Their investment decisions are often based on panic, fear, or greed, resulting in more losses than gains. Talk of a recession at the end of 2000 caused many to panic and unload investments at rock bottom prices—a definite no-no according to the philosophy that investors should buy low and sell high.

John Brennan, chairman and CEO of Vanguard, remembers the market correction of 2000 when many people had much of their savings sitting in aggressive growth and technology funds. "It's true," says Brennan, "that you can win big by putting all your money into one good stock, a handful of individual stocks, or securities in just one sector. But you can also lose catastrophically, as the year 2000 demonstrated."[2]

Responding to a down day in the stock market, Dave Kolkebeck simply says "The market tanked again. So what?" David feels protected by his fixed investments and believes they provide a cushion against market volatility. "No matter what the market does," says Dave, "I will always continue to invest."[3] Dave's attitude toward market downturns is based on a strong belief in dollar cost averaging. By investing regularly in his 403(b) plan, Dave can't lose. His dollars buy more shares in a down market so when the market rises, he owns more shares to cash in on the upswing.

Balance also plays a big part in successful budgeting. Without a balanced budget, you're not likely to have money left over to save or invest. With a budget that's balanced, however, you're more likely to live within your means and practice safe saving strategies. Dave, our exemplary 403(b) investor, has been a saver all his life. He says, "a budget keeps you looking forward, not backward. It helps you fulfill goals by forcing you to plan ahead." Dave is also convinced that you need a budget before you can begin saving and investing. "You have to see where the money is going before you can begin to control it."

Dave credits his parents with teaching him the value of a dollar early on. He learned the importance of setting aside even small sums of money and his "fear of going under" keeps his spending in check.

## Financial Balance

An informed investor is a calm one who doesn't panic at market twinges or let media hype influence his long-term investing decisions. He or she is able to distinguish between short-term economic cycles and long-lasting secular factors. His or her investments are selected not on recent performance but on how they fit into long-

---

**Financial Knowledge Helps You . . .**

- Understand the market and the media
- Differentiate between short and long-term cycles
- Practice safe investing strategies

---

term objectives and tolerance for risk. This section will explore the positive effects of knowledge in investing.

### Understanding the Market and the Media

The market rises; the market falls. Like molten lava, it's always flowing in one direction or another. And the truth is, we have no idea where the market is going on a given day. At 9 A.M. the Nasdaq might be drowning; by noon it's picked itself up because of a merger between two blue chips, an announcement of better-than-expected earnings from IBM, or a televised pep talk from a financial pundit. But even the most prolific pundits don't have crystal balls, and educated long-term investors know that. They pay little attention to market moves or the media hype that surrounds them. They know better than to get caught up in market spins that lead them to follow the pack.

Investors who listened to tech noise and bought on momentum were sadly disappointed. When tech stocks took a plunge in 2000, many hard-earned investment dollars disappeared, teaching some investors a lesson they'll never forget. On the other hand, educated investors stay on the sidelines and stick with their original asset allocations, boring though they may seem. If they decide to spice up their portfolio with a touch of tech, it's never enough to upset the balance.

### Information Overload

Paul Farrell, *CBS MarketWatch* columnist, refers to the media, collectively, as the "Great American Financial Advice Machine."[4] The machine has amazing capabilities. Picture the Great Oz working wonders in the Emerald City. According to Farrell, "The Great American Financial Advice Machine generates enormous data on individual funds and stocks. Analyzes your goals. Creates an ideal portfolio. Monitors it. E-mails breaking news about companies and industry trends. But The Great American Financial Advice Machine doesn't answer the big questions: The future of the market? The economy? Your future?"[5] Because it can't.

Although we're living in the information age, we've made few advances in the field of fortune telling. There will always be a financial wizard who predicts disaster and another who swears by never-ending prosperity. An educated investor is able to shut out these background noises and not get distracted by market hype. And there's no shortage of it. According to a study done by Oxbridge Communications, in 1998 there were 162 financial Web sites, 187 financial publications, and 5 television stations dissecting and delivering financial information 24 hours a day.[6]

In early 2001, financial gurus were asked to make predictions about investments for a successful portfolio in 2001. Eric Kobren said, "I would be careful about getting too heavily weighted in technology."[7] John Rekenthaler said his portfolio theme would be "cheap and classy," meaning he'd stick with reasonably-priced old reliables. Reckenthaler also said, "If you bought a technology fund on March 10, I think that's God's way of saying 'never, never buy a sector fund again.'"[8] Both experts are obviously in agreement on cutting back on tech.

Bob Markman, however, remains gung-ho on technology. Believing that the communication and Internet revolution will continue, he told investors to "stick with a portfolio that is significantly growth weighted, significantly tech weighted."[9]

And then there's the controversy over index funds. Rekenthaler likes indexing as an investment strategy but thinks "it's more fun not to pick index funds."[10] Roseanne Pane encourages investors to buy both index and non-index funds.[11] Bob Markman believes the real question isn't whether you should buy index funds but, rather, which of those funds should you buy. "Are you going to balance a growth index, a value index, an international?"[12] asks Markman.

So how does one deal with so much advice—much of it conflicting? Is growth the way to go or is value better? Are you really supposed to buy on the dips? What if the Dow isn't done dipping?

Between July and October of 1998, for example, the market lost 15 percent. That's a scary "correction", especially if you had jumped into the market in June. It's tempting to cut your losses and run, but those who did missed out on a 50 percent gain in the market over the next two quarters. In that scenario, investors who didn't bail out fared better.

### Know When to Fold 'Em

Most successful 403(b) investors practice "buy-and-hold"—but not forever. They know there are times when it makes sense to sell a fund. For instance, it may be time to say good-bye when

- a fund in a particular sector continues to underperform other funds in the same sector.
- the fund manager leaves, taking the fund's hot performance record with him or her.
- your portfolio is overweighted in one sector or asset class and you have to sell something to regain balance.

Dave Kolkebeck is a devoted buy-and-holder who rarely sells or trades. He's weighed the options and decided to stay with his original mix, at least for the time being. With a portfolio of 45 percent equities, 45 percent fixed income investments, and 10 percent cash, Dave is happy with the balance he's achieved and the funds he's chosen.

Knowing he has a low tolerance for risk, Dave isn't tempted by media hype that promises to make him a millionaire. His primary concern is safety, so volatility is a big turn-off to him. He's always believed that "slow and steady wins the race"—not media-driven decisions that have investors moving in and out of sectors.

Dave's realistic approach to investing includes the financial goals he's set for himself. He thinks that "setting too high a goal can paralyze people and make them want to give up." Dave hopes to have $1,000,000 stashed away for retirement, and his lifestyle goal is "to be working less earlier and working less longer." Retiring at the traditional age of 60 or 65 is not where Dave's headed. He plans to enjoy a lot more years on his terms, so he'll work less for a longer period of time. Dave likes his teaching job and has no desire to give up the contact with kids. His mortgage is paid off, his financial house is in order, and he's set goals based on life-long saving habits. That he'll meet his goals is practically a sure thing, as Dave doesn't intend to deviate from the financial principles by which he lives.

### Differentiating between Short- and Long-Term Economic Cycles

People who jump on the bandwagon of the hottest sector seem to treat investing like a trip to the casino. Day traders click their mouse as if it were a slot machine lever, hoping for short-term profits and instant gratification. Fortunately, 403(b) investors can't play the day trading game. Rules and regulations that govern 403(b) investing don't allow for quick trading of individual stocks; long-term investing is built into the plan. However, when the words "short-term" or "long-term" are applied to economic cycles, they take on a different meaning.

Knowledgeable 403(b) investors know the difference between short-lived cycles in the economy and other more permanent cycles that can take years to fully evolve. Economic slowdowns occur on a regular basis, depending on various factors such as the unemployment rate, the value of the dollar, and the rate of inflation. These are considered short-term cycles and they can fluctuate rapidly. For example, if a glut of new construction occurs in Pleasanton, the law of supply and demand kicks in. More available real estate usually means lower prices. But if Pleasanton becomes the "in" place to live, more people will want to move there, so the cycle is reversed. People buy Pleasanton properties, the supply of available homes dwindles, the price of real estate in Pleasanton skyrockets—and a relatively short-term economic cycle has gone full circle.

Long-term cycles take more time to play out and can have a permanent impact on market trends. Technology is a prime example. We've experienced a full-blown tech explosion; it is the tool that drives the information age. The economy runs on technology and that's not likely to change.

An investor who has done some homework is able to distinguish between the short-term effects of technology and those with longer lasting impact. Internet companies were weeded out by the thousands when the dot-com bubble burst. Those that remained in business did so because they had some substance behind them. Astute investors saw the difference and entrusted their money to mutual fund managers investing in technology-driven companies with real earning potential.

## Successful Investing Strategies

There's no shortage of investment strategies and they can be either right or wrong, depending on how they're applied. Successful investors know that the most important thing is simply having a strategy and sticking to it. They focus on proven long-term strategies that fit their particular lifestyle and that have the staying power to see them through to retirement.

### Safety First

Dave prefers a safe investment strategy. While he may find some Internet funds intriguing, he doesn't want to own them. He has a conservative attitude toward money, so flashy funds are not his style. The funds Dave picks fit his low tolerance for risk and his personal comfort level.

There are many investment choices and more than one way to manage a portfolio. Dave, for example, isn't a fan of index funds and prefers to depend on the expertise of active managers. He believes a reliable manager with extensive tenure can beat the performance of most index funds. Dave also has an aversion to sector funds because he believes they're not diversified enough and tie a manager's hands by limiting him to equities in only one sector.

Therefore, Dave's strategy is to stay in the mainstream, avoiding sector and index funds. It may not be yours. You may be an index fund fan or like the spice that sector funds can bring to a portfolio. The bottom line is that almost any sound strategy will work as long as you stay with it.

### Low Cost

Another strategy that can make or break a portfolio's success is the cost of the funds in it. Educated 403(b) investors keep an eye on the bottom line. They know that returns are reduced by the cost of owning a fund. So before they buy, they look for funds that meet the following criteria:

- No-load funds
- Low expense ratios
- No 12b-1 fees

### Diversification

No fund makes it into Dave Kolkebeck's portfolio if it doesn't fit his asset allocation mix. Like other successful 403(b) investors, Dave wants the balance of different categories. Diversification gives him protection and a feeling of security in both bull and bear markets and will always be at the top of his list of investment strategies.

## Strategic Wisdom

An important thing to remember about strategies is that they're based on past performance, not future outcomes. They can't guarantee success in the stock market—nothing can. Strategies are simply a means to an end, a way of channeling the investment process and converting it to a manageable form. Without a strategy you may as well throw darts at a Wall Street board. With them, you have some control, but still no guarantees.

No matter how hard you try or how many strategies you apply, you won't always get it right. Sometimes you'll stay in a fund too long; sometimes you'll sell too soon. In either case, you may feel cheated because you didn't make as much money as you thought you could. Don't beat yourself up and don't abandon your strategies. That the stock market will always be unpredictable is a given, but a few good strategies can work wonders in coping with volatility.

### Confidence

It's not surprising that investors who employ successful strategies often have the confidence that comes with positive results. If you always do what you've always done, then you'll always get what you always got. So if your investment methods resemble gambling, chances are your returns will be haphazard: a few good hits along with many losses. But if you've taken the time to implement strategies, you're likely to be a confident investor with a portfolio that's under control.

Dave is confident to the core. He's comfortable with an investing style that works for him and has no plans to change it. He has clearly-defined financial goals and the strategies in place to achieve them. Dave's stringent saving and investing habits assure him of always having enough assets to meet his needs. And his confidence level is high because he knows he's financially prepared and equipped to manage his own investments.

However, even successful investors make mistakes. Dave wishes that he had taken better advantage of recent bull markets. However, he also knows his own limitations, and one of them is that he's not a risk taker. While hindsight tells him he could have made more, logic tells him aggressive investing is not his style.

In the stock market, mistakes usually mean lost money, and even the most confident investor hates to take a loss. We feel dumb for having bought a loser in the first place and we agonize over lost dollars and what they might have bought. In short, we're only human. A confident investor isn't thrown by the fact that there will always be winners and losers in the investing game. Millions of dollars have probably been lost by investors holding onto a stock until they could at least break even. Figure 14.1 shows how hard it is to do that. Confident investors cut their losses and move on.

Peter Lynch of Fidelity fame urges you to have confidence in your ability to manage your own investments and "stop listening to professionals. Twenty years in this business convinces me that any normal person using three percent of his brain can pick stocks just as well, if not better, than the average Wall Street expert."[13] As a 403(b) investor, you don't even have to worry about individual stock picking. You just have to pick a good fund manager to do the job for you.

### Realistic Expectations

Another key indicator of successful investing is having realistic expectations about money. People who set goals that are too high often have trouble managing their investments, while those

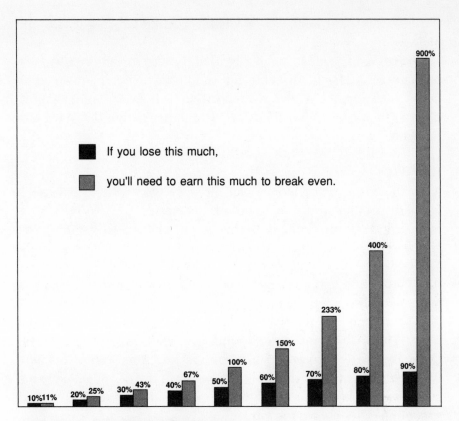

**FIGURE 14.1** Recouping Investment Loss.
Copyright 2000, *USA TODAY*. Reprinted with permission.

with a more balanced perspective generally have more success. The financial arena is particularly susceptible to disappointment, but investors with realistic goals are better able to handle unmet expectations; they continue to persevere and aren't put off by minor setbacks.

Someone whose goal is to become a millionaire by age fifty but who has only managed to save $80,000 and a few collectibles may be tempted to give up. If goals are too pie-in-the-sky, it's easy to abandon them because they weren't real to begin with. Dave's goal to work less earlier and longer is reflected in his financial expectations. By planning to work into retirement at his own pace, Dave feels he won't require as much of a nest egg. And chances are he's right, although he'll probably accumulate a sizeable one anyway.

Setting realistic goals and doing what it takes to achieve them is a big part of successful investing, but simply writing them down won't make them happen. A successful portfolio is the result of a commitment to financial responsibility and to the realization that it's a lifetime job.

### Respect for Money

A healthy respect for money can often be traced back to lessons learned in childhood. Wise parents encourage their kids to save money and set an example by being savers themselves. They set aside assets for that proverbial rainy day and won't do the credit card shuffle, borrowing from Visa to pay MasterCard. They pay themselves first and don't count on phantom dollars that might not be there at the end of the month.

There are plenty of twenty-somethings capable of saving just $1.50 a day. That's $45 a month and at an average return of 12 percent, could be worth almost a million by the time they retire. But few twenty-year-olds learn this lesson. Stores are full of appealing items and they want them *now*. Saving money is put off until later. And sometimes later comes too late.

Twenty-somethings who have developed a healthy respect for money, however, are able to give up immediate gratification in exchange for future rewards. They don't postpone saving until they finish school or get that big raise. Somewhere along the line they learned that wealth is produced by time and lost time cannot be recovered. Bottom line: start saving early, invest wisely, and enjoy the peace of mind that is part of that package.

### Investment Style

This chapter has focused on developing investment styles based on strategies that help you prepare for that inevitable market volatility. Having a style you're comfortable with can help you cope with inevitable market gyrations and tune out background noises.

Successful 403(b) investors know that sticking to an investment style takes discipline. Investment portfolios are never stagnant.

They need constant monitoring to maintain balance and diversification. Within the framework of your own personal style, you'll be able to make a multitude of choices with confidence. You can choose to buy and hold and go for the gold; you can buy index funds or avoid them entirely. Whatever works for you will become your own personal style. Dr. Gottenfurcht sums it up nicely by saying "an investment style that includes realistic expectations and investment knowledge places individuals in powerful territory for attaining their investment goals."[14] Rest assured, you now have the right stuff to make that happen.

## The Last Word: Patience

If I could give you one gift to take on your investment journey, it would be the gift of patience. Understanding the complexities of a 403(b) plan doesn't happen overnight. It's a financial learning curve that develops over time. Slowly the pieces will start to fit and what seemed so baffling at first will eventually make perfect sense.

Educators strive for metacognition—that point when what you've learned becomes a part of you—where you've reached the deepest level of comprehension and are no longer struggling to understand. But you can't get there without patience.

Mastering the market is a slow process that can't be rushed. As soon as you figure out one piece, other questions will pop up. Sometimes you'll need a truckload of patience just to keep going. The important thing is to stay focused on the journey and not become distracted by detours along the way.

No one ever said long-term investing was easy. There's no instant gratification; the goal of a secure retirement seems very far away, and that's why you need patience. It takes a lot of it to put up with slow moving funds when you're itching to play in hot sectors. It takes still more fortitude to wait on the sidelines while your perfectly balanced portfolio is moving at the speed of a glacier. Trust me, that patience will pay off in the end. So keep the faith, hold onto the belief that "slow and steady wins the race," and twenty, thirty, or forty years from now, you'll be glad you did.

## Chapter 14 Homework

Here is some worthwhile Internet information to help round out your 403(b) research.

GO TO: www.coffeehouseinvestor.com
CLICK ON: 403(b) and 401(k) Corner
The following links are a good source of up-to-date information on 403(b) plans.

### Teachers and Money

Written by a teacher for teachers and contains general information on compounding, investment plans, do-it-yourself investing, and so forth.

### 403(b) Rip-offs

Good links to 403(b)-related newspaper and magazine articles such as

"Fighting for 403(b) Funds" (*Kiplinger's*)

"Costly Lessons for Teachers" (*Bergen County Record*)

### Internal Revenue Service

Publication 571, "Tax sheltered Annuity Programs for Employees of Public Schools and Certain Tax-exempt Organizations"

### GO TO: www.investorwords.com

Every definition of every word you ever wanted to know on the subject of investing. A great tool to have on hand when trying to decipher a fund prospectus.

### GO TO: www.maxfunds.com

An investment tracking Web site similar to Morningstar, but more fun. Its risk rating tool, for example, is called the "Fat Fund index". Maxfunds also has a unique rating system correlated to traffic lights.

### GO TO: www.fundalarm.com

Fundalarm is yet another way to examine fund performance, your personal wake-up call for funds that are in trouble. If one of your funds has a three alarm signal, it may be time to sell.

# New Tax Legislation and What It Means

## "Comprehensive Retirement Security and Pension Reform Act of 2001"

### 403(b) Plans

**Minimum Contribution**—The minimum contribution to 403(b) plans will gradually increase to $15,000 by 2006.

**Changing Plans**—Eliminates much of the "red tape" in transfers from one retirement savings plan to another when changing jobs, such as from a 403(b) to a 401(k).

**Income Tax Reduction**—Offers additional tax credit for low-income workers who contribute to a retirement plan. This goes into effect in 2002 and gives a tax refund of 50 cents for each dollar contributed, up to a maximum of $2,000 in contributions. This means that if you contribute $2,000 to your plan, you will reduce income taxes owed by $1,000. In order to qualify, joint filers must make under $50,000 combined income, and single filers $25,000 or less.

**A Roth 403(b) Choice**—In 2006, there will be a Roth option available for contributors to 403(b) plans. Employees will be able to choose either plan A: a Roth-like savings tool in which the taxes on 403(b) contributions are paid upfront in order to receive tax-free distributions during retirement, or plan B: the traditional approach in which contributions are tax-deferred now with taxes due at withdrawal.

**Catchup Provisions**—The new legislation simplifies the catchup provision enabling 403(b) plan participants to make up for years in which they could have contributed more and offering a special catchup provision to all participants over age 50.

**Increased Competition in the 403(b) Marketplace**—A growth in 403(b) providers can be expected under the new tax law because it encourages new vendor participation by simplifying IRS regulations and reducing liability. While the 401(k) market is somewhat saturated, the 403(b) market is quite open and its participants are growing steadily. Hopefully, other players will enter the field, increase the competition, and benefit 403(b) holders with lower costs and better service.

## Traditional and Roth IRA

The maximum amount that can be contributed to both IRAs will be increased gradually from the current $2,000 to $5,000 by 2008, after which maximum contribution amounts will be adjusted for inflation. The good news for those 50 and older is that they can contribute the full $5,000 to an IRA beginning in 2002.

## Education

**Education IRA**—The new name for an education IRA is "Education Savings Account." Under the old law, only $500 could be contributed annually. That limit has been increased to $2,000. Like the Roth IRA, contributions to an education savings account are made with after-tax dollars, but there is no tax on withdrawals and they can be used to pay educational expenses at all levels, from elementary through college. At the K-12 level, distributions can be used for everything from uniforms and transportation to computers and extended day care. An additional benefit to Education Savings Accounts is that they offer direct investing wherever you choose.

**Section 529 Plans**—Distributions from these plans will now be totally tax-free and can be used to fund private, as well as state universities. They are designed to offset taxes at the state, rather than the federal level.

**College Tuition Deduction**—Under the new legislation, in 2002 and 2003 single filing taxpayers making less than $65,000 and joint filers with a combined income of less than $130,000 can take a $3,000 deduction for college tuition. In 2004 and 2005, that deduction increases to $4,000.

## Marital Taxes

The new law has provisions for eliminating the "marriage penalty" tax that often results in couples paying more taxes than if each were single and filing separately. Married couples will see an increase in their standard deduction and the 15 percent tax bracket will be adjusted to benefit married couples filing jointly. The provisions won't take effect until the year 2005 and will be phased in gradually over a five year period.

## Tax Rates

The new legislation provides for six income tax brackets ranging from 10 percent to 35 percent. Under the old law, there were five brackets with a range of 15 percent to 39.6 percent. In 2001, tax payers in the 28 percent, 31 percent, 36 percent, and 39.6 percent can look for a half point reduction in their rates. The introduction of a new 10 percent tax rate will take effect in 2002, while additional rate cuts will be implemented gradually through the year 2005. The IRS is required to adjust withholding tables to reflect the lower rates.

## Estate Tax

Perhaps the most complicated new legislation concerns estate taxes and, specifically, the exemption factor. In 2001, the estate tax exemption applied to estates valued at $675,000 or less. The new law provides for an increased exemption on estates valued at $3.5 million through 2009. At the same time, the rate on taxable estates will slowly decrease from 55 percent to 45 percent. In 2010, the entire estate tax will be repealed for a one-year period only.

# IRS Publication 571

**Publication 571**
Cat. No. 46581C

Department
of the
Treasury

Internal
Revenue
Service

# Tax-Sheltered Annuity Programs for Employees of Public Schools and Certain Tax-Exempt Organizations

For use in preparing

## 1999 Returns

**Get forms and other information faster and easier by:**
**COMPUTER**
• World Wide Web • www.irs.gov
• FTP • ftp.irs.gov
**FAX**
• From your FAX machine, dial • (703) 368-9694
See *How To Get More Information* in this publication.

## Contents

## Important Change for 1999

**Photographs of missing children.** The Internal Revenue Service is a proud partner with the National Center for Missing and Exploited Children. Photographs of missing children selected by the Center may appear in this publication on pages that would otherwise be blank. You can help bring these children home by looking at the photographs and calling 1–800–THE–LOST (1–800–843–5678) if you recognize a child.

## Important Reminders

**Includible compensation.** Your includible compensation for purposes of figuring your exclusion allowance includes:

1) Elective deferrals (your employer's contributions made on your behalf under a salary reduction agreement),

2) Amounts contributed or deferred by your employer under a section 125 cafeteria plan, and

3) Amounts contributed or deferred under a section 457 plan (state or local government or tax-exempt organization plan).

Your exclusion allowance is the amount of employer contributions (including elective deferrals) to your tax-sheltered annuity contract or account that you can exclude from income. For more information on includible compensation, see *Includible Compensation*, later.

**Contributions—employed ministers.** If you are a minister and if in the exercise of your ministry you are employed by an organization with which you share common religious bonds, but which is not a certain type of tax-exempt organization, you may not have to include contributions made on your behalf to a tax-sheltered annuity plan. You do not have to include contributions to a church plan if you would have been able to exclude them had you been an employee of a church.

For more information, see *Special Rules* under *Includible Compensation*.

## Introduction

This publication explains the federal tax provisions that apply to tax-sheltered annuity (TSA) plans offered to employees of public schools and certain tax-exempt organizations. The discussions primarily cover employer contributions (elective deferrals) made under a salary reduction agreement. The publication is for employees who participate in TSA plans. It is not for custodians or plan administrators because it does not cover many of the operating requirements of these plans.

A tax-sheltered annuity plan, often referred to as a "403(b) plan," "tax-deferred annuity plan," or simply "TSA plan" (which is used in this publication), is a retirement plan that, if operated properly by a qualified employer, is tax-exempt.

A qualified employer can purchase TSA contracts or accounts for eligible employees. Three types of employers qualify: public schools, certain tax-exempt organizations, and certain employers of ministers. Your employer may be able to help you determine whether you are an eligible employee.

The most common way to contribute to TSA plans is through a salary reduction agreement. This is an agreement under which an employee agrees to take a reduction in salary or to forego a salary increase and the employer contributes that amount to a TSA plan for that employee. These employer contributions made on your behalf are called "elective deferrals." A TSA plan can also be funded through nonelective employer contributions, after-tax employee contributions, or a combination of these contributions.

There is an annual limit on elective deferrals. Generally, you cannot defer more than $10,000 for 1999 for all plans covering you, including TSA plans. If elective deferral contributions on your behalf are more than the allowable amount, you must include the excess in your gross income.

Limits are placed on the contributions that can be made by an employer to TSA plans. Special rules may apply in determining the limit on employer contributions for you to a TSA plan if you also are covered by a qualified plan.

The exclusion allowance is the amount of employer contributions (including elective deferrals) to your TSA contract or account that you can exclude from income. You pay tax on these excluded amounts when you receive a distribution from the TSA.

Employees of public schools and public school systems, hospitals, home health service agencies, health and welfare service agencies, churches, and certain church-related organizations can make a "catch-up" election to increase the limit on employer contributions for the exclusion allowance.

The *Other Rules* section includes a discussion of the cost of insurance under a TSA plan and a discussion of social security and Medicare taxes on employer contributions.

In most cases, the payments you receive, or that are made available to you, under your TSA contract or account are taxable in full as ordinary income. In general, the same tax rules apply to distributions from TSA plans that apply to distributions from other retirement plans. These rules are explained in Publication 575, *Pension and Annuity Income*. If you transfer all or part of your interest from a TSA contract or account to another TSA contract or account, the transfer may be tax free. You can generally roll over tax free all or any part of a distribution from a TSA plan to a traditional IRA or another TSA plan.

You can use the worksheets at the end of this publication to figure many of the limits that apply to your TSA plan.

### Useful Items
You may want to see:

**Publication**

☐ **15A** Employer's Supplemental Tax Guide

☐ **575** Pension and Annuity Income

☐ **590** Individual Retirement Arrangements (IRAs) (Including Roth IRAs and Education IRAs)

**Form (and Instructions)**

☐ **W-2** Wage and Tax Statement

☐ **1099-R** Distributions From Pensions, Annuities, Retirement or Profit-Sharing Plans, IRAs, Insurance Contracts, etc.

☐ **5330** Return of Excise Taxes Related to Employee Benefit Plans

See *How To Get More Information*, near the end of this publication for information about getting these publications and forms.

## What Is a Tax-Sheltered Annuity (TSA) Plan?

A tax-sheltered annuity plan, often referred to as a "403(b) plan," "tax-deferred annuity plan," or simply "TSA plan" (which is used in this publication), is a retirement plan that, if operated properly by a qualified employer, is tax-exempt.

The TSA plan can invest funds for participating employees in:

• Annuity contracts,

• Custodial accounts holding mutual fund shares, or

• Retirement income accounts (defined contribution plans maintained by churches or certain church-related organizations).

Throughout this publication, wherever "TSA contract" appears, it refers to any one of these

funding arrangements, unless otherwise specified.

**Tax advantage for employees.** Generally, you can exclude from current income contributions by a qualified employer to purchase a TSA contract for you under a TSA plan. You do not have to include the contributions (and any earnings on them) in your taxable income until you begin to receive annuity payments from your TSA plan, usually after you retire. Because of this tax postponement, these plans are described as 'tax-deferred' or 'tax-sheltered' annuities.

## Qualified Employer

A qualified employer can purchase TSA contracts for eligible employees. Three types of employers qualify — public schools, certain tax-exempt organizations, and certain employers of ministers.

### Public Schools

A state or local government or any of its agencies or instrumentalities can be a qualified employer. However, employers are qualified employers only for employees who perform (or have performed) services, directly or indirectly, for an educational organization, such as a public school. For this purpose, an Indian tribal government is a state government.

**Educational organization.** An educational organization is one that normally maintains a regular faculty and curriculum and normally has a regularly enrolled body of students in attendance at the place where it regularly carries on educational activities.

### Tax-Exempt Organizations

Generally, a qualified employer includes an organization that is tax-exempt because it is organized and operated exclusively for religious, charitable, scientific, public safety testing, literary, or educational purposes. A qualified employer also includes a tax-exempt organization that is organized and operated exclusively to encourage national or international amateur sports competition (but only if no part of its activities involve the provision of athletic facilities or equipment), or for the prevention of cruelty to children or animals. The organization can be a corporation, community chest, fund, or foundation.

**Government instrumentalities.** Wholly-owned instrumentalities (other than public schools) of state or municipal governments generally are not qualified employers. However, a separate instrumentality that has been recognized as tax-exempt by the Internal Revenue Service because it is organized and operated exclusively for one or more of the exempt purposes described earlier is a qualified employer. A separately organized school, college, university, or hospital may qualify if it is not an activity essential to and conducted under a branch or department of a state or municipal government.

**Cooperative hospital service organization.** A cooperative hospital service organization that meets certain requirements is a qualified employer.

**Uniformed Services University of the Health Sciences.** This is a federal organization authorized to train medical students for the uniformed services. The rules in this publication apply to TSA contracts purchased for civilian faculty and staff for work they performed after 1979.

**Indian tribal governments.** Any TSA contract purchased by an Indian tribal government for its employees is treated as having been purchased by a tax-exempt organization that is qualified to provide TSA contracts for its employees. An Indian tribal government includes any political subdivisions, agencies, and instrumentalities of it, as well as any corporations that are chartered under federal, state, or tribal law and owned by it.

## Certain Employers of Ministers

A qualified employer of a minister can be either the minister (if self-employed) or an organization with which the minister shares a common bond. A self-employed minister is treated as employed by a tax-exempt organization that is a qualified employer. An organization, other than a qualified tax-exempt organization of the type described earlier under *Tax-Exempt Organizations*, is a qualified employer of a minister if the organization and the minister share common religious bonds.

# Eligible Employees

A qualified employer can purchase TSA contracts only for eligible employees. If you are subject to the will and control of a qualified employer regarding what work you do and how you do it, you are an eligible employee. If you are subject to the control or direction of another as to the result only, and not how you do the work, you will generally be an independent contractor, and not an eligible employee.

The employer who pays you for services you perform may be able to help you determine whether you are an eligible employee.

## Employees of Public School Systems

You are an eligible employee if you perform services as an employee, either directly or indirectly, for a public school system.

For example, if you are a principal, clerical employee, custodial employee, or teacher at a public elementary school, you are an eligible employee because you are performing services directly for a public school.

If you are involved in the operation or direction of an education program carried out through public schools, you are an eligible employee because you are performing services indirectly for those public schools. See *Elected or appointed to office,* later.

If you are an employee participating in an in-home teaching program, you are an eligible employee since these programs are merely an extension of the activities carried on by public schools.

**Employees of a state's Department of Education.** If you are a janitorial, custodial, or general clerical employee appointed by a state commissioner of education, you are an

eligible employee because you indirectly perform services for the public schools.

If you were appointed by a state commissioner of education to a position involving a significant degree of executive or policy making authority, and your appointment is based on required training or experience in the field of education, you are an eligible employee because you indirectly perform services for the public schools.

***Elected or appointed to office.*** If you occupy an elective or appointive office, you may be an eligible employee. You are an eligible employee if your office is one to which a person is elected or appointed only if he or she has received training, or is experienced, in the field of education.

A commissioner or superintendent of education generally is considered an employee performing services for an educational organization. However, a university regent or trustee, or a member of a board of education, is not an eligible employee.

**Employees of a state teachers' retirement system.** If you are an employee of a retirement system set up to administer a state teachers' retirement program, you are not an eligible employee because you are not performing services, either directly or indirectly, for a public school.

## Employees of Certain Tax-Exempt Organizations

Certain tax-exempt organizations (described under *Qualified Employer,* earlier) can purchase TSA contracts for their employees. Employees of these tax-exempt organizations include individuals who perform services as social workers, members of the clergy, teachers, professors, clerks, secretaries, etc.

For more information on who is an employee, see Publication 15A.

### Ministers

If you are a duly ordained, commissioned, or licensed minister of a church and are working as a minister or chaplain, you may be an eligible employee. You are an eligible employee if, in connection with the exercise of your ministry, you are either self-employed or working for an organization with which you share common religious bonds, but which is not a qualified tax-exempt organization of the type described earlier under *Tax-Exempt Organizations.*

# Contributions

A TSA plan can be funded by the following contributions:

- Elective deferrals,
- Nonelective employer contributions,
- After-tax employee contributions, or
- A combination of the above.

**Elective deferrals defined.** Under a salary reduction agreement (defined later), your employer's plan may permit your employer to contribute part of your pay to a retirement fund, rather than pay it to you. These employer contributions are called "elective deferrals" because:

1) You choose (elect) to set aside part of your pay, and

2) Tax on that part of your pay is postponed (deferred) until it is distributed to you.

**Nonelective employer contributions defined.** An employer contribution to a TSA plan is treated as a nonelective contribution if employees are not required to choose the contributions. The employer chooses to make these contributions to the TSA plans. The employer must be a qualified employer (defined earlier) for the contributions to be excluded from the employee's gross income. These contributions are subject to the limit on employer contributions discussed later.

**After-tax employee contributions.** If the plan permits these contributions, an employee contribution made with funds on which income taxes have already been paid is treated as an after-tax contribution. A salary payment on which income tax was withheld is an example of such funds. These contributions are subject to the limit on employer contributions.

## Exclusion From Gross Income

Generally, if you are an eligible employee (defined earlier), you can exclude from gross income your qualified employer's (defined earlier) contributions to your TSA contract.

**TIP** *Contributions made by a self-employed minister or chaplain who is treated as employed by a qualified tax-exempt organization to a retirement income account that is treated as a TSA contract are deductible (rather than excludible) up to the exclusion limits for TSA plans (discussed next). This is true unless the contributions are made by the employer of a chaplain and excluded from the chaplain's income as discussed under Specials Rules under Includible Compensation, later.*

### Exclusion Limits

Generally, the amount of contributions you can exclude for a tax year is the smallest of the following limits:

1) The limit on elective deferrals (discussed later) for the year.

2) The limit on employer contributions (discussed later) for the limitation year (discussed later) ending with or within your tax year.

3) The exclusion allowance (discussed later) for your tax year.

**Alternative limits.** You may be able to use an alternative limit to increase the amount you can exclude. See *Catch-up Election — Alternative Limits for Certain Employees,* later.

**TIP** *The worksheets at the end of this publication are designed to help you determine the contribution limits that apply to you. To determine the exclusion allowance, use* Worksheet 1; *for the limit on employer contributions, use* Worksheet 2; *and for the limit on elective deferrals, use* Worksheet 3. *If you qualify to choose an alternative limit, use* Worksheet 4, 5, or 6, *whichever applies. See* Catch-up Election — Alternative Limits for Certain Employees, *later.*

Page 3

**Rollover contributions.** For purposes of determining the exclusion allowance, your employer's contributions do not include a rollover contribution from another TSA contract or a traditional individual retirement arrangement (IRA). A traditional IRA is any IRA that is not a Roth, SIMPLE, or education IRA.

**Only elective deferrals.** If all of the contributions are elective deferrals, the total must not be more than the smallest of the three limits in the preceding list.

**Only nonelective contributions.** If all of the contributions are nonelective contributions, only limits (2) and (3) apply.

**Both elective deferrals and nonelective contributions.** If the total contributions include both elective deferrals and nonelective contributions and limit (1) is the smallest of the limits in the preceding list, the elective deferrals minus limit (1) is an excess deferral and is included in your gross income. The total of all contributions (including the elective deferrals) minus the smaller of limit (2) or (3) is an excess contribution.

**More than one TSA contract.** If for any tax year elective deferrals are contributed to more than one TSA contract for you (whether or not with the same employer), you must combine all the elective deferrals to determine whether the total is more than the limit for that year. See *Limit on Elective Deferrals*, later.

### Treatment of Excess Contributions

If the contributions to your TSA contract for a year are more than any of the limits discussed above under *Exclusion Limits*, you must include the excess in your income for that year. Further, if you have an excess because the contributions are more than limit (2), that excess reduces the amount of your exclusion allowance for future years, even though the excess has already been included in your income.

For more information on the treatment of excess contributions, see *Excess Deferrals, Limit on Employer Contributions*, and *Tax on Excess Contributions to a Custodial Account*, later.

## Salary Reduction Agreement

The most common way to contribute to TSA contracts is through a salary reduction agreement. This is an agreement between the employer and employee under which the employee agrees to take a reduction in salary or to forego a salary increase and the employer contributes that amount to a TSA contract for that employee. These employer contributions are called "elective deferrals" and excluded from the employee's income when made and included in the employee's income when withdrawn. See *Limit on Elective Deferrals*, for more information.

 *You can enter into more than one salary reduction agreement during a tax year. In addition, for salary reduction purposes, you must use compen-*

Page 4

sation that has not yet been made available to you. (However, to determine what compensation can be used to figure the maximum exclusion allowance, see Includible Compensation, *later, under* Exclusion Allowance.)

**Treatment of contributions.** Amounts contributed by your employer under a salary reduction agreement and invested in a TSA contract for you are generally treated as elective deferrals (defined under *Contributions*, earlier).

*Exemption.* An employer contribution to your TSA contract is not treated as an elective deferral if it is made as a condition of employment or as a one-time choice by you when you first become eligible to participate in the agreement. But, if you can change or end the election to participate in the agreement, the election is not a one-time choice and the contributions are elective deferrals.

## Limit on Elective Deferrals

As defined earlier, elective deferrals are employer contributions made under a salary reduction agreement to your TSA contract. There is an annual limit on the amount of elective contributions that you can defer. To determine the limit on elective deferrals, use Worksheet 3.

**Deferrals subject to limit.** The limit applies to the total of all elective deferrals contributed for the year on your behalf (even if by different employers) to:

- Cash or deferred arrangements (known as section 401(k) plans) to the extent excluded from your gross income,

- Section 501(c)(18) plans created before June 25, 1959, and only to the extent excluded from your gross income,

- SIMPLE plans,

- Simplified employee pension (SEP) plans, and

- Tax-sheltered annuity (TSA) plans.

**Dollar limit.** Generally, you cannot defer more than an allowable amount each year for all plans covering you, including TSA plans. For 1999, the allowable amount (limit) is $10,000. This limit applies without regard to community property laws. If you defer more than the allowable amount for a tax year, you must include the excess in your gross income for that year. See *Excess Deferrals*, later.

*Increase for 15-year employees.* If you have a TSA contract and you have completed at least 15 years of service with a public school system, hospital, home health service agency, health and welfare service agency, church, or convention or association of churches (or associated organization), the $10,000 limit is increased each tax year. The limit is increased by the *smallest* of the following:

1) $3,000,

2) $15,000, reduced by increases to the $10,000 limit you were allowed in earlier years because of this rule, or

3) $5,000 times the number of your years of service for the organization, minus the total elective deferrals made by the organization for you for earlier years.

For example, if you qualify, you may increase your elective deferrals to $13,000. For the computation, see Step 2 of Worksheet 3.

*Cost-of-living adjustment.* Under current law, the $10,000 limit is to be increased to reflect any increases in the Consumer Price Index in future years.

## Excess Deferrals

Excess deferrals are total elective deferrals for the year minus the limit on elective deferrals.

### Tax Treatment

**General rule.** If the total you defer for a tax year is more than the limit for the year, you must include the excess in your gross income for that year on line 7 of Form 1040.

**Distribution of excess.** If the plan allows you to receive the excess amount and that is what you choose to do, you must notify the plan as explained next.

*One plan.* If only one plan is involved, you must notify the plan by March 1 after the end of the tax year that an excess amount was deferred. The plan must then pay you the excess, along with any income on that amount, by April 15.

⚠ *Because you are responsible for notifying the plan, you must monitor contributions to the plan.*

*More than one plan.* If more than one plan is involved, you must notify each plan by March 1 of the amount to be paid from that particular plan, and the plan must then pay you that amount, along with any income on that amount, by April 15.

*Distribution of excess by the required date.* If you receive the excess amount by April 15, do not include it again in your gross income and do not subject it to the additional 10% tax for premature distributions. However, any income earned on the excess deferral that is distributed to you is taxable to you in the tax year paid but is not subject to the additional 10% tax for premature distributions.

If you receive part of the excess deferral and the income earned on it, you must treat the distribution as if ratably received from the excess deferral and the income earned on it.

*Example.* Assume that your excess deferral is $1,800 and the income earned on it is $200. If your distribution is $1,000, $900 ($1800/2000 x $1,000) is from the excess deferral and $100 ($200/2000 x $1,000) is from the income earned that must be separately reported.

**Excess left in the plan.** If you leave the excess deferral in the plan, you must include the excess amount in your gross income for the tax year in which the amount was deferred. You cannot treat the excess amount as an investment in the contract (tax-free return of cost) when you figure the taxable amount of any future benefits or distributions. Thus, an excess deferral left in the plan would be taxed twice, once when contributed and again when distributed.

# Limit on Employer Contributions

There is a limit on employer contributions to tax-sheltered annuity (TSA) plans for each limitation year (defined later). TSA plans are treated as defined contribution plans for purposes of this limit (which is also called the "general rule"). Under the general rule, an employer's contributions (including elective deferrals) to an employee's account under a defined contribution plan should not be more than the lesser of:

1) $30,000, or

2) 25% of the employee's compensation (defined later) for the year.

This limit is in addition to the exclusion allowance (discussed later) and the limit on elective deferrals (discussed earlier). To determine the limit on employer contributions under the general rule, use Worksheet 2. Also, see *Catch-up Election — Alternative Limits for Certain Employees,* later.

**Limitation year.** Generally, your limitation year is the calendar year. However, you can elect to change to a different limitation year consisting of any period of 12 consecutive months by attaching a statement to your individual income tax return for the tax year you make the change.

**Contributions in excess of employer limit.** An excess employer contribution must be included in your gross income in the tax year when it is made.

For future tax years, the exclusion allowance (see *Exclusion Allowance,* later) must be reduced by this excess contribution even though it was not excludable from your gross income in the tax year when it was made.

**TSA plan and qualified plan.** If the limit is exceeded because you must combine a TSA plan with a qualified plan, the same rule applies. You must include the excess in your gross income for the tax year the excess contribution is made and reduce your exclusion allowance for any future years in which you are a participant in a TSA plan.

If you are a participant in both a TSA plan and a qualified plan, see *Limit on Employer Contributions to More Than One Plan,* later.

**Excess contribution in earlier years.** If in earlier years your employer made annual contributions to a TSA plan for you that were more than the annual maximum permitted under this limit on employer contributions, your exclusion allowance is reduced by the excess.

**Reduction procedure.** The exclusion allowance is reduced by including the excess contributions from prior years in amounts previously excludable (discussed later under *Exclusion Allowance*). Include prior years' excess contributions in amounts previously excludable only if the limit was exceeded for a tax year beginning after January 24, 1980.

**Compensation.** Generally, for purposes of the 25% of compensation limit (item (2) at the beginning of this discussion), compensation *includes:*

• Wages, salaries, and fees for personal services with the employer maintaining the plan, even if excludable as foreign earned income,

• Certain taxable accident and health insurance payments,

• Moving expense payments or reimbursements paid by your employer, if such payments are not deductible by you,

• The value of nonqualified stock options granted to you that are includible in your gross income in the year granted,

• Elective deferrals, and

• Amounts contributed or deferred by your employer for a cafeteria plan, or a section 457 plan.

Generally, compensation *does not include:*

• Contributions toward a TSA contract (other than elective deferrals),

• Contributions toward a deferred compensation plan if, before applying the limit on employer contributions, the contributions are not taxable,

• Distributions from a deferred compensation plan,

• Proceeds from the disposition of stock acquired under a qualified stock option, and

• Certain other amounts that are excludable from your income, such as group term life insurance premiums that are not taxable.

**More than one TSA contract.** For each year you apply this limit, you must combine the contributions to all TSA contracts made on your behalf by your employer. This is done whether or not you elect one of the alternative limits discussed under *Catch-up Election — Alternative Limits for Certain Employees,* later. You may also have to combine contributions to qualified plans of the same employer or an employer that you contribute to (for purposes of applying this limit). See *Limit on Employer Contributions to More Than One Plan,* later.

**More than one employer.** If more than one qualified employer contributes to a TSA contract for you, you must figure a separate exclusion allowance for each qualified employer. Do not include amounts contributed, compensation, or years of service for one qualified employer in the computation for another qualified employer. Special rules apply to church employees, as discussed under *Years of Service,* later.

**Employer must remain qualified.** The exclusion allowance applies only to those contributions made while your employer was a qualified employer. If, for example, your employer loses tax-exempt status and is no longer qualified, your exclusion allowance will not apply to the employer's contributions made during period(s) that the employer is not qualified.

**Catch-up election for certain employees.** Certain employees can elect to substitute the limit on employer contributions for the exclusion allowance under an alternate rule called the "overall limit" (explained under *Catch-up Election — Alternative Limits for Certain Employees,* later). Only employees of public schools, hospitals, home health service agencies, health and welfare service agencies, churches, and certain church-related organizations can make the election.

**Minimum exclusion allowance for church employees.** If you are a church employee (defined later under *Years of Service*) and your adjusted gross income (figured without regard to community property laws) is less than $17,000, you are entitled to exclude from your gross income a certain minimum amount called a minimum exclusion allowance. The minimum is your exclusion allowance figured as explained earlier, but not less than the smaller of:

1) $3,000, or

2) Your includible compensation (defined later).

## How To Figure

To determine your annual exclusion allowance, you will need to know the following:

• Includible compensation,

• Years of service, and

• Amounts previously excludable.

You can determine the exclusion allowance at the end of your tax year by using Worksheet 1 at the end of this publication.

**Reduction of the exclusion allowance.** You must reduce your exclusion allowance by the excess of your employer's contributions (for tax years beginning after January 24, 1980) over the limit on employer contributions for those years. (See *Contributions in excess of employer limit* under *Limit on Employer Contributions,* earlier.)

For future years, treat the excess as though it were an amount previously excludable.

## Includible Compensation

For purposes of figuring your exclusion allowance, includible compensation generally is the amount of pay that you received from the employer who made contributions to your TSA contract and that you must include in income for the most recent period (ending no later than the end of your tax year) which you can count as one year of service. It does not include your employer's contributions to your TSA contract. You determine the amount that must be included in income without taking into account the foreign earned income exclusion. See *Most Recent One-Year Period of Service,* later.

## Exclusion Allowance

The exclusion allowance is the amount of employer contributions (including *elective deferrals*) to your TSA contract that you can exclude from income. To figure the amount of the exclusion allowance, see *How To Figure,* later. You pay tax on the excluded amount when you receive a distribution from the TSA contract.

**More than one TSA contract.** If, during any tax year, you have two or more TSA contracts, custodial accounts, or retirement income accounts maintained by your employer, figure only one exclusion allowance for the TSA contracts because they are considered as one TSA contract.

Page 5

For purposes of figuring your exclusion allowance, the following amounts are includible compensation. Generally, these amounts are not included in income.

- Elective deferrals (employer's contributions made on your behalf under a salary reduction agreement).
- Amounts contributed or deferred by your employer under a section 125 cafeteria plan.
- Amounts contributed or deferred under a section 457 nonqualified deferred compensation plan (state or local government or tax-exempt organization plan).

**Self-employed ministers.** If your are a self-employed minister treated as an employee of a tax-exempt organization, your includible compensation is your net earnings from your ministry minus the contributions made to the retirement plan on your behalf and the deduction for half of the self-employment tax.

### Special Rules

When figuring your includible compensation, you should examine the following exceptions and definitions.

**Employer not qualified.** Only the compensation earned from the employer purchasing your TSA contract is includible compensation. Do not include compensation earned while your employer was not a qualified employer. However, your employer's status when you actually receive the compensation does not matter.

*Other employers.* Compensation from employers who are not purchasing your TSA contract and compensation from other sources generally is not includible compensation. However, see *Service with one employer* under *Years of Service*, later.

**Contributions for a TSA contract.** Contributions by your employer for a TSA contract are not part of includible compensation.

*Foreign missionary.* However, if you are a foreign missionary during the tax year, your includible compensation includes contributions by the church during the year toward your TSA contract.

You are a foreign missionary if:

1) You are a lay person or a duly ordained, commissioned, or licensed minister of a church,

2) You are an employee of a church or a convention or association of churches, and

3) You are performing services for the church outside the United States.

**Contributions to a church plan on behalf of a minister.** If you are a duly ordained, commissioned, or licensed minister and, in the exercise of your ministry, you are employed by an organization with which you share common religious goals, but which is not a qualified tax-exempt organization of the type described earlier under *Tax-Exempt Organizations*, contributions made to a church plan on your behalf are excluded from your gross income to the extent they would have been excluded had you been an employee of a church.

For purposes of this rule, a minister of a church also includes:

Page 6

1) A self-employed minister, and

2) A minister employed by an organization other than a tax-exempt organization that shares a common religious bond with the minister.

**Contributions to a TSA contract and a qualified retirement plan.** If your employer makes contributions for you toward both a TSA contract and a qualified retirement plan, your employer's contributions to the qualified retirement plan that you can exclude from income are not part of includible compensation for figuring your exclusion allowance.

**Contributions that are more than your exclusion allowance.** Contributions that are more than your exclusion allowance are not part of compensation for figuring your exclusion allowance, but they must be included in your gross income.

*Example.* After taking a reduction in salary to pay for your employer's contribution to a TSA contract during your first year of employment, you received a salary of $12,000. According to your agreement, $2,800 ($400 more than your exclusion allowance) is contributed for your contract. Use $12,000 as includible compensation in figuring the exclusion allowance, even though you must include $12,400 in gross income.

**The cost of incidental life insurance.** The cost of incidental life insurance provided under a TSA contract is not includible compensation even though the cost is taxable to you. This part of the cost of your TSA contract is treated as contributed by you, rather than by your employer, and is part of your cost (basis) in the contract.

**Foreign earned income exclusion.** Excludable foreign earned income is part of includible compensation.

### Most Recent One-Year Period of Service

When determining your includible compensation for purposes of figuring the exclusion allowance, first take into account the services you performed during the tax year for which you are figuring the exclusion allowance. Keep in mind that your most recent one-year period of service may not be the same as your employer's most recent annual work period. This can happen if your tax year is not the same as that of your employer.

**Tax year different than that of employer.** If your tax year is not the same as that of your employer, your most recent one-year period of service is made up of parts of at least two of your employer's annual work periods.

*Example.* A professor who reports her income on a calendar year basis is employed on a full-time basis by a university that operates on an academic year (October through May). For purposes of computing her exclusion allowance for 1999, the professor's most recent one-year period of service consists of her service performed during January through May of 1999 and her service performed during October through December of 1999.

**Part-time or employed only part of year.** If you are a part-time employee, or a full-time employee who is employed for only part of the year, your most recent one-year period of

service consists of your service this year and your service for as many previous years as is necessary to total one full year of service. (See *Full year of service*, later, under *Rules for Figuring*.) You add up your most recent periods of service to determine your most recent one-year period of service. First, take into account your service during your tax year for which the exclusion allowance is being determined. Then add your service during your next preceding tax year and subsequent tax years until your total service equals one year of service.

*Example.* You were employed on a full-time basis during the months July through December 1997 (1/2 year of service), July through December 1998 (1/2 year of service), and October through December 1999 (1/4 year of service), your most recent one-year period of service for purposes of computing your exclusion allowance for 1999 is the total of your service during 1999 (1/4 year of service), your service during 1998 (1/2 year of service), and your service during the months October through December 1997 (1/4 year of service).

**Not yet employed for one year.** If at the close of your tax year, you have not yet worked for your employer for one year (including time you worked for the same employer in earlier tax years), use the period of time you have worked for the employer as your most recent one-year period of service.

## Years of Service

For purposes of figuring your exclusion allowance, your years of service depend on your employment status with the employer who maintains the TSA plan for the current tax year and earlier tax years. How you figure your years of service depends on whether you were a full-time or a part-time employee, whether you worked for the full year or only part of the year, and whether you have worked for your employer for one year.

### Definition

Your years of service are the total number of years you worked for your employer figured as of the end of the tax year for which you are figuring an exclusion allowance. The service need not be continuous.

### Rules for Figuring

Take the following rules into account when figuring your years of service.

**Less than one year of total service.** Your years of service cannot be less than one year. If at the end of your tax year, you have less than one year of service (including service in any previous years), figure your exclusion allowance as if your years of service is one year.

**Status of employer.** Your years of service will only include periods during which your employer was a qualified employer, defined earlier.

**Service with one employer.** Generally, you cannot count service for any other employer. *Church employee.* If you are a church employee, treat all of your years of service with related church organizations as years of service with one employer. If during your church career you transfer from one organization to another within that church or to an associated organization, treat all this service as service with a single employer. When these organizations make contributions to your TSA contracts, treat them as made by the same employer.

A church employee is anyone who is an employee of a church or a convention or association of churches. This includes an employee of a tax-exempt organization controlled by or associated with a church or a convention or association of churches.

**Self-employed ministers.** If you are a self-employed minister, your years of service include full and part years in which you have been treated as employed by a qualified tax-exempt organization.

**Full-time employee for full year.** Count each full year during which you were employed full-time as one year of service. In determining whether you were employed full-time, compare the amount of work you were required to perform with the amount of work normally required of others who held the same position with the same employer and who generally received most of their pay from the position.

**How to compare.** You can use any method that reasonably and accurately reflects the amount of work required. For example, if you are a teacher, you can use the number of hours of classroom instruction as a measure of the amount of work required.

In determining whether positions with the same employer are the same, consider all of the facts and circumstances concerning the positions, including the work performed, the methods by which pay is determined, and the descriptions (or titles) of the positions.

*Example.* An assistant professor employed in the English department of a university will be considered a full-time employee if the amount of work that he is required to perform is the same as the amount of work normally required of assistant professors of English at that university who get most of their pay from that position.

If no one else works for your employer in the same position, compare your work with the work normally required of others who held the same position with similar employers or similar positions with your employer.

**Full year of service.** A full year of service for a particular position means the usual annual work period of anyone employed full-time in that general type of work at that place of employment.

*Example.* If a doctor works for a hospital 12 months of a year except for a one-month vacation, the doctor will be considered as employed for a full year if the other doctors at that hospital also work 11 months of the year with a one-month vacation. Similarly, if the usual annual work period at a university consists of the fall and spring semesters, an instructor at that university who teaches these semesters will be considered as working a full year.

**Part-time or employed only part of year.** You include a fraction of a year of service for each year during which you were a full-time employee for part of the year or a part-time employee for the entire year or for a part of the year.

*Full-time for part of year.* If you worked full time for part of the year, you figure the fraction of a year of service to include by dividing the number of weeks (or months) during which you were a full-time employee by the number of weeks (or months) considered the usual annual work period for the position you held.

*Example.* If you were employed full time as an instructor by a university for the 1999 spring semester (which lasts from February 1999 through May 1999) and the academic year of the university is 8 months long, (from October 1998 through May 1999), you completed 4/8 of a year of service.

*Part-time for full year.* If you worked part time for a full year, you figure the fraction of a year of service to include by dividing the amount of work required of you by the amount of work normally required of someone holding the same position on a full-time basis. You can use any method that reasonably and accurately reflects the amount of work required. You can use the number of hours of classroom instruction as a measure of the amount of work required.

*Example.* A practicing physician teaches one course at a local medical school 3 hours per week for two semesters. Other faculty members at the same school teach 9 hours per week for two semesters. The practicing physician is considered as having completed 3/9 of a year of service.

*Part-time for part of year.* If you worked part time for part of the year, you figure the fraction of a year of service to include by multiplying two fractions. Figure one fraction as if you worked full time for part of the year and figure the other fraction as if you worked part time for the full year.

*Example.* An attorney teaches a course for 3 hours per week for one semester at a law school. The full-time instructors at that law school teach 12 hours per week for two semesters. The fractional part of a year of service for the part-time instructor is computed as follows:

1) The fractional year of service if the instructor was a part-time employee for a full year is 3/12 (number of hours employed divided by the usual number of hours of work required for that position).

2) The fractional year of service if the instructor was a full-time employee for part of a year is 1/2 (period worked or one semester, divided by usual work period, or 2 semesters).

These fractions are multiplied to obtain the fractional year of service: 3/12 times 1/2, or 3/24 (1/8).

## Amounts Previously Excludable

To figure your exclusion allowance, you must know the amounts previously excludable from your income.

### Definition

Amounts previously excludable is the total of all contributions for retirement benefits made for you by your employer that you could exclude from your gross income. It does not include amounts for the tax year for which the current exclusion allowance is being figured.

Amounts previously excludable include contributions in earlier years by your employer to:

• A tax-sheltered annuity (TSA) plan,

• A qualified annuity plan or a qualified pension, profit-sharing, or stock bonus trust,

• A qualified bond-purchase plan,

• A retirement plan under which the contributions originally were excludable by you only because your rights to the contributions were forfeitable when made, and which also were excludable by you when your rights became nonforfeitable (This does not apply to contributions made after 1957 to purchase an annuity contract if your employer was an exempt organization when the contributions were made.), or

• An eligible deferred compensation plan (under Code section 457) of a state or local government or tax-exempt organization, even if maintained by a separate employer.

You must treat contributions to a state teachers retirement system made for you in earlier tax years, up to the amount that was excludable, as amounts previously excludable.

You must treat employer contributions and other additions in earlier years (beginning after January 24, 1980) that were more than the limit as if they were amounts previously excludable. See *Limit on Employer Contributions,* earlier.

# Social Security Online: Frequently Asked Questions

SocialSecurityOnline
The Official Website of the Social Security Administration

## Frequently Asked Questions

**Answers to your questions about Social Security**

[Home] [Top 10 Services] [Search Site] [Site Map]

- **Check Out the May Issue of eNews**
  This month we've got important news for you: Whether you're looking for some extra cash, or want to file for benefits, we've got it covered. If it has to do with Social Security, you'll hear it here first.
  Subscribe Today; It's FREE!

- **Consumer Price Index Fix**
  If you currently get Social Security benefits or Supplemental Security Income , we'll be sending you a payment of $12 to $19 dollars sometime in July. We're doing this to remedy a small error in the way the Bureau of Labor Statistics calculated the 1999 cost-of-living adjustment.

**Find Answers**
Start here! We store all frequently asked questions and answers in a database. Search by category, keywords, or phrases. If you are unable to find an answer, you will be given an opportunity to ask a question.

**My Notification Requests**
You can be notified when certain questions change. Use this area to create an account, or to modify the selection of questions you wish to be notified about, or to change the e-mail address where we will send the notification.

Powered by
RightNow Web

[home] [top 10 services] [search the site] [sitemap] [privacy policy]

SocialSecurityOnline
The Official Website of the Social Security Administration

# Frequently Asked Questions

Answers to your questions about Social Security

[Home] [Top 10 Services] [Search Site] [Site Map]

◿FAQ Home ◢   ▶◿ **My Notification Requests** ◿                                   Hel

**Category**
| All Categories ▼ |
| All Subcategories ▼ |

**Search Text (optional)**

**Search by**
| Phrases ▼ |

**Sort by**
| Default Sort ▼ |

Search Tips?

| Search |

◉ Powered by
RightNow Wel

◁

◁

**574 Answers Found**                    Page: | 1 ▼ | of 29 | Go |  ▶

| | Category ▼▲ | Subject | | Questions Answered ▼▲ |
|---|---|---|---|---|
| 1 | Social Security Numbers and Cards | How do I replace a lost Social Security card? | | 393884 |
| 2 | Benefits | Can I apply for retirement benefits on the Internet? | | 9279 |
| 3 | Benefits | What are the disability requirements for an adult? | | 365763 |
| 4 | Web Site Questions | Why does Social Security have a Web site targeted to women? | | 351600 |
| 5 | Social Security Numbers and Cards | How do I change my name on my Social Security card? | | 191662 |
| 6 | Social Security Numbers and Cards | How do I obtain a Social Security number? | | 78794 |
| 7 | Social Security Numbers and Cards | How do I replace a lost Social Security card? | | 60218 |
| 8 | Benefits | How are my retirement benefits calculated? | | 39850 |
| 9 | Social Security Numbers and Cards | What do I need to do to get a Social Security number for my baby? | | 38899 |
| 10 | Miscellaneous | What are the tax, benefit and earning amounts for 2001? | | 37546 |
| 11 | Social Security Numbers and Cards | If I submit form SS-5 to a local office, will I get a card immediately? | | 37062 |
| 12 | Social Security Numbers and Cards | How does a non-citizen obtain a Social Security number to get a drivers license? | | 36621 |
| 13 | Social Security Numbers and Cards | I just got married and want to change my name; how do I do this? | | 29846 |
| 14 | Social Security Statement | I want to apply for my benefits. What do I do? | | 23313 |
| 15 | Social Security Numbers and Cards | I have lost my Social Security card. Must I replace it? | | 22506 |
| 16 | Checks and Payments | Are my retirement benefits figured on my last five years of earnings? | | 22465 |
| 17 | Benefits | How much can I earn and still receive Disability benefits? | | 22391 |
| 18 | Social Security Numbers and Cards | What do I do if someone else is using my Social Security number? | | 20900 |
| 19 | Social Security Numbers and Cards | How do I change my name on my Social Security records? | | 20859 |
| 20 | Miscellaneous | How do I change my address? | | 20172 |

◁

[home] [top 10 services] [search the site] [sitemap] [privacy policy]

# How to Read a Mutual Fund Prospectus— Simplified

All mutual fund companies are required to provide a prospectus to investors. This collection of information, in booklet form, can be a daunting read because it's filled with facts, figures, charts, and tables. Many investors may prefer to skim the fine print and concentrate, instead on the following most important sections:

**Investment Objective**—*Identifies the fund's goals and objectives such as long-term growth combined with protection of principal.*

**Investment Policies**—*Highlights strategies used by the fund manager to meet the fund's objectives.* This section will also explain the types of securities held by the fund. For instance, the fund might diversify assets among stocks, bonds, and money markets or may be totally invested in only one asset class.

**Investment Risk**—*Explains risk factors specific to the fund.* The infinite variety of equities available have different risks associated with them. If the fund invests in emerging markets, for example, the prospectus should point out the risks associated with investments in developing countries. And a sector fund prospectus should emphasize the risks of confining an investment to a specific sector.

**Fund Fees and Expenses**—*Reveals the costs associated with owning the fund, including possible sales charges (loads)*. A fund with a 6 percent load, for example, means that each time you make a $1000 investment in that fund, you're paying $60 to do that. That $60 fee compounds, but not to your benefit; over time it will subtract thousands of dollars from your returns. It's also important to remember that a fund deducts its fees and expenses before declaring earnings, so a fund with a 6 percent load has to earn 6 percent before it can break even and begin to show a profit (positive return).

**Financial Highlights Table**—*Gives the financial history of the fund on a year-by-year basis for the past ten years or since the fund's inception if it's been in existence for less than ten years*. For those seeking current income, the financial highlights table is the place to look for both past and present dividend results.

The fund's expense ratio, also found in the financial highlights table, gives the cost of managing the fund. Like loads, expense ratios are taken off the top before the fund calculates its return.

**Turnover Rate**—*Indicates how frequently the fund buys and sells equities*. The more trades a fund makes, the higher the impact on returns and the greater the likelihood for capital gains. These are passed onto the shareholder in the form of lower returns and/or capital gains taxes. Fortunately funds held in a 403(b) plan are not subject to capital gains tax.

**Manager**—*Presents a brief profile of the fund's manager including qualifications and how long he or she has been at the helm*. This is important information because a fund's performance is a reflection of its management and can be adversely affected by a change.

**Shareholder Services**—*Highlights the services a fund offers to its investors including telephone and Internet trading, availability of automatic investment programs such as 403(b) plans, policies on trading funds within the family, and any minimum investment requirements*.

# How to Read a Morningstar Quicktake Report

The Morningstar Quicktake Report (www.morningstar.com) is a snapshot of important highlights of a specific mutual fund. Its condensed format enables prospective investors to quickly review relevant information. Refer to the Morningstar Web site for the corresponding terms and up-to-date values.

## How Has This Fund Performed?

Growth of $10,000

*Fund:* name of the fund

*Category:* investment class (i.e., large growth, small value, index, sector, etc.)

*Index:* the benchmark index to which this fund can be compared (i.e., S&P 500)

**Annual returns**—for the last four years displayed graphically and in chart form.

**Category rating**—numerical comparison of this fund to others in its category. For example, a fund that has a "3" rating has average risk combined with average reward (5 being the highest and 1 being the lowest).

## Fund Details

**Sales Charge Percentage**—cost to buy that fund, not including management fees.

*Front*: percentage of investment paid as an upfront sales charge deducted from each investment (front load).

*Deferred*: percentage of investment paid when shares are sold (back load).

**Expense Ratio Percentage**—cost to manage the fund. Add this figure to the sales charge (above) to calculate the total costs of owning this fund.

**Manager Name**—name of current manager.

**Manager Start Date**—date when manager began tenure.

## Quick Stats

**NAV**—net asset value (cost to buy one share of the fund).

**Day Change**—change in price from previous day's NAV.

**YTD Return**—increase or decrease in the fund's value from the beginning of the year to the present date.

**Morningstar Rating**—Morningstar's star system of rating funds with five stars being the highest possible.

**Morningstar Category**—asset class to which this fund belongs (i.e., large growth, mid-cap value, international, etc.).

**Net Assets**—total amount the fund has invested in all of its holdings combined.

**Inside Scoop**—brief summary of the positive and negative aspects of the fund.

## What Does This Fund Own?

**Style Box**—graphic illustration of the type of equities in which the fund invests.

**Asset Allocation Percentage**—The percentage of fund assets held in various categories such as cash, stocks, bonds, and other.

**Top 3 Stock Sectors**—The three sectors in which the fund is most heavily invested. (This can be found next to the asset allocation column.)

## Top 5 Holdings

**Name of Holding**—names of the five holdings in which the fund has the most money invested.

**YTD Return Percentage**—amount returned by that equity from the start of the year to the present.

**Percentage of Net Assets**—weight occupied by each of the five top funds expressed in percent.

**News**—headlines of the most recent news articles that contain a reference to that fund. Click on the headline of any article you wish to read. Click on "View all news stories related to this fund" to see a backlog of relevant articles.

**Conversations**—various chat room communications about this fund including the name of the author. Click on the conversation headline to read it in its entirety. Click on "View all conversations in this fund's forum" to see the entire collection of conversations.

Following is a summary of some categories that may prove especially helpful.

**Trailing Returns**—explains how the fund compares to its peers in both the short and long term, going back to the fund's inception.

**Top 25 Holdings**—lists the fund's top 25 holdings.

**Sector Weighting**—gives a more complete picture of the sectors this fund favors and those it avoids.

**Fees and Expenses**—offers a detailed account of every cost associated with ownership of the fund and makes sense out of the fund's expense ratio by translating it into dollars and cents.

# Helpful Web Sites

## Financial News and Current Commentary

### *Wall Street Research Net*

www.wsrn.com
Recent articles about the stock market, in general, with more emphasis on individual stocks than on mutual funds.

### *The Street.Com*

www.thestreet.com
Various articles from different financial experts who present well-written, informative views on topics of concern to all investors.

### *Third Age*

www.thirdage.com
Web site devoted to mature investors with interesting how-to articles about money and investing such as when to hire a financial advisor, how to simplify the investing process, and how to evaluate a portfolio.

### CBS MarketWatch

www.cbs.marketwatch.com

The strength of this Web site lies in its collection of market analysis reports and indepth articles on specific industries written by financial experts.

## Mutual Fund Specific

### MAXfunds

www.maxfunds.com

Fund tracking information presented in a unique style with creative icons and catchy headlines in an uncluttered format.

### ICI Mutual Fund Connection

www.ici.org

General information about mutual funds including fund legislation, fund regulation, and mutual fund shareholder demographics.

### Mutual Fund Investor's Center

www.mfea.com

Basic articles about investing that even a novice can understand such as model investment strategies and a guide to automatic investing.

### Mutual Fund Café

www.mfcafe.com

General fund information delivered in a coffeehouse atmosphere with a clever food theme featuring menu choices like Top Bananas, Blue Plate Special, and Legal Stew.

### Index Funds Online

www.indexfundsonline.com

Information about all major indices, including weekly performance and a list of funds that track each index.

### Index Funds

www.indexfunds.com

Index fund information highlighting the relationship risk to return in index funds and including basic statistics on over 150 funds such as targeted benchmark, expense ratio, and minimum investment.

### Armchair Millionaire

www.armchairmillionaire.com

A Web site from the authors of the book of the same name offering an entertaining approach to portfolio building with index funds using their " 5 Easy Steps" plan.

### Vanguard Mutual Funds

www.vanguard.com

A treasury of everything you always wanted to know about mutual fund investing in simulated classes at the Vanguard University.

## General Investing

### The Motley Fool

www.fool.com

General information about investing with a home page divided into three sections: news & investing, featured services, and personal finance with an especially helpful Q & A section.

### Invest-O-Rama

www.investorama.com

Good source for timely stock market commentary, financial calculators, and other Web sites with investment information.

## Current Legislation

### U.S. Securities and Exchange Commission

www.sec.gov

Contains all legal documents that mutual fund and other public companies are required to file with the government.

### Free Edgar

www.freeedgar.com

Offers SEC documentation on a well-organized, user-friendly, easy-to-navigate Web site with categorized sections and detailed explanations of what each contains.

## Portfolio Tracking and Analysis

### Morningstar

www.morningstar.com

Good site for daily tracking of portfolio holdings and for "snapshot" profiles of specific funds.

### Fund Alarm

www.fundalarm.com

Gives well-defined advice on when to sell a fund, rather than when to buy it, using an easy to understand "alarm" system.

### Yahoo!Finance

www.yahoo.com

A good tracking tool enabling users to view the daily investment performance of their funds in a table format, followed by a list of current articles in which those investments were mentioned.

### BigCharts

www.bigcharts.com

Contains a wealth of financial information on stocks and funds in chart and graph format.

## 403(b) Specific

### Mpower Café

http://403b.mpower.com

Contains current information and articles specifically relating to 403(b) plans with a very helpful FAQ section.

### 403(b)wise

www.403bwise.com
A comprehensive collection of 403(b)-related articles from various sources that include information on annuities, current legislation and lawsuits, and links to other 403(b)-focused Web sites.


## Glossaries

### Superstar Investor

www.superstarinvestor.com
A site with links to just about every financial site on the Worldwide Web categorized according to investor supersites, superstar stock analyzer, the top 100 investing sites, along with a sidebar on the top-performing mutual funds.


### Investor Words

www.investorwords.com
Contains the definition of any word imaginable regarding money, investing, and finance.

# Notes

## Chapter 1   Ten Questions to Ask about Retirement

1. "Social Security . . . a foundation for building a secure retirement," Social Security Retirement Planner, ssa.gov/retire/ (undated).
2. Dr. Don Taylor, "30-Something Investor on Track to Retire at 55," TheStreet.com, October 19, 2000.

## Chapter 2   What is a 403(b) and How Does It Compare to Other Retirement Plans?

1. Jeanne Sahadi, "Take advantage of a 403(b)," CNN Financial Network, February 16, 2000.

## Chapter 3   403(b) Plan Secrets

1. Dan Otter, "Wealth Building Tool for Teachers," 403bwise.com, August 28, 2000.
2. Mary Doclar and Mike Lee, "Retirement Savings Plan Costs Teachers, Lawsuits Say," 403bwise.com, *Fort Worth Star-Telegram*, September 17, 2000.

3. Alan Feigenbaum, "The fleecing of 403(b) participants," *CBS Market-Watch*, May 30, 2000.

4. Mike Diersen, "Annuities vs. Mutual Funds within a 403(b)," 403bwise.com, February, 2001.

5. Ibid.

6. Larry Putnam, "A Tale of Two Hospital 403(b) Plans," 403bwise.com, January, 2001.

7. Christine Dugas, "Evolving economy sparks growth, change in 401(K)s," *USA TODAY*, August 28, 2000, 01.B.

8. Keith L. Alexander, "New TV dramas make a big deal of Wall Street lives: Forget cops, lawyers—stock trades are sexy," *USA TODAY*, August 31, 2000, 06.B.

9. Morningstar Forum, conversation #699, Morningstar.com, November 7, 1998.

10. Mary Doclar and Mike Lee, "Retirement Savings Plan Costs Teachers, Lawsuits Say," 403bwise.com, *Fort Worth Star-Telegram*, September 17, 2000.

### Chapter 4    Choosing the Best 403(b) Vehicle

1. Christine Dugas, "Annuities: Worth a look—a good, hard look," *USA TODAY*, May 29, 1998, 03.B.

2. Joseph Loschiavo, "An Annuity in a 401(k)?" *Mutual Funds*, February 1998, 73.

3. Walter Updegrave, "One (small) Cheer for Variable Annuities," *Money*, January 2000, 91.

4. Ellen E. Schultz, "Your Annuity's 'Death Benefits' May Be Overkill," *Wall Street Journal*, June 3, 1998, C1.

5. Alan Feigenbaum, "The Fleecing of 403(b) Participants," *CBS Market-Watch*, May 30, 2000.

### Chapter 5    Mutual Funds 101

1. Robert Frick, "Why Mutual Fund Expenses Matter," Kiplinger.com, *Kiplinger's Personal Finance*, May 4, 2001.

2. Sheldon Jacobs, "Mutual fund fees aren't necessarily a big rip-off," Honoluluadvertiser.com, *USA TODAY*, October 22, 2000.

3. From a speech given by Arthur Levitt to Investment Company Institute, Washington, DC, May 15, 1998.

4. "Nothing Fails Like Success: the Investment Implications of the Great Mutual Fund Boom," speech given by John Bogle to the Contrary Opinion Forum, Vergennes, Vermont, October 3, 1997.

## Chapter 6 Planning and Saving for Retirement

1. Harry S. Dent, *The Roaring 2000s Investor: Strategies for the Life You Want,* (New York: Simon & Schuster, 1999), 63.
2. Dr. Paul B. Farrell, "Live like a millionaire—without a million bucks," *CBS MarketWatch,* June 7, 2000.
3. Ibid.
4. Joint Statement of Treasury Secretary Lawrence H. Summers and Labor Secretary Alexis M. Herman, *Treasury News,* July 18, 2000.
5. "What problem is the coalition addressing?" Mission Statement, National Partners for Financial Empowerment (NPFE), November 9, 2000.
6. Gary Schatsky, "Fine Tuning in Semi-Retirement," worldlyinvestor.com, August 17, 2000.
7. "Upgrading Strategy," NoLoad Fund*X, DAL Investment Company newsletter.
8. Paul B. Farrell, "Retirement Boot Camp—too tough," *CBS MarketWatch,* October 11, 2000.

## Chapter 7 Managed versus Index Funds

1. The Vanguard Group, "Comparing Actively Managed and Index Funds," *Facts on Funds,* June 30, 2000.
2. John Bogle, "The Debate Goes On: Use Brains or Indexes?", Businessweek.com, *BusinessWeek,* February 22, 1999.
3. Christopher Farrell, "The Real Decision," Businessweek.com, *BusinessWeek,* February 22, 1999.
4. The Vanguard Group, "Plain Talk: Five Myths About Indexing," Vanguard.com/educ/lib/plain/5myths, 1998.
5. Dagen McDowell, "Keep Swimming in that Index Pool," TheStreet.com, March 14, 2000.
6. Anne Tergesen and Peter Coy, "Who Needs a Money Manager?" *BusinessWeek* Online, February 22, 1999.

## Chapter 8 Buy and Hold or Go for the Gold?
## Investing in Bull and Bear Markets

1. Lawrence Cunningham, *How to Think Like Benjamin Graham and Invest Like Warren Buffett,* (New York: McGraw-Hill, 2001), 82.
2. Invesco Mutual Funds, "The Great American Wealth Transfer," *Of Mutual Interest,* Spring 2000.
3. Michael Molinski, "Health funds not just short-term stars," *CBS MarketWatch,* September 28, 2000.

4. Harry S. Dent, *The Roaring 2000s Investor*, (New York: Simon & Schuster, 1999), 53.

5. Dr. Paul B. Farrell, "Why 'Joe America' bets on Nasdaq," *CBS Market-Watch*, March 17, 2000.

6. Iana Polyak and Penelope Wang, "10 Best Mutual Funds for 2001," Money.com, January 8, 2001.

7. Sandra Block, "Tech funds stumble, tumble Bruised investors need to take long view, experts say," *USA TODAY*, October 4, 2000, 05.B.

8. Adam Shell and Matt Krantz, "Optimism gets rubbed out," *USA TODAY*, April 14, 2001, 01.B.

9. Speech given by Alan Greenspan to the Chamber of Commerce, "The Implication of Technological Changes," Charlotte, NC, July 10, 1998.

10. Dr. Paul B. Farrell, "Tech recovery! Get ready to rock 'n' roll," *CBS MarketWatch*, May 24, 2000.

11. Ibid.

12. Invesco Mutual Funds, "Should You Invest in Technology," *Of Mutual Interest*, Winter 2000.

13. Dr. Paul B. Farrell, "Stealth bull market, triple-digit funds," *CBS MarketWatch*, August 14, 2000.

14. Ibid.

15. Ibid.

16. Sandra Block, "Tech funds are great, but don't invest blindly," *USA TODAY*, March 14, 2000, 03.B.

17. Vern Hayden, "Practice Safe Sector Investing," TheStreet.com, May 31, 2000.

18. Rick Bloom, "Nasdaq mutual funds a good investment." *Detroit News*, February 6, 2000, 5D.

19. Dr. Paul B. Farrell, "Fourth of July: Nasdaq 10,000 by 2005," *CBS MarketWatch*, July 3, 2000.

20. Adam Shell and Matt Krantz, "Nasdaq in second-worst bear market ever," newsbytes.com, *USA TODAY*, February 26, 2001.

21. Ibid.

22. Henry Pearson, "Old financial advice holds true today," *USA TODAY*, February 26, 2001, 06.B.

## Chapter 9   Creating a Balanced Portfolio

1. Harry S. Dent, *The Roaring 2000s Investor*, (New York: Simon & Schuster, 1999), 117.

2. Vern Hayden, "Practice Safe Sector Investing," TheStreet.com, May 31, 2000.

## Chapter 10   Tried-and-True Investment Strategies

1. The Vanguard Group, "An Interview with Morningstar Research Director John Rekenthaler," *In the Vanguard*, Autumn 2000.

2. Jonathan Clements, "When the Street's Wisdom Doesn't Work," *Wall Street Journal*, May 5, 1999, C1.

3. The Vanguard Group, "Diversification Deficit Plagues Many Investment Programs," *In the Vanguard*, Spring, 2000.

4. Investment Company Institute, "Frequently Asked Questions About Mutual Fund Fees," 1998.

5. Bill Schultheis, *The Coffeehouse Investor—How to Build Wealth, Ignore Wall Street and Get On with Your Life*, Longstreet Press, (Marietta, Georgia: November, 1998), 68.

## Chapter 11   Hired Help

1. Dr. Paul B. Farrell, "Future millionaire? You may need help," *CBS Market Watch*, August 4, 2000.

2. The Vanguard Group, "An Interview with Morningstar Research Director John Rekenthaler," *In the Vanguard*, Autumn, 2000.

3. Jane Bryant Quinn, Making the Most of Your Money, (New York: Simon & Schuster, 1997), 32.

4. John Waggoner, "Fund fee report arms both sides," *USA TODAY*, January 11, 2001, 03.B.

## Chapter 12   Changing Choices Changing Jobs

1. Hap Bryant, "What to Do with Your 403(b)," Morningstar.com, May 5, 2000.

2. Gary Schatsky, "Liberating Funds Trapped in an Annuity," worldlyinvestor.com, November 2, 2000.

3. Richard A. Oppel Jr., "For Teachers, Object Lessons From the 401(k)," *New York Times*, June 13, 1999, 11.

4. Mary Doclar and Mike Lee, "Retirement Savings Plan Costs Teachers Lawsuits Say," 403bwise.com, *Fort Worth Star-Telegram*, September 17, 2000.

5. Ibid.

6. Jack VanDerhei and Craig Copeland, "The Changing Face of Private Retirement Plans," ebri.org, Employee Benefit Research Institute (EBRI), April, 2001, No. 232.

## Chapter 13   The Retirement Years

1. Telephone interview with Ken Deptula, Vanguard Mutual Funds, Retirement Division, November 5, 2000.

2. Paul Merriman, "Paul Merriman Answers Your Questions," FundAdvice.com, January, 2001.

## Chapter 14   Profile of a Successful 403(b) Investor

1. Invesco Mutual Funds, *Of Mutual Interest*, "The Psychology of Money," Winter 2000.

2. The Vanguard Group, "The Chairman's Corner," Vanguard Chairman John Brennan, Vanguard.com, *Quarterly Column for Investors*, January 2, 2001.

3. Dr. Paul Farrell, "The Great American Financial Advice Machine," *CBS MarketWatch*, December 4, 2000.

4. Ibid.

5. Ibid.

6. John Waggoner, "Panelists try to ride market's pendulum," *USA TODAY*, December 14, 2000, 10.E.

7. Ibid.

8. Ibid.

9. Ibid.

10. Ibid.

11. Ibid.

12. Ibid.

13. Peter Lynch, *One Up on Wall Street—How to Use What You Already Know to Make Money in the Market,* (New York: Simon & Schuster, 1989) 26.

14. Invesco Mutual Funds, *Of Mutual Interest*, "The Psychology of Money," Winter 2000.

# Glossary

**asset allocation**  Portfolio division among stocks, bonds, and cash.

**balanced portfolio**  A collection of diversified investments with a combination of stock, bond, and cash components.

**bear market**  Period in which the stock market experiences a strong and prolonged decline.

**beta**  Measurement of a fund's risk. The higher the beta, the more volatile the fund.

**blue-chip stocks**  Stocks of stable, long-established companies such as General Electric, IBM, and Proctor & Gamble.

**bond**  A loan made by an investor to a corporation or the government.

**bull market**  Period in which the stock market has a strong and prolonged upward swing.

**capital appreciation fund**  Aggressive growth funds that can be very risky.

**capital gains**   Taxable events that occur when a fund or stock is sold and realizes a profit. 403(b) holders pay no capital gains taxes on their investment while contributing to it.

**compounding**   Process by which investment dollars generate their own growth.

**core fund**   Funds invested in both growth and value stocks.

**dividends**   Portion of company profits paid directly to shareholders.

**dollar cost averaging**   Investing equal amounts of money in the stock market at regular intervals.

**Dow Jones Industrial Average**   An index that tracks thirty of the largest actively-traded stocks in U.S. corporations.

**emerging markets fund**   Funds investing in stocks of countries whose economies are small but appear to be growing.

**equity income fund**   A conservative type of mutual fund investing in stocks with steady dividends.

**expense ratio**   Annual operating expenses and management fees of a mutual fund company.

**403(b) plan**   A retirement account for employees of non-profit organizations in which contributions are taken directly from the employee's salary. The money grows tax-deferred and does not become taxable until it is withdrawn.

**401(k) plan**   Similar to a 403(b) but for employees of for-profit companies.

**global fund**   Mutual funds that invest in both American and foreign stocks.

**growth fund**   A mutual fund that invests in stocks of companies with the potential for continued growth and earnings.

**growth and income fund**   A fund that invests in companies expected to show respectable earnings (growth) along with steady or rising dividends.

**index fund**   A mutual fund that includes an assortment of companies from a particular index such as the S&P 500 or the Russell 2000. Index funds do not have an active fund manager.

**inflation**   The term for a gradual increase in the cost of goods and services.

**international fund**   Invests in companies outside the United States.

**IRA**   An individual retirement account with tax-deferred growth available to anyone with earned income.

**large-cap fund**   Invests in large companies with a net worth of several billion dollars.

**loaded fund**   A mutual fund that charges a fee for purchase and/or redemption.

**micro-cap fund**   Mutual funds that invest in small companies with market capitalization under $300 million. Can be extremely volatile.

**mid-cap fund**   Invests in stocks of midsize companies.

**Morningstar**   A company whose sole business is to track and rate mutual fund performance.

**mutual fund**   An investment vehicle that pools money from shareholders and invests in a variety of securities including stocks, bonds, and money market instruments.

**net asset value (NAV)**   The price of one share of a mutual fund. The figure is determined by taking a fund's total assets, deducting liabilities, and dividing by the number of shares outstanding.

**no-load fund**   A fund that sells shares without any sales or redemption charges.

**portfolio**   An individual's stock holdings and other financial investments.

**price/earnings ratio (P/E)**   The ratio of a stock's current price to its per-share earnings during the previous year.

**risk tolerance**   Ability to tolerate market swings. People with a high risk tolerance will typically invest in more aggressive funds.

**Roth IRA**   An individual retirement account with tax-free growth on the investment earnings.

**sector fund**   A mutual fund that invests in one specific industry, such as health, financial, technology, and so on.

**small-cap fund**　Invests in stocks of companies with a net worth of $500 million or less.

**Social Security**　A government program in which retired workers receive monthly allotments based on various factors including the amount they paid into the system.

**stock**　Ownership in a company in the form of shares.

**turnover rate**　Indicates how frequently the fund manager buys and sells equities. High turnover means more trades and usually higher transaction costs passed on to the investor as capital gains.

**unit investment trust (UIT)**　A form of index investing, much like a mutual fund in its variety of equities, but trades like a stock.

**value fund**　Invests in stocks that are selling at bargain prices because they're temporarily out of favor.

**variable annuities**　Mutual funds within an insurance policy. The earnings in annuities grow tax-deferred until they are withdrawn; investors pay insurance company fees along with fees of funds held within the annuity.

**yield**　Fund returns over a given period. Can be positive or negative.

# Index